ITALY

The Unfinished Revolution

ITALY

The Unfinished Revolution

MATT FREI

SINCLAIR-STEVENSON

To Penny

First published in Great Britain 1996
by Sinclair-Stevenson
an imprint of Reed International Books Ltd
Michelin House, 81 Fulham Road, London SW3 6RB
and Auckland, Melbourne, Singapore and Toronto

A CIP catalogue record for this title
is available from the British Library

ISBN 1 85619 571 6

Phototypeset by Intype, London
Printed and bound by Clays Ltd, St Ives Plc

Contents

Acknowledgements

I am indebted to many people who have helped in the creation of this book: my colleagues and friends at the BBC in Rome – Patti Partee, Cecilia Todeschini, Claudio Tondi, Jon Dumont, John Arden, Sean Salsarola, David Willey and Derek Wilson – encouraged me and provided entertaining company throughout. Thanks also to Charles Richards, Alan Cowell and Robert Fox for the same. In London my editors Jenny Baxter, Chris Wyld and Malcom Downing were kind enough to let me off the leash. Special thanks to my friend Robert Graham from the *Financial Times* who found time to comb through the manuscript and pointed out some of the more glaring errors; and to Francois and Shirley Caracciolo for providing an idyllic setting in which to plug in my Toshiba. Piero Ottone, Franco Pavoncello, Franco Ferrarotti, Franco Venturini, Sergio Romano, Gianfranco Pasquino, Rodolfo Brancoli, Roberto Lasagne, Livio Caputo, Luigi Berlinguer, and many others all provided great wisdom and insight, while tolerating the musings of a foreigner. I am also grateful to the scores of journalists from RAI and numerous regional Italian newspapers for their expertise and help in ushering me through tickets of bureaucracy. Finally I would like to thank my editors Neil Taylor and Katie Green for their patience, my agent Bill Hamilton for his enthusiasm, my friend Tom Weldon for his advice and my parents Anita and Peter for their encouragement. My Penny I thank for all the above and much more.

Matt Frei, Rome, 17 July 1995

Author's Note

Most of us have been caressed by Italian culture at one time or another but few of us have been initiated into the heady pleasures of Italian politics. This book is neither a history of modern Italy nor a purely political chronicle. This is an idiosyncratic portrait of a very eccentric democracy in one of its greatest periods of upheaval and revelation. The country is still in transition and some events may have been too late to be captured in print. I apologise for dwelling too little on the Italian left; an omission which is justified by the fact that the most novel developments have been on the right. I recall the warning words of my history tutor at university who told me not to lose my readers in the thicket of too much dense detail. All I can say is that covering Italy for the BBC and writing a book about this extraordinary and wonderful country has been a very pleasurable experience. It goes without saying that all errors of fact or judgement are entirely my responsibility.

Cappuccino By-Laws:
a Prologue

The Italians have a reputation for flouting the law, breaking the rules and conducting their daily lives in a manner that is infuriatingly haphazard but charmingly individualistic. Their easygoing Mediterranean lifestyle is the envy of pent-up Protestants in more sober climates. Yet when I first moved to Italy in 1991 I discovered to my horror that the Italians had been misunderstood and that I had been misled. Italy turned out to be hair-splittingly legalistic, a country slavishly obsessed with petty rules and officialdom. Tourists do not stay long enough to get entangled in the legal web of opening a bank account, getting a phone line, a parking permit, a residence permit or a mushroom-picking permit. They have probably never had the degrading experience of sending a package in the Italian postal system or paying a gas bill, both of which involve hours of queuing and paperwork. Overawed by the colourful and noisy theatre of street life, they are blissfully unaware of the fact that it is they, not the Italians, who are breaking the rules. Take even the enjoyable and deceptively simple act of drinking a cappuccino. This ritual is a minefield of regulations.

Rule Number 1: never have a cappuccino after eleven in the morning. It is only intended as a morning meal, accompanied by a croissant (*cornetto*) or a brioche. If you do order a cappuccino after the deadline make sure you give the person behind the bar a reason. For instance, you could say that you woke up late because you were working until the early hours of the morning. *Do not* say that you are hungover. Getting inebriated in public or private is very un-Italian and frowned upon.

Rule Number 2: never order a cappuccino after lunch or dinner. How can your pour all that hot milk on a stomach filled with pasta, meat and cheese? A post-prandial cappuccino will immediately brand you as a foreigner. This can lead to an increment on the bill. If you walk into a café and the waiter asks you in broken English if you would like a cappuccino – whether before or after eleven o'clock – leave immediately! The café probably only caters for tourists and is therefore neither good nor cheap.

Rule Number 3: never have your cappuccino sitting down unless you want to pay large amounts of money to be served outside on the terrace in summer.

Rule Number 4: when you have found the right café at the right time, don't just order your cappuccino without knowing what *kind* of cappuccino you want. Italians are very particular about whether they drink it *bollente*, literally boiling hot; *sensa schiuma*, without foam; *con cioccolate*, with a sprinkle of chocolate; or indeed *in vetro*, in a glass, as opposed to in a cup. This is one of the more puzzling rules, because the barman often actually prepares the cappuccino in a cup only to then pour it into a glass.

Rule Number 5: you can drink an espresso all day long. The question again is *what kind of expresso*: *lungo*, long with a dash of water; *macchiato*, with a dash of milk; *lungo macchiato*, with dashes of both; or *coretto*, with grappa. This is allowed before 11.30 a.m.

Rule Number 6: never leave the bar without your receipt, even if it's for the trifling sum of 800 lire. You are obliged by law to take the receipt. Not taking it makes you an accessory to tax evasion. The receipt is proof that a purchase has been made and that the purchase will be registered in the till, and therefore eventually on the bar's tax returns. In 1992 a young boy was fined for leaving a grocer's shop with an apple but without a receipt. The fact that the shop was owned by the boy's father did not impress the Guardia di Finanza, Italy's much-loathed Financial Police, recognisable by their grey uniforms and the emblem of a small yellow flame flickering on their peaked caps.

Italy has a genius for complication, which is exemplified by the byzantine ritual of drinking coffee as much as by the country's four competing police forces. The Guardia di Finanza deals only with fiscal abuse and contraband, leaving theft, rape or murder to the Polizia. Crimes against the state, such as Mafia killings, flag burning and attempted *coups d'état*, are on the whole dealt with by the Carabinieri, who answer to the Ministry of Defence as opposed to the Ministry of the Interior. The Cavalry branch of the Carabinieri have been entrusted with the stylish protection of historic monuments such as the Senate or the Forum in Rome. With their long capes, swords and knee-high boots they are the world's most over-dressed police force and are uninterested in any crimes that do not directly concern their narrow brief. They are also too decorative to stoop to the undignified act of making an arrest or running after a suspect.

Traffic offences in cities are the exclusive domain of the Vigili Urbani, whose lowly status in the law-enforcement hierarchy is compensated for by a splendid white pith helmet. All the police forces take pride in their dress code and in 1988 the Carabinieri commissioned Giorgio Armani to design their lightweight summer uniform. Indeed, the art of surviving in Italy depends to a degree on knowing what crimes to commit in the presence of which uniform. An officer of the Carabinieri or the Guardia di Finanza is unlikely to intervene in a traffic offence. For fear of stepping on a colleague's toes, a traffic cop is unlikely to touch a serious crime without deferring to the Carabinieri or the Polizia. Italy's multifaceted police apparatus exists to enforce a myriad of laws, inscribed in one of the world's longest and most complex legal codes.

Why then have they done such a terrible job? Why has Italy experienced the most rampant and systematic corruption of any post-war democracy? Why has an entire political élite been toppled from decades of uninterrupted power because of widespread abuse of public office? Why is tax dodging a national sport in Italy? Greed and power are only two reasons. Another is that Italy's laws are too complicated to be followed and too contradictory to be respected. The country, which invented Roman law and therefore helped to lay the foundations of modern society, seeks refuge in illegality. But even within the realms of illegality rules are all-important. For instance, the billions of lire in bribes that were collected by many of Italy's ruling parties were distributed according to a strict rule where the size of the kickback was proportional to the number of seats a party occupied in parliament. The bribes, or *tangente*, took into account the competing faction within a party. Even the opposition was given a slice, so as not to feel left out.

The Mafia too is governed by a strict set of rules. 'Men of Honour' are initiated into Cosa Nostra with an initiation ceremony that involves pledging adherence to seven commandments, from the notorious *omertà*, or vow of silence, to marital fidelity. Breaking the rules carries the death penalty. The Mafia's hierarchy, from the ruling *commissione* to the *platoons* of ten foot-soldiers from a single family, is a strict pyramid. Cosa Nostra's obsession with title and rank resembles that of the stuffiest British officers' mess. In his confessions the Mafia supergrass and 'executioner' Giovanni Drago described how he stamped out petty crime like pickpocketing and mugging. In his diligent pursuit of law and order he killed thirty-five 'criminals'. Thanks to his concept of neighbourhood watch the Mafia's backyard is clean and to this day you can leave your car unlocked in a notorious Sicilian town like Corleone or Gela without fear of a break-in. What makes the Mafia unique is not the amount of money it extorts, the volume of drugs it ships or the number of people it has killed – the Medellin cartel or the Moscow mafia are scoring higher on that front – but the fact that Cosa Nostra is criminal civilisation in its most sophisticated form.

There is nothing chaotic or haphazard about Italian society. Every clan, party, family, village, city guild, Masonic lodge or trade union is governed by a complex set of rules and by-laws. To know them is to understand Italy. But the one thing they all have in common is that they distrust the Italian state and despise *its* laws as an attempt to enforce uniformity. As he was wallowing in self-pity on the shores of Lake Garda in the final months of his life, Mussolini made the bitter realisation that 'Italy is not a serious nation, but an aggregate of individuals'. He was in a position to know. No one had tried harder – and failed more humiliatingly – than the Duce to impose his will on the Italians.

After fifty years of democracy, unprecedented stability and wealth, Italy is still a nation in the making. Today the project has gone back to the drawing board and the systematic corruption of the so-called First Republic has unleashed a crisis of democracy. The Italian state is still looking for recognition from its citizens. In December 1994 I interviewed Giuliano Ferrara, the government spokesman, about the fact that Silvio Berlusconi, the media tycoon/Prime Minister, had come under criminal investigation for tax fraud. The investigation should have been acutely embarrassing for a Prime Minister who had swept to power on promises of cleaning up politics. Ferrara, a former talk-show host with an astounding girth, puffed on his cigar and said: 'In this country you are a nobody if you haven't been investigated. To be a suspect in Italy is something like belonging to the House of Lords in your country.'

The Cleaning Contractor,
His Wife
and Her Alimony

It all started in Milan in February 1992 with the cleaning contractor, the head of the old people's home, his wife and her alimony. Mario Chiesa ran the Pio Albergo Trivulzio, Milan's oldest and most venerable retirement home, a beautiful nineteenth-century palazzo with an ornate garden. He was also a member of the Socialist Party of the former Prime Minister Bettino Craxi, who had turned Milan into the party's stronghold. For someone occupying a relatively humble position in the civil service, Signor Chiesa had a remarkably luxurious lifestyle. He lived in a spacious apartment on the Via Monte Rosa, was often seen dining out at Savini's, Milan's most expensive restaurant. He had several holiday homes and dressed expensively. Nevertheless Chiesa could also be stingy, especially towards his ex-wife. Lara Sala was not only aggrieved by the fact that her estranged husband had jilted her for a woman twenty years her junior, she was also annoyed that he had not been paying the alimony. So she complained to the police. Her *denuncia*, or denunciation, would surely have been buried in a mountain of yellowed paper at the civil dispute section of the city's Palazzo di Giustizia had it not been for the fact that Mario Chiesa had also become the subject of another complaint.

Luca Magni ran an industrial cleaning firm and was negotiating with Chiesa about a contract to clean the Pio Albergo Trivulzio. What annoyed Signor Magni was that Mario Chiesa asked for a ten per cent 'commission', payment of which would have halved the cleaning contractor's profits. Signor Magni also went to the police. They referred the case to a medium-ranking investigating magistrate called Antonio Di Pietro, who had spent several years looking into a local bribery racket. Chiesa, with his wealth, his secure job, his 'commissions' and his connections in the Socialist Party, was the man they were looking for. Di Pietro told Magni to go back to the old people's home and hand over the 'commission'. Only this time he would be wired with a tiny microphone hidden in his ball-point pen and a High 8 camera concealed in a black briefcase.

Magni met Chiesa in his ornate office decorated with red leather armchairs and old master paintings, and handed over the arranged sum of seven million lire, about £3000. The wadge of notes included ten marked 100,000 bills, an old trick that Di Pietro, the magistrate, had learnt while working as a policeman and a detective. The meeting, which was watched and overheard by the police, went smoothly and shortly afterwards Chiesa was arrested. When he heard from the porter at the front gate that policemen had entered the old people's home, Chiesa suspected that something was wrong. He was caught while flushing 100,000-lire notes down the toilet.

A year later the political establishment that had ruled Italy for almost five decades collapsed; whole political parties with their deputies, prime ministers and pretensions were flushed into one of the grubbier dustbins of history. Chiesa's arrest helped to unthread a whole regime.

Further investigations revealed that Chiesa had deposited at least 12 billion lire in bank accounts belonging to his secretary, who was also his girlfriend. He turned for help to the people who had always acted as his benefactors and protectors, the Socialist Party. After all, Chiesa had friends in high places, friends like Paolo Pilliteri, a former mayor of Milan and brother-in-law to the autocratic leader of the Socialist Party Bettino Craxi. He was also on first-name terms with Bobo, Craxi's twenty-eight-year-old son, who was the head of the party in Milan. But help wasn't forthcoming. Chiesa was on his own. Taking revenge, he decided to spill the beans. What he told the investigators went well beyond their most lurid expectations. It emerged that every contract at the old people's home, from the funeral arrangements to the cut flowers for the dining room, had been subject to a fixed commission, or what the Italians in a wonderful example of verbal obscurantism call *una tangente*, a tangent, a sideways approach, in other words: a bribe. *Tangentopoli*, 'bribesville', the scandal to beat all Italian scandals, was born. For it wasn't only the old people's home that was run on bribes. Chiesa gave the magistrates a floppy disk containing the names of 700 people who had been involved in the systematic exchange of kickbacks for business in Milan. Chiesa himself had acted as a kind of middleman, a broker of bribes.

The disk confirmed that the Socialist Party and the other mainstream parties that had ruled Milan were lining their pockets with *tangente* from the business community vying for public works projects. No flyover, hospital, ring-road, airport, underground, or sewage plant could be built in Milan without a bribe.

At first most of the investigations concentrated on Milan, a galling fact for the rich, hard-working city that had always considered itself to be a bastion of honesty in an otherwise dishonest country. The magistrates who made up the investigative pool involved in *Mani Pulite*, or 'Clean Hands' – one of several names for the scandal – didn't have to dig for further evidence, they were showered with it. Confession became fashionable, as one businessman after another saw which way the wind was blowing and turned themselves in with their tales of *tangente*. Those who were reluctant to talk were softened up with a spell in Milan's notorious San Vittore jail. Preventive custody, one of the many sweeping powers bestowed upon Italian investigating magistrates by the Penal Code, became a widely used and controversial means of extracting confessions. People more used to seeing each other at La Scala or Savini's were now bumping into each other at San Vittore jail. Isolation cells which had not been used for years were opened up to make room for the new breed of white-collar criminals.

It transpired, however, that Chiesa was one of the very few to be tried and sentenced. He got six years and had to pay a fine of six billion lire, which would have left him with another six when his sentence was over. But the great majority of those arrested were nothing more than suspects, who had not been formally charged or tried, let alone found guilty. Many spent up to six months in jail, being questioned. Several, like Gabriele Cagliari, the former head of ENI, the state's energy giant, committed suicide.

The spectacle of seeing Italy's great and good dragged in hand-cuffs from their elegant restaurants and luxurious holiday villas was mesmerising. The viewing figures of nightly news bulletins shot up as the roll-call of suspects became longer and more illustrious. American soap operas were eclipsed by programmes like *Un Giorno in Preturn* (*A Day in Court*), which had previously only attracted a small audience of trial junkies. Italy now had its own home-made soap opera about the decline and fall of the rich and famous. As a foreign correspondent who had just arrived in Italy and who initially spent much time in the former Yugoslavia, it was almost impossible to keep up with events. A week's absence from Italy meant missing several instalments of the *Tangentopoli* drama. The Italian newspapers would have discovered new scandals and new names, which they didn't always bother to explain. The media and the country were becoming totally self-absorbed. And who could blame them? Italy, a place where politics had become tediously predictable, was being rattled by one bombshell after another.

No one and nothing, it seemed, were untouchable. Carlo De Benedetti, the head of the computer and office equipment giant Olivetti and one of the country's most flamboyant businessmen, decided to go to the judges before they came to him. He confessed to taking billions of lire in illegal payments and exposed what he described as 'the systematic extortion imposed on the business community by Italy's political parties'. But it was a system of extortion that also helped De Benedetti to earn 832 million dollars in profits. The scandal even reached the factory gates of Fiat, Italy's largest company, producing everything from cars to arms and accounting for almost five per cent of the country's gross national product. Fiat's construction company Cogefar-Impresit was accused of paying bribes to political parties for the building of Milan's metro. Cesare Romiti, Fiat's second in command after the imperious Gianni Agnelli – one of the few business leaders not to be touched by the scandals – was hauled in for questioning. He too blamed 'the system'. It became a common refrain in a country where the buck never stops anywhere and where the Catholic concept of universal temptation has helped to quash any sense of personal culpability. Meanwhile the Milan judges, led by Antonio Di Pietro, the ex-cop, and Francesco Saverio Borelli, his softly-spoken, sophisticated boss, became Italy's Jacobin judges, leading the revolution against the corrupt *palazzo*. A rash of graffiti declaring *Grazie Di Pietro* covered walls, monuments and lavatory doors all over the country. When Di Pietro walked in the streets of Milan or Rome, surrounded by his posse of bodyguards wielding machine-guns, he was celebrated like a pop or soccer idol. Gradually the magistrates became as powerful as the ruling parties they had helped to topple.

The scandal quickly crept up the political ladder. Bettino Craxi, the former Prime Minister who was once hailed by *Time* magazine as the Italian 'Maestro' for presiding over the economic boom of the 1980s, was suddenly cast as a villain. The boom had not only been forgotten in the recession of the early 1990s, it now also appeared that much of it had been financed by corruption. Craxi became the subject of seventeen different inquiries into bribery and fraud and was finally forced to resign from the leadership of his party in February 1993, booed and pelted with coins by passers-by as he left the Socialist Party headquarters in Rome for the last time. The 'Maestro' took refuge in his holiday villa in Tunisia, fleeing a string of court cases and an irate public. Other former Prime Ministers followed suit. Ciriaco De Mita, a Christian Democrat, came under investigation for channelling billions of lire earmarked for an earthquake relief fund in his native Irpinia region to the bottomless coffers of his party. The third former Prime Minister to come under investigation and eventually face trial was Giulio Andreotti. The friend of four Popes who had helped to write the Constitution of the post-Second World War republic and who had served in twenty-three cabinets, Andreotti embodied the bizarre mixture of stability and byzantine intrigue that was Italy's political system. Now he was accused of the ultimate political crime. Don Giulio, as he was known to his friends, was charged with being – amongst other crimes – the Mafia's Godfather in Rome. Although he has repeatedly protested his innocence the 'uncle' has become another figure of dislike and derision. It seemed as if a biblical plague was spreading through the ranks of Italian politics. Over a hundred city councils were disbanded because of corruption and by 1994 one-third of parliament had come under criminal investigation.

The voters reacted accordingly. Parties that had ruled Italy without pause since 1945 were being deserted. The Socialists, who had taken part in every government since 1963, plummeted to barely one-per cent in regional and national elections. The Christian Democrats, for four decades the single largest party, halved their share of the vote. Eventually the party was disbanded and its shrivelled rump reborn under a different name with a new leader. Then, in May 1993, Carlo Azeglio Ciampi became Prime Minister. It was an indication of the acuteness of the crisis and the popular disgust with politics that Ciampi, the former governor of the Bank of Italy, had never even been a member of a political party, let alone an elected deputy. His government of 'technicians' was, however, surprisingly successful and some Italians even began to ask themselves whether the country needed to bother with elections if these unelected politicians were more competent and spent less time feuding with each other.

The once rigid tectonic plates of Italian politics had been blasted, burying the old rulers and giving birth to a bizarre new generation. The Northern League may have taken its inspiration and emblem from a twelfth-century rebellion against the Holy Roman Empire, but now it rode the wave of political protest to become the largest party in Italy's rich industrial north. Like a poltergeist from the darkest corner of Italy's history, the neo Fascists burst from the lunatic fringe of Italian politics. Their party, the MSI, once marginalised for worshipping the wartime dictator Mussolini, became the biggest political force in the poor south, absorbing millions of voters who had been left homeless by the collapse of the Christian Democrats. Eventually it even became a party of government. It was the first time in Europe that the ideological right-wing forces which everyone thought had been buried at the end of the Second World War returned to power. Was Italy experiencing a revolution, a counter-revolution or neither?

No one knew quite what to call the extraordinary upheavals

and contortions of Italian politics. I remember sitting together one balmy summer evening with friends trying to come up with the right description. One thought of *la dolce rivoluzione*, 'the sweet revolution'. But there were victims too. Giovanni Falcone and Paolo Borsellino, two leading anti-Mafia judges, had been assassinated in Palermo. Car bombs exploded in Milan, Rome and Florence, killing civilians and destroying part of Italy's cherished cultural heritage – a twelfth-century church in Rome, part of the Uffizi Gallery in Florence, home to some of the most famous Renaissance paintings. As the evening got livelier and the bottles emptier, another thought of 'the sweet and sour revolution'. Then we moved into textiles. The velvet revolution? No, there was a Czech copyright on that. The cashmere revolution, because of the smooth and expensive nature of the material? But that sounded too much like an upheaval in the rag trade, rather than political change. The drunken conclusion of the evening was that the events in Italy defied description, partly because they were so unique and still evolving. Moreover in the warm embrace of a Roman evening in May, with fountains playing to the baroque façades of a piazza full of attractive people, revolution just seemed the wrong kind of word. Life for Italy's Armani-clad *sansculottes* wasn't so miserable after all. The events seemed more like a vendetta by the electors against the elected, than a revolution.

But the events continued. By the end of 1993 everyone was preparing for general elections, the second in two years under a new electoral system, in which a ragtag alliance of the right would be pitted against a well-organised party and its allies on the left. The PDS, successors to Italy's Communist Party, once the biggest in the West, were confident of victory. They too had been embroiled in the system of corruption, but with much smaller amounts than the ruling parties. Now with the Cold War over and Communism a thing of the past, the PDS was no longer worshipping at the shrine of Marx but of Mammon. After four decades in the opposition the party finally seemed *papabile*. Three months before elections that everyone hoped would breathe new life into the political system, the PDS was poised for power. Ladbrokes, the London bookmakers, gave it the best odds to win. Unbeknown to them and everyone else the script of Italy's political drama was being rewritten in a way that no one had expected.

In January 1994 a man entered the political stage out of the blue and declared that he would save Italy from Communism, even though Communism had ceased to exist. Instead of being laughed off stage he was taken seriously and became brazenly confident of winning. His confidence, some called it arrogance, may have had something to do with the fact that he owned most of the country's commercial television channels, controlled one-third of its advertising, owned its biggest real estate empire, its most popular chain of supermarkets, several magazines and publishing houses and the national soccer champions, AC Milan. The man was a master of mass psychology and a brilliant salesman. He launched a political movement the way that you would launch new deodorant, and called it 'Forza Italia,' or 'Go For It, Italy', a rallying cry borrowed from football. It was a catchy title and appealed to millions of voters who were bored and confused by names like Christian Democrat, Liberal, Socialist or Social Democrat. The man then turned his company into a party, using his managers to orchestrate the election campaign and to run as candidates. He boasted that none of his candidates had ever sat in parliament. A new form of politics was born, one that was overtly anti-political. A new genre of politics came into effect, articulating the widespread disgust with old-style politicians and their parties which was spreading all over the West but which was particularly virulent in Italy. All over the country people were beginning to mutter the mantra of Forza Italia: *Old is bad: new is good.* They didn't seem to notice that the tycoon was not that new himself, and that one of the country's most hated and discredited political leaders was the godfather of his daughter. But Silvio Berlusconi knew about seducing an audience – he'd once been a nightclub singer on cruise ships – and in April 1994 he became Prime Minister.

To his supporters he was the man of providence who would restore Italy to greatness, to his detractors he was a salesman who hijacked the country's revolution with cheap promises of wealth and was hell-bent on self-preservation. In any case, Italy had embarked on another political adventure. In two years a curious alliance of voters and judges had staged one of the most remarkable political rebellions for any modern democracy, they had rewritten the rules of modern politics and given the world its first tycoon prime minister. Was this an eccentric aberration Italian style or had Italy once again become 'the laboratory chamber of politics', a role which it had played in the early 1920s when the collapse of its democracy and the onset of Fascism preceded similar developments in Germany and Spain? Had Italy become the first in a long line of nations to reject traditional politics, in an era when governments could no longer meet the expectations of their electorates and when the traditional post-war parties seemed to have buried ideology? The whiff of *fin de siècle* decadence was everywhere: in the television/soccer politics of Silvio Berlusconi, in the byzantine plotting of the ruling coalition – lurid even by traditional Italian standards – in cute eccentricities such as the election of a porn queen to parliament, in the widespread disgust and derision felt for politics of all kind. Where better to stage the opening scene of the end of an era than amongst the moss-covered ruins of ancient Rome?

Political voyeurs have flocked to Italy to prod the body politic for answers and left even more confused. The lava of change is still hot, the 'revolution' still unfinished. As for the Italians themselves, many of them had expected their political experiment to yield more. They had seen this as the big chance to turn Italians into real citizens and redefine the meaning of 'Italy', a country whose very existence is still under debate more than a century after it was founded. But then, had ordinary Italians not voted for the politicians that ruled them? After all, they had also been on the take, dodging taxes, subverting the state in a myriad of different ways. Italy had managed to separate the state from the people, so much so, that when the state crumbled, the people continued, willy-nilly, to do business as usual. Had this separation not-existed Italy's 'revolution' may have turned out to be a lot less sweet. Like many of my friends and colleagues I have been bowled over by Italian politics. The scandals seemed to be more far-fetched than anywhere else in the western half of the Northern hemisphere, the bribes bigger, their receivers more illustrious, the corruption more systematic, politics more outlandish and the backdrop more beautiful. In the words of the Italian playwright Ennio Flaviano, who died in 1972: 'Things are tragic but not serious!'

2

Poggiolini's Pouffe

Did Pierr di Maria Poggiolini, the wife of the head of the Pharmaceutical Department of Italy's Health Ministry, get an upholsterer to stuff the treasury bills worth ten million dollars into her living-room pouffe, or did she do it herself? The brown leather pouffe, stuffed to the point of explosion, was discovered by the police when they raided her villa on the outskirts of Rome. It was sitting near the coffee table on the Poggiolinis' shagpile carpet. Signora Poggiolini had never dabbled in upholstery. The pouffe showed no signs of having been slit open, clumsily stitched back together or generally tampered with. So how did the neatly bundled bills get into the pouffe? It must have been a professional job, the police concluded: the search for the upholsterer continues.

After Dr Poggiolini's arrest, it was important, too, to trace the origins of the money. Why had it been hidden in the first place? And how did it relate to the other 120 million dollars found in the Poggiolinis' three homes and fourteen Swiss bank accounts? How, above all, was it possible for a civil servant to steal so much money without the connivance of others? Although the Poggiolini case turned out to be one of the most lurid examples of corruption, it was typical in many other ways: Professor Poggiolini remained convinced of his own innocence. As he told his investigators: 'I was merely bending the rules a little.' Poggiolini, like so many other suspects in the corruption scandals, saw himself as little more than the average tax-dodging Italian, forced to live a life of petty illegality by a terrifyingly complex and cold-blooded *stato*. The fact that Poggiolini was himself a representative of the much-loathed state didn't seem to bother him. What the Italians

who congested the phone lines of the Ministry of Health or wrote stinging letters to the newspapers hated him for wasn't the fact that he *took* money – that was almost taken for granted. It was the amount that riled. Poggiolini, like hundreds of other politicians or civil servants, broke the thieves' honour of Italian society by being too greedy.

The pouffe was not the only piece of evidence that the Guardia di Finanza, the state's financial police, had stumbled across in the Poggiolinis' luxury villa in EUR, a fascist-built Milton Keynes between Rome and the polluted Mediterranean. During their search they also came across a collection of sixty paintings, including several canvases by Modigliani and De Chirico. One of the works, a small sixteenth-century canvas attributed to the German painter Hans Rottenhammer, had, as it later turned out, been stolen from the private collection of a Florentine business-man in 1992. How the painting ended up in the hands of Professor Poggiolini is still a mystery. There is no suggestion that he stole the work himself, merely, according to the investigators, that he had bought it with stolen money. Despite their value and beauty the Poggiolinis' paintings were not proudly displayed on the walls but packed away in cardboard boxes.

Three weeks earlier the police had searched another Poggiolini residence in the centre of Rome. This had turned out to be an Aladdin's cave of riches: the family safe contained hundreds of krugerands, old Roman coins, diamonds (cut and uncut) in small pouches and cash worth 30,000 dollars in a bizarre array of cur-rencies: dollars, Deutschmarks, francs, Dutch guilders and ECUs. The latter, one newspaper mused, may have been given to Pro-fessor Poggiolini in his capacity as a member of the European Union's Pharmaceutical Commission.

Next to the safe the police found a pyramid of shoe boxes. The beginnings of a footwear collection, inspired by Imelda Marcos perhaps? Not so. The boxes didn't contain shoes but over 100 neatly stacked gold ingots. 'Forty years of personal savings,' Pro-fessor Poggiolini told the investigating magistrates. They didn't believe him. Nor did they believe his wife who dismissed a current account containing lire worth 300,000 dollars as 'shopping money'. And what about the other fourteen accounts, most of them in Swiss banks? All in all the Poggiolinis had squirrelled away 130 million dollars, worth – according to the most conservative estimate – well beyond the savings capacity of an official in the Italian Health Ministry, even one as high-ranking as Professor Diulio Poggiolini.

As the head of the Health Ministry's Pharmaceutical Department, the professor was in charge of approving medicines, fixing their price and putting them on the national register. In his ten years in office he sat in judgement over hundreds of medicines which had to receive his stamp of approval in order to be sold in Italian pharmacies. His pricing policy, approved by the Health Minister Francesco De Lorenzo, determined how many lire the man or woman in the piazza had to pay for medicines. Professor Poggiolini was arrested in September 1993 on charges of taking bribes, as well as of approving medicines that were faulty or not thoroughly tested. Magistrates believed that the 130 million dollars in accumulated assets were the fruits of years of graft – the professor's reward for helping the drug companies.

Newspaper cartoonists had a field-day depicting the professor as a Dracula figure, sucking the blood out of his victim, the Italian consumer of medicines. Caricaturists were helped by Poggiolini's stoop, his thin hooked nose that hails from Etruscan cave murals, his subtly crossed eyes and crest of grey hair on top of a very high forehead. His wife, who is gaunt and wears thick spectacles, was depicted at various stages as Dracula's bride, Lady Macbeth or a very large rodent. The Poggiolini case seemed to owe more to Transylvanian legends than to European public administration.

What particularly puzzled the investigators was that the couple hardly spent their ill-gotten gains. The millions could easily have elevated the Poggiolinis to the jet-set status enjoyed by so many other grandees of corruption. Villas in Capri or in Porto Ercole, yachts or private planes, expensive hotel suites. Instead most of their treasures were stashed away where even they couldn't see them. The couple's lifestyle was parsimonious and dull. They lived frugally, did their shopping in the cheapest supermarkets and department stores and redeemed coupons. 'Why,' the investigators asked Mrs Poggiolini, 'did you *need* so many billions of lire if you weren't spending them?' 'Billions?' the professor asked. 'I don't even know how many zeros that is!' The investigators pressed on until Mrs Poggiolini, who came from a wealthy Sicilian family, relented. 'We did it for our son!' she said, weeping. Perhaps this was an attempt to soften the hearts of her inquisitors, by appealing to their sense of filial love. Giovanni, the Poggiolinis' son, is physically handicapped and nursed at home by one of his aunts. The money the couple had 'saved' was meant to provide a secure future for their only off-spring.

The couple were kept in separate Neapolitan jails for six months without appearing in court. Italian magistrates have wide-reaching powers and can keep a suspect in 'preventive custody' for over a year without filing charges. This is frequently used as a way of extracting confessions. In the Poggiolinis' case it worked. Every week the location and number of another secret bank account was revealed. Professor Poggiolini – dubbed the King Midas of the Italian health system – even offered to pay back a sizeable fraction of his 'savings'. Unlike his cell-mate, a garrulous engineer who had been accused of fiddling the state over an earthquake relief fund, the professor never acclimatised to the dank austerity of the infamous Poggioreale jail in Naples. He complained of cataracts, high blood pressure and couldn't understand why he wasn't allowed to leave even though he had cooperated so willingly with the police. He told reporters that all the blame was being loaded onto his shoulders when the real culprit, his boss, the former Health Minister Francesco De Lorenzo, was allowed to escape arrest. (In fact, magistrates arrested De Lorenzo in April 1994, though just as the minister went to jail the professor was released.) The investigators were satisfied that Poggiolini had confessed everything he knew and his health was beginning to deteriorate. Soon afterwards the former head of the Pharmaceutical Department of the Italian Health Ministry was discovered queuing up for his pension in a social security office in Rome – this despite the fact he had millions of dollars stashed away in various bank accounts. He was wearing sunglasses, cowboy boots and a blue teddy-boy suit. But no disguise, however ridiculous, could hide the distinctive features of this professorial fraudster and when the professor was spotted by one of the officials behind the counter he was hounded out of the office by an angry crowd.

Similar acts of public humiliation were meted out to those whose guilt or innocence had yet to be proven in court. Hitherto syco-phantic waiters in exclusive restaurants refused to serve an Interior Minister under investigation; Gianni De Michelis, the former Foreign Minister of Falstaffian girth, was pelted with eggs and tomatoes in his own hometown, Venice; and the former Prime Minister Bettino Craxi was hit by a barrage of coins and insults outside his Rome residence, the exclusive Hotel Raphael.

Yet Professor Poggiolini wasn't a single villain acting alone. His pricing policy was fully endorsed by De Lorenzo, a leading member of the now defunct Liberal Party. De Lorenzo, who was still languishing in the Poggioreale jail in December 1994 awaiting trial for corruption and fraud, was accused of receiving millions of dollars in kickbacks from drugs companies whose products he had helped to put on the market with the help of Poggiolini. It takes at least two to bribe and, as was widely expected, the pharmaceutical industry also became embroiled in the scandal. Senior executives from at least three leading pharmaceutical com-panies were also arrested for allegedly paying the bribes that allowed their products to be sold at inflated prices. Although Italian medicines are heavily subsidised by the state – up to ninety per cent for the most essential drugs – the number of products available is relatively small. In 1987 Italian pharmacies were allowed to have 5455 products on their shelves. In Germany the figure was 70,000. In Britain 35,000. In the US well over 50,000. The Italian Health Ministry was far more restrictive about which medicines it would release on the official list. A bribe was one way of securing a place.

As soon as the scandal erupted the arguments started about who corrupted whom first. Did the pharmaceutical companies tempt the civil servants at the Health Ministry with a bribe or were they the victims of extortion, forced to pay up when faced with the prospect of being banned from the Italian market? This argument would become a leitmotif of the corruption scandal.

Italian political scandals like the Poggiolini saga frequently border on the unbelievable. As plots of modern fiction they would probably be dismissed for their lack of verisimilitude. But they are fact, or at least treated as fact by everyone from the public to the judiciary. The case of Diulio Poggiolini, his wife and the Health Minister shocked a nation that had already become hardened to the flagrant abuses of public office. This may have been due to the fact that although there was a sort of world record of alleged corruption, very little of it was proven in court. Yet almost all allegations were taken seriously enough to file criminal charges, led to arrests, ended political careers, produced suicides, and persuaded millions of Italian voters to turn their backs on the parties that they had re-elected year after year for four decades.

Considering the number of people under investigation and the extent of abuse, it is baffling that Italy's 'revolution' is considered to have been so 'sweet'. The list of *indagati* – those under investigation – included not only politicians, but businessmen, administrators, civil servants, journalists, academics, judges, football managers, insurance brokers, spies, doctors, game-show hosts and opera singers. The 5000 or so suspects in the *tangentopoli* saga – it is impossible to keep up with the exact number – represent a cross-section of Italy's élite. In fact the Italian *Who's Who* has struck 1800 names from its 1994 edition, including such grandees as Mr Craxi, Mr De Michelis and the Ferruzzi family, celebrated as one of the country's most glamorous business dynasties two years ago, investigated but not subsequently charged by the judiciary as an *associazione a delinquere*, a delinquent organisation. This label is normally reserved for Mafia families. It's as if the entire cast-list of *Hello!* magazine had suddenly ended up on the criminal register. Roberto Mongini, a cynical Milanese lawyer and former Christian Democratic Party hack, who was escorted in police handcuffs from one of the smartest restaurants in Milan – he had been accused of collecting bribes for the Malpensa airport project – put it like this: 'You never meet anyone at La Scala these days. That's because they're all serving time in San Vittore jail.' VIP has come to mean *visti in prigione*, or spotted in prison. In the summer of 1992 a blue-chip PR firm tried to cash in on the new population of inmates that was overcrowding Italian prisons. It advised them to take smart casual clothes – 'stretchy trousers for many hours spent sitting down on uncomfortable chairs' – several good long books – 'to avoid brooding', enough shaving foam and razors – 'you might be released at any moment and have to look decent for the cameras waiting outside the prison gates'. No tie – 'it may tempt you to hang yourself'. The joke turned sour when Gabriele Cagliari, the former head of ENI, the state's chemical giant, took his life by suffocating with a plastic bag, one day before he was due to be let out of 'preventive detention'. Although the main judge in his investigation had decided to release Cagliari, another judge felt it necessary to continue with the questioning and cancelled the release order indefinitely. The bureaucratic blunder had tragic consequences and Cagliari's suicide briefly created a wave of public indignation against the judiciary, who were accused of abusing their powers. But in general the Italian public cherished the nightly televised spectacle of seeing the rich and famous in disgrace or handcuffs. The Italians feasted on *schadenfreude*.

Hundreds of politicians were involved in the 'system'. But because they were protected by a parliamentary immunity from prosecution, they could not be arrested. Like so many other pieces of legislation in Italy, the immunity law was introduced with the best of intentions in 1945 as a safeguard for democracy. Mussolini had frequently arrested politicians who refused to toe the Fascist line. Gradually, however, the immunity law became a shield of impunity, behind which hundreds of deputies could take refuge from the law. Lifting the parliamentary immunity was a lengthy process, involving an application from the judiciary, consideration by parliament's Immunity Commission, a report, a recommendation, and finally a vote in the chamber against which the subject in question could appeal. Every count of an indictment required a new application by the judiciary to lift the immunity. It was a laborious procedure, especially in the case of someone like Bettino Craxi who was investigated under sixteen separate counts.

As the corruption scandal gathered pace the law on parliamentary immunity increasingly caused outrage. Indeed, in May 1993 the chamber of deputies voted to maintain the immunity of Bettino Craxi over corruption charges and the anti-immunisation cause looked doomed. To the Italian public it was as if the former Prime Minister, the chief villain in the scandal, was being protected by his chums. The Palazzo Montecitorio, the home of the lower chamber, and the lavish Hotel Raphael, where Craxi used to reside with his travelling court of sycophants and advisers, were besieged by demonstrators. Carlo Azeglio Ciampi the prime minister at the time, immediately began to prepare legislation to scrap parliamentary immunity.

The corruption scandal unfolded during Italy's eleventh parliament, which turned out to be the shortest in the country's postwar history. By the time the country went to the polls again in March 1994 both chambers of parliament had received 619 different requests from the judiciary to lift the immunity from prosecution. Parliament's information office had become so used to inquiries about which deputy was being investigated for what crime that they compiled a list which they regularly updated. On request the information officer would now deliver two heavy tomes which make hair-raising reading. For instance, Severino Citaristi, a Christian Democrat senator who had been accused of acting as the party's principal collector of bribes, occupied fifteen pages in the catalogue of crimes. He was being investigated in no fewer than 75 cases. Most of them concerned 'an act of corruption that contravenes the duties of office' and 'violation of the law on the public financing of political parties', that is to say, collecting bribes on behalf of the party. Out of 630 deputies in the lower house 228 had received an *avviso di garanzia*, the warrants which notify a suspect that he is under investigation by the judiciary. In the senate the count was 93 out of 315.

A particular feature of Italy's *consociativismo*, the system of government whereby the opposition is given a share of power in return for its acquiescence, was that the Communists – once the biggest Communist Party in the West – were also tainted. As an opposition party the Communists were able to corrupt less easily, but their boast that they were the only squeaky-clean party in Italian politics was absurd. In fact the only political parties still believed to have been immune to the system of corruption were the Radicals of the maverick politician Marco Pannella, the Greens and the neo-Fascist MSI.

There seem to be few, if any, political virgins in Italy. Temptation is always nigh. Even the Northern League, a relatively new party which had established itself as the alternative to 'politics as usual', was investigated for taking bribes from the Montedison conglomerate, the prime temptress of the *tangentopoli* scandal. The sums involved were relatively small – 350,000 dollars – but the way they were handled was amateurish and squalid. The League's treasurer Alessandro Patelli first denied that he had received the money from Carlo Sama, the disgraced chief executive of the Ferruzzi empire, then admitted it but said that the money had been stolen from party headquarters. The episode became farcical when the League's fiery leader Umberto Bossi appeared in court with a cheque for one billion lire, and tried to foist it upon one of the judges. Cheque-book absolution has been tried by numerous politicians and revealed a perturbing misunderstanding not only of the rule of law but of the notion of personal responsibility.

Many Italians I have met in recent years have combined a loathing for their own corrupt system with a sense of indignation that Italy has been singled out as the most corrupt country in 'the democratic world'. It goes without saying that Italy doesn't have a monopoly on sleaze. In Germany, where the same coalition of Christian Democrats and Free Democrats has been in power for thirteen years, accountability has festered, the fungus of corruption has blossomed. In Spain the Socialist Workers' Party of Felipe González has also contributed lavishly to the annals of European corruption. The former deputy Prime Minister Alfonso Guerra used airforce jets to fly him and his family to their holiday destinations. His brother ran a business empire from an office provided free of charge by the party. And last year a woman who worked as a secretary for the Socialists and whose mother had been a housekeeper in the party headquarters rose through the ranks to become the linchpin in a network of bribery. The owner of a number of precious fur coats stored in a special refrigerator at just the right temperature, Señora Aida Alvarez is today a fugitive from justice, accused of having pocketed millions of pesetas in kickbacks for major arm contracts. In 1994 the political élite in France became implicated in a corruption scandal with dramatic consequences. Several ministers were forced to resign and one was arrested because of bribes allegedly paid by industry.

Some reasons for the corruption were no doubt universal. The longer a party stayed in government, clearly the greater the temptation it had to misbehave. This rule has applied to all ruling political parties across the globe. The Italian Christian Democrats first came to power in 1947 and stayed there until 1993, precisely forty-nine years. Corruption had a long time to flourish. The Socialists, the second party of government, deserted the Communists in 1963 and joined the ruling coalition soon afterwards. As we shall see, the Italian political system did not allow for an alternation of power between government and opposition because the Vatican, the United States and the ruling parties worked together to keep the Communists out of office during the Cold War. But in Italy corruption was compounded by other factors.

One was the all-pervasive disrespect for the state and the rule of law. The Italian state, which is only just over a hundred and twenty years old and was abused for twenty years by the Mussolini dictatorship, has never earned the respect from its citizens that it enjoys in France or the United States. In Italy the state is either feared or flouted. It is not the sum of all its citizens but an alien power imposed from above on a society of individuals, families, clans or cliques. This is perhaps one reason why personal contacts, family ties or other social bonds are much more important in Italy than adherence to the laws imposed by the state for the benefit of society. One reason is that the legalistic Italians have produced so many contradictory laws that breaking them is often the only way to escape the tangle. Flouting the law has its down side – the whimsical terrorism of Italian bureaucracy, the unreliable judiciary and other malignant state organs – and can be a nerve-racking business. The solution has always been to take refuge in the tribe. Even politicians see themselves primarily as members of a political party rather than representatives of the state. In Italian politics the party became an extended family or tribe for whose survival, well-being and power it was justified to break the laws of state. This is part of what the Italians call *partitocrazia*, partyocracy or the supreme rule of the parties.

The most common crime of which the suspects in the *tangentopoli* scandal were accused was illegal financing of political parties. They were charged with pocketing millions of dollars in bribes from business to supplement the income of their parties from members' subscriptions. In the United Kingdom, by comparison, there are no laws forbidding the financing of parties through private donations. Had this been Britain, Italian politicians like Bettino Craxi wouldn't even have committed a crime – at least not on this account. But the fact is that in Italy the illegal system of party financing became so costly that it distorted the state's budget. The Enaudi Economic Research Institute in Turin calculated that fifteen per cent of Italy's vast budget deficit – in percentage of gross national product terms, the second largest in the European Union after Belgium, in real terms half as big as the national debt of the United States – was created by *tangente*, or bribes. Almost every business dealing with the state, whether to build a hospital, a motorway or to secure a cleaning contract for an old people's home, was forced to pay a bribe of ten to fifteen per cent of the value of the contract. Naturally the companies marked up the price so as to make up the difference. The ruling parties, which borrowed money at a ludicrous rate, simply paid the inflated prices from which they themselves had benefited. The prices and the system of bribery spiralled out of control until the Italian state could no longer afford it. Meanwhile the distinction between bribes that were destined for party coffers and those that disappeared into personal pockets became increasingly blurred.

As the bitter-sweet perfume of *fin de siècle* decadence wafts through one Western democracy after another, corruption scandals of even greater proportions than Italy's may be in the offing. But for now the Italians have the Gold Medal of Sleaze. The number of people and the sums involved were, so far at least, unique in a Western democracy. So was the political fall-out. No country has dealt with its corrupt politicians in as ruthless a way as Italy did. An entire governing class has been toppled as a result of *tangentopoli*. Political parties went from omnipotence to oblivion in a matter of months. It was the collapse of a regime. But there was one other way in which Italy distinguished itself in the field of corruption: this is the complete lack of personal responsibility exhibited by nearly all the suspects in the scandal. Japanese politicians caught with their hands in the till gave tearful resignation speeches in parliament and committed political hara-kiri in front of their colleagues. French, British and German politicians under investigation all withdrew, overcome by shame or bitterness that they had been more sinned against than sinning. The Italians blamed 'the system' and claimed they were the victims of original sin and universal temptation.

Accusations, charges and sentences that would have been enough to shame politicians elsewhere into a low profile brought out the fighting spirit of some of the most notorious villains in the scandal. Bettino Craxi preferred to stay in his holiday home in Tunisia rather than face an eight-and-a-half-year sentence for fraudulent bankruptcy or a corruption trial over funding of the Milan metro. But from his sumptuous seaside villa at Hammamet in Tunisia the former Prime Minister battled the courts and public opinion by firing off faxes and giving interviews in which he threatened to 'reveal all'. Giulio Andreotti, another former Prime Minister, was preparing to go on trial in September 1995 for Mafia charges, but he still found the time and the serenity of mind to edit a religious monthly called *30 Giorni* (*Thirty Days*). Before he was investigated the former Foreign Minister Gianni De Michelis was well known for enlivening dreary EU summits with his sense of humour. He had also written a guide to the best discothèques in Italy. De Michelis left his position as a chemistry professor at Venice University to enter politics. Following traditional steps he built up a regional power base in his native Veneto and used this to exert his influence on the Socialist Party to which he belonged. At the height of his power De Michelis was revered as the 'Doge' in his native Venice. He married and later divorced a member of one of the most prominent Venetian families, the Bernabaus. De Michelis still lives in a palace on the Grand Canal which happens to be the same palazzo in which Casanova once resided.

In July 1995 De Michelis was found guilty of corruption and got a four-year sentence from a court in Venice. He had been charged with receiving a bride of 500,000 dollars for the construction of a motorway near Venice airport.

Other charges still pending concern the alleged 'rechannelling' of millions of dollars of Third World aid money into the Socialist

Party's coffers. Every business contract that needed the approval of the state and therefore of the political parties required a 'commission'. This was the rule at home as well as abroad. If a company wanted to take part in a lucrative overseas project financed by Italian State Aid it had to pay a *tangente* to the appropriate party. Businessmen thus found themselves in the unenviable position of having to pay bribes not only to the relevant authorities in the country where the project was being funded but also to the political party at home that funded it.

This had less to do with an aggressive Italian trade policy and more with the parties' greedy need to siphon off from business, even if it meant going to the far-flung corners of the world. The system of rake-offs was fair, ensuring that all the major players would get their share and no one was left out. For these purposes the Italian Foreign Ministry had its own imaginary map of neo-colonial influence. Sitting in one of the drafty marble-clad rooms of the Farnesina, the Fascist-built Foreign Ministry, officials carved up the world for the parties they represented. The Christian Democrats controlled most of Latin America. The Socialists were 'allocated' North Africa and much of the Middle East, apart from Libya which was traditionally a fiefdom of the Christian Democrats. The Communists were given Nicaragua, Mozambique and Angola. In each of these fiefdoms a political party not only had the right to appoint its ambassador and other senior diplomatic staff, it also called the shots over aid policy. An Italian business project to China or Chile would most likely have meant a bribe for the Christian Democrats. A contract with 'Socialist' Tunisia benefited the Socialists. The system had been well established by the time Gianni De Michelis became Foreign Minister. He merely perfected it.

The Horn of Africa was one example of Italian aid policy at work. Since Mussolini invaded Abyssinia in 1935 Italy has had a special interest in the region. Ethiopia was given to the Christian Democrats, Somalia to the Socialists. Italian is still widely spoken in Somalia and during the American-led 'Operation Restore Hope' in the country the Rome government took the most unusual step of not toeing Washington's line over the treatment of General Aideed, the renegade warlord who repeatedly escaped

American arrest and finally contributed to the US's swift and clumsy departure from Somalia. But Italy's claims that it knew what was best for Somalia became ridiculous in the light of Italian aid policy towards the country in the 1980s. Between 1981 and 1990 Italy backed 114 projects in Somalia costing a total of one billion dollars. But few of the projects ever took off or served any real purpose other than to generate a 'commission' for the Socialist Party. A 300-mile motorway built in the middle of the desert was occasionally used by zigzagging nomads. A hospital in Mogadishu equipped with state-of-the-art machines soon sank into disrepair. The list of wasted projects is probably as long as in many other developing countries receiving the wrong kind of aid. The difference with Italy was that the conspicuous expenditure was fuelled by the parties' desire for funds. During his four-year stint as Foreign Minister Gianni De Michelis, as we have seen, is accused of having syphoned off hundreds of millions of dollars. His tactical mistake was that he became too greedy. De Michelis started 'colonising' countries that had traditionally belonged to other parties. He appointed his favourites to prestigious ambassadorial postings, flouting the time-honoured rules of seniority, experience and party-political affiliation. Much like the party he belonged to, De Michelis was too greedy and therefore upset the delicate balance of the system. In 1993 the 'Doge' became another grandee fallen from grace. When he emerged from his first pre-trial hearing in Venice he was greeted by a crowd of angry Venetians and excited cameramen, who filmed him getting pelted with tomatoes and insults. The 'Doge' was seen dodging the crowd and scuttling from one canal to the next in search of a water taxi.

The first time I interviewed him was in the lobby of his Rome residence, the Plaza Hotel. Many of Italy's prominent politicians, especially those who were not from Rome, used the capital's luxury hotels like lavish headquarters for their travelling entourage. De Michelis was billeted in the Plaza, Craxi in the Raphael. The Christian Democrats used the Grand and the Excelsior. When the scandal spread, the funds dried up and the parties became impoverished, the apparatchiks moved from five-star to four-star hotels. The Popular Party, the shrivelled successors to the once omnipotent Christian Democrats, held their founding meeting at the humble Santa Chiara Hotel, just round the corner from the papal tailor in the Piazza Minerva. It was also here that the original Popular Party had been founded in 1911 by Dom Sturzo, a Catholic priest. In choosing the grandiose and rather moribund Plaza on the busy Corso, Gianni De Michelis had chosen the ideal backdrop for a guest who embodied the excesses and demise of an old era. I interviewed the former Foreign Minister two weeks before his first encounter with the judges who had charged him.

'Are you still dancing?' I asked the former groover of the European Community Foreign Ministers' Conference. 'This is not a time for dancing,' he replied lugubriously. What did he make of all the charges against him? I asked. 'Absolute rubbish,' he replied in perfect English. 'There was never any corruption, not in my case, at least . . . Yes, we received contributions from business. But that was necessary to run the campaigns, to pay for all the advertising, the posters, the badges, the television. How else were we to compete in elections?' The former Foreign Minister was indignant. His large round face was getting redder. Pearls of perspiration glistened on his nose. 'The only thing we were guilty of was to violate the law on the financing of political parties.' This law allowed for only limited public financing of political parties, which meant that the remaining funds had to be sought elsewhere. The charges arose because of the amounts involved, the methods of extraction, which in many cases amounted to downright extortion.

'Did all the money you received from business end up in the party coffers, or did any of it make its way into a Swiss bank account or into your own pocket?' I asked him. There was a second's silence while I waited for him to combust. When it came, the answer was a simple 'No', an avuncular smile and an explanation. 'You see, Mr Frei, there has been a conspiracy against us,' he went on. 'There is a plot against the Socialists all over Europe, not just in Italy.' He listed a number of his Socialist friends from other countries who had been toppled by corruption allegations. Then he leaned back in the deep armchair, let the Chopin wash over him and, looking me straight in the eye, said: 'Mr Frei, there is an unfortunate appetite for justice in Europe these days!' The underlying theme of Gianni De Michelis's arm-chair discourse on corruption was that justice belongs to those who can get away with it. They were all just 'average sinners'.

3

Average Sinners

A devout Catholic with a knack for witty one-liners, Giulio Andreotti, the seven-time former Prime Minister, once said: 'In Italy there are neither angels nor devils, only average sinners.' The remark seems particularly cynical coming from a politician who has been charged with Mafia collusion, something that could hardly be described as an average sin. Andreotti's wise comment was only possible in a country where not scores but thousands of people had been embroiled in a systematic culture of corruption. The conclusion was: If six thousand people were guilty, then no one was guilty. Italy's corruption suspects enjoyed the safety of numbers and the tolerance of a Catholic society nurtured on the concept of original sin and universal temptation. The rituals of confession, penitence and absolution provided the time-honoured solutions.

The sleaze that flourished in Italy was as varied as the people who benefited from it. The most common category involved the payment of bribes by businesses who wanted to secure public works projects. When you land at Milan's unfinished Malpensa airport you have to think of the billions of illicit lire mixed into the fresh cement. The taste of a cappuccino in Verona is soured by the *tangente*, the bribe that was necessary to build the milk-processing plant. Venice has a water purification plant thanks to murky money. A motorway tunnel in Genoa, which took five years to build and was essential for relieving the city's congested traffic, was finally completed in March 1993. The project had cost 14 million dollars. Unfortunately the tunnel was too low for the lorries that rely on the motorway. Other examples abound and, indeed, it seems no public works project was started anywhere in Italy without someone paying a bribe. The system was straightforward. If a municipal or regional government decided that a new motorway, sewage plant or rail link had to be built, the bidding for the contract was based not on who could present the most competitive deal but who could come up with the biggest bribe.

For companies selling to the state, the bribe was as uneventful as a corporate tax. The difference is that it was one of the few Italian taxes that couldn't be dodged. The system of virtual extortion was described in detail by one of Italy's most famous businessmen, Carlo De Benedetti, the chief executive and main shareholder of the computer giant Olivetti. De Benedetti tried – unsuccessfully as it turned out – to avoid arrest by going directly to the judges with an eleven-page dossier in which he described the payment of bribes. It was a rare admission of personal culpability, albeit one designed to get De Benedetti off the hook. In his dossier he described how party henchmen from the Socialists and the Christian Democrats browbeat, cajoled and blackmailed his company into paying *tangente*.

The message from both parties was: Pay up or no business! De Benedetti pointed out that the Christian Democrats behaved like gentlemen thieves. The Socialists, less burdened by moral pretensions, were gruff extortionists. Much of the Italian economy is owned by the state and therefore controlled by the parties. Before it embarked on a programme of privatisation Italy had the biggest state-sector economy in the European Union. The threat to uncooperative businesses therefore wasn't idle. For those who could afford the bribe, corruption had its rewards. In his confession De Benedetti described how the turnover of one of his office equipment companies with the Post and Telecommunications Ministry increased from 1 billion to 100 billion lire a year in 1984 after paying a bribe of 10 billion lire. Olivetti thus acquired an exclusive contract to supply the ministry with typewriters, photocopiers, computers and other office equipment. Magistrates questioned De Benedetti, who did go to jail in November 1993 – for half a day. As Sergio Romano, a historian and former high-ranking diplomat, pointed out in his book on the roots of corruption in Italy: 'the exchange of bribes for contracts fits neatly into the long-established pattern of relations between Italian industry and politics. These relations were based on compromise: industry helped the rulers of the day to stay in power, the rulers helped private industry to make money.'

The genius of Italian corruption was its pluralism. The bribes were shared out amongst a large number of parties. If possible no one was made to feel left out. This was corruption based on consent; very democratic and strictly in accordance with the country's electoral system of proportional representation. The size of the bribe often corresponded uncannily to the electoral strength of the party that received it. Roberto Mongini, the 'collector' for the Christian Democrats in the Malpensa airport project in Milan, told me how his party had received twenty per cent of the money; the Socialists, who ruled Milan, thirty per cent; the Republicans, who were a small but loyal coalition ally, ten per cent, and so on. The Enimont 'superbribe' of 100 million dollars paid to the political parties in 1991 even took into account the feuding factions of the Christian Democratic Party: 4750 million lire were paid to the faction headed by Arnaldo Forlani, the Secretary of the party; 5000 million lire to Paolo Cirino Pomicino, a former Industry Minister and a leading figure of the Neapolitan faction of the party; 2477 million lire went to the *corrente*, or party-political current, of Giulio Andreotti, whose power base was in Lazio and Sicily. The smaller parties weren't ignored either. The Liberals got 205 million, the Republicans and the Social Democrats each 300 million, and so that the newcomers, the anti-corruption Northern League of Umberto Bossi, could also join the ranks of 'average sinners' they too were given the relatively small but nevertheless compromising sum of 200 million lire, about 120,000 dollars. The bribes were paid by Raul Gardini, head of the Ferruzzi agro-industrial empire. Their purpose was to ensure that he could cancel out all the losses incurred by the merger of his chemical company Montedison with the state's chemical giant ENI. Gardini was Italy's paymaster of bribes. By paying off as many parties and factions as possible, he tried to broaden the base of complicity. Once the racket was unmasked, Gardini, a passionate sailor and playboy with a perpetual tan, preferred to take his own life rather than face the judges and the humiliation of arrest.

The pluralist system of kickbacks mirrored the consensus in parliament. Despite their sense of moral rectitude the Communist opposition also transgressed. Although their corruption was quantitatively smaller than that of the ruling parties they were a minority shareholder in *tangentopoli*. The Communists received bribes but used them to supplement party finances. They were much less prone than politicians from other parties to line their own pockets. The Communists also controlled RAI 3, one of the three-state run television channels, just as the Christian Democrats and the Socialists did. They provided the Speaker of the lower house of deputies. This is an important constitutional position, since the two speakers of the two houses automatically assume the role of heads of caretaker administrations in the protracted absence of a government, a fairly common occurrence in Italy. Business cooperatives set up by the Communist Party shared in lucrative state contracts. Their connivance in, or at least tolerance of, malpractice could be bought. But because they were not in power and therefore not in a position to commission as many public works projects as the Christian Democrats or Socialists, they were forced to be less corrupt. The fact that their reputation was 'cleaner' than that of the other parties may have had more to do with lack of opportunity than with moral rectitude.

The system of corruption was based on a mutually beneficial contract between the political parties and business. The parties needed to pay for election campaigns, party workers and, most importantly, the increasingly lavish lifestyle of the party bosses. In the heyday of *tangentopoli* the party secretaries and their armies of flunkies lived like princes. In her kiss-and-tell account of life with the Italian Socialists the actress Sandra Milo describes the dreary routine of orgiastic parties in exclusive Roman hotels, luxury apartments for hangers-on and the state's executive jets used for private purposes. Businesses didn't mind financing this lifestyle as long as they could increase their yield. The system collapsed not because of moral outrage but because of lower profit margins. At its annual conference in 1992, Confindustria, the Italian Employers' Federation, a naturally conservative body which had shown a self-interested loyalty to the government, turned its back on the parties it had supported for five decades.

There were two reasons. Firstly in a recession the companies could no longer afford to pay the ten to fifteen per cent bribe on major contracts nor ask for the equivalent mark-up in their own prices. Secondly the Italian budget deficit – at 115 per cent of GDP – was no longer just embarrassing. It had become unviable and posed a serious threat to Italy's place in the first division of the European Union. The Maastricht Treaty had just been signed, committing its twelve signatories to a reduction of the budget deficit of six per cent per annum by 1997, in preparation for monetary union. For Italy this meant halving the debt in five years, an impossible task. Facing the prospect of Italy, the wunderkind of the 1980s, lumbering somewhere in Europe's second division with Britain, Spain and Greece, the grandees of Confindustria panicked. They saw their own businesses losing out. Ironically the devaluation of the lira which was one of the consequences of the international dismay with Italy's inability to whittle down its public expenses, led to an export boom. Italian products had become much cheaper. But the damage that had been done by the system of corruption was lasting.

The cost to the taxpayer and to the country's economic health was enormous. It was calculated that between 1980 and 1992 20 billion dollars had been paid out in bribes. Because businesses were allowed to mark up the price the 20 billion were added on to the state's bills for public works projects. The figure corresponds to about fifteen per cent of Italy's colossal budget deficit. The state in turn made up the shortfall by increasing prices for the consumer. A motorway that should have cost 10 billion lire ended up costing 11.5 billion lire. This not only increased Italy's mountain of debt, naturally it also had a trickle-down effect ordinary Italians, who had to pay a higher motorway toll, or an extra 2000 lire to see the Uffizi Gallery in Florence, or an exorbitant electricity bill. The man or woman in the piazza had nothing to gain from the bribes circulating at the top of the pyramid. They were in a different league to Bettino Craxi.

There were two other economic reasons which precipitated the collapse of the system. The international community had lost faith in Italy's ability to get its accounts in order. The American credit ratings institute Moody's downgraded Italy from the top AAA category reserved for the members of the G7 club of indus-trialised powers to the second group, which included countries like Spain and Portugal. The reaction from a country that had always prided itself on being the world's fourth or fifth richest nation, depending on whom you believed, was one of indig-nation.'Who is this Moody, anyway?' snapped the *Repubblica* newspaper. For a whole week columnists and politicians heatedly debated the merits of Moody as if he were some cocky *agent provocateur*.

The fact was that Italy was becoming less creditworthy. In September 1992 the lira was taken out of the European Exchange Rate Mechanism and devalued by approximately twenty per cent. The government of Prime Minister Amato was staring bankruptcy in the face. Stefano Micossi, the head of Confindustria's planning and research staff, told me at the time that the government had been gripped by sheer panic. 'Something had to be done. They had to save money, otherwise we would have faced financial collapse and a massive crisis. You can imagine the social conse-quences.' In fact the government of Giuliano Amato had already begun to cut public spending. But the crisis of the lira left no one in any doubt that the party was over.

The domino effect was dramatic. Unable to borrow more and more money, the ruling parties could no longer afford to finance the system of political patronage which they had set up. They could no longer build motorways, office blocks, tunnels, hospitals or car parks whose sole purpose had been to generate bribes and power. In short they could no longer buy their votes. The other great source of money, especially for the depressed south, was the European Community. The flow of money was reduced by twenty per cent between 1991 and 1993 because of German unifi-cation. The German government spent billions on restructuring the east German economy and reduced the amount of money it was sending to Brussels. As a consequence the European Com-munity's regional development fund, from which the poor and most Mafia-ridden areas of Italy had benefited in the past, sud-denly became no more than a trickle. Money was running out everywhere. The system of corruption hadn't just consisted of a few hefty bribes. It had lubricated the whole machinery of politics from the upper echelons of the parties to the lower ranks where loyal party workers were paid off with jobs, flats or cash. The illicit money even trickled down to the voter in regions like Sicily or Campania where reluctant electors were simply bought off by the parties. For instance during the 1992 national elections the price of a vote the Christian Democratic Party in Naples was 50,000 lire, about 35 dollars. As the party got more desperate in subsequent elections the price of a vote increased but the ability to pay had declined. The party's share of the vote in the Naples municipal elections of November 1993 crashed to five per cent. The *tangente* were the lifeblood of the *partitocrazia*. Without them its metabolism simply packed up. Corruption was largely killed off by its own excesses.

The 'system' had several unhealthy consequences. The first was to undermine Italian democracy. The second was to prevent a freer market and fairer competition. Some would say that it took Italy's instinctive distrust of the free market to create a system based on deals and kickbacks. In that sense the *tangente* was more than a bribe, it was a peace offering to a potential enemy, the modern equivalent of a feudal tithe. Those who couldn't afford to pay it were excluded from the market.

In April 1992 I went to Milan to see one such outcast. Giancarlo Gadola was the owner of Italy's oldest construction company, founded in 1857. The offices of this diminutive but immensely proud entrepreneur were located in a nondescript housing block. The yellowed walls were decorated with photographs of the company's projects: a small sandal factory, an office block, a footbridge. The company clearly wasn't doing very well. Anywhere else in Europe this fact would have been put down to the firm's own failings, but Signor Gadola came up with a different explanation. 'Our business isn't thriving,' he lamented, 'because we haven't got the funds to pay the *tangente* that get you the big projects. All the lucrative public works projects in Milan demand a *tangente*.' Gadola, who was perched on a huge swivel chair, then became angry. 'My family refuses to take out loans to pay bribes.' The construction industry was one of the most difficult sectors for an honest entrepreneur to thrive in, since the most lucrative contracts came from the state, and therefore from the greedy parties. But the point was that this company had probably been denied its share of the market because it wasn't corrupt.

It has become a common refrain in Italian industry to lament the absence of a genuine free market. Carlo De Benedetti, for instance, has frequently lamented the lack of a free market in Italy. In an interview in 1992, well before he was himself sucked into *tangentopoli*, he told me: 'We Italians dislike genuine competition amongst ourselves . . . in politics as well as in economics.' This was ironic since De Benedetti was one of those who had benefited from the system of kickbacks. More recently ex-Prime Minister Silvio Berlusconi based part of his election campaign on promises to create a genuine free market 'that would allow small businesses, the backbone of this country's economy, to prosper'. To prove the point, Berlusconi brought some prominent Italian free marketeers into government. Antonio Martino, the Foreign Minister, was a professor of economics and a discipline of Milton Friedman, the Free Market guru. Lamberto Dini, the Treasury Minister, another economics professor and former central banker, was also a committed free marketeer. But none of these appointments, nor any of the campaign rhetoric, could fudge over the fact that Berlusconi's own business empire had thrived on the absence of a free market. The media tycoon controlled a virtual monopoly of commercial television. His supermarket and retail chain Standa had caused the death of thousands of the small corner shops and businesses for whose prosperity Berlusconi had vowed to fight. At heart Berlusconi either misunderstood or mistrusted the free market. For example, when his government ran into trouble, thanks to problems largely of its own making, the financial markets gave the lira another beating. Berlusconi, however, preferred to blame the decline in the currency's value on a conspiracy against his government rather than on the cut and thrust of the market.

The lack of a free market may have been a misfortune for small businesses, but it didn't hinder the Italian economy from blooming. Compared to the United Kingdom or Germany, Italy's recession was short-lived. By mid-1994 growth rates had risen above two and a half per cent; and thanks to the low value of the lira, Italian exports were booming. To some this proved that Italy was still a success story despite its widespread corruption. But to say this is to ignore the upheaval created by the collapse of the old regime. This created genuine political instability and rattled the brittle foundations of Italian democracy. It also left visible scars on Italy's spectacular landscape and cultural heritage. This is a sad and lengthy catalogue of mutilation. The story of ancient Rome was told in marble, granite and travertine, that of modern Italy in reinforced concrete, cement and asphalt. A whole coffee-table book could be filled with tales of the motorway stumps, the unused canals, the abandoned building sites that litter the Italian landscape.

The further south you head, the less harmless the abuses. En route from Rome's Fiumicino airport to the centre, an uncompleted clover-leaf sprouts out of a cabbage field, next to the existing motorway, like some luxuriant cement triffid. This excrescence of modern civic engineering has been there for ten years. It is a building site without builders. The roads look like amputated stumps. Metal girders stick out at odd angles like bristles. Meanwhile the never-ending construction site on the existing motorway creates a nerve-racking traffic jam. Beyond the stranded clover-leaf is a collection of what look like futuristic grain silos. In fact these are housing blocks. The protest banners and flags hanging from the windows next to lines of washing denounce the local housing authorities and plead for better accommodation. The silos are inhabited by humans. Most Italian cities are ringed by housing developments that have never even experienced a bat's squeak of *dolce vita*.

The stunning coastlines of Calabria, Puglia and Sicily are likewise scarred with unfinished multi-storey car-parks or tower-blocks. One of the most shocking examples of the surreal genius of overconstruction is the bay of Palermo. At the end of a sweeping valley that hangs like a hammock between two mountain ranges, this bay was once one of the most beautiful in Italy. Even allowing for the urban expansion of Palermo, a city of one and a half million inhabitants, there is no excuse for the abandoned housing estates that stick to the mountainside like solidified lava.

The houses, built on a perilous slope, were never meant to be lived in. Their *raison d'être* was to generate business for the local construction company in the hands of the Mafia and a bribe for a politician, also in the hands of organised crime. The superstrada from Palermo to San Giuseppe Iato that traverses the bay is built on five-metre pylons, even though it crosses no rivers or valleys. The motorway could just as well have been built on the ground. The pylons were an ingenious way of using more cement and therefore generating more money and bigger bribes. Cement also rules in Sicily. Just two hundreds yards from where the anti-Mafia judge Giovanni Falcone, his wife and their five bodyguards were killed by a car bomb in May 1992 is a sign put up by the Sicilian cement company, bidding visitors welcome to the island. The bomb, which had been planted in a drainage shaft under the motorway, left a crater that was two metres deep and thirty wide. Within days the crater was filled, the motorway patched up. The Mafia, they say, is in construction. The bomb not only removed the country's leading anti-Mafia judge, it also created more demand for cement.

Broadly speaking, what distinguishes Southern Italy from the north is that the bribe was not only used as a lubricant for business, it was often its sole purpose. Since 1992 more than 400 city and town councils have been dissolved in Italy because of corruption charges. In almost every case the charge concerned construction projects. It was an epidemic that infected every part of the country, the self-consciously moralistic north, as much as the self-abasingly derelict south. In the city of Varese, in the foothills of the Alps, the entire assembly of forty councillors, Socialists and Christian Democrats, were suspended and ended up spending a brief spell in the very object of their alleged greed: the municipal jail, built with billions of lire in bribes. In this case, at least, corruption did create genuine demand.

Much of Italy is littered with what the Italians call *catedrali nel deserto*, cathedrals in the desert, the white elephants of construction that swallowed billions of dollars in public money only to be abandoned. The St Peter's amongst these cathedrals is the European container port at Gioia Tauro in Calabria. This is a monument to corruption, mismanagement, delusions of grandeur and misplaced hopes amongst the local population. What was once one of Calabria's most fertile agricultural plains filled with orange orchards and with some of the peninsula's oldest olive trees is now a vast expanse of concrete, empty and desolate. The trees were mowed down in 1969 to make room for fifty square kilometres of industrial park. The centre-piece was going to be one of Italy's largest steel mills. Gioia Tauro was selected over eleven other potential sites against all technical advice. The area had no port, it was predominantly and profitably agricultural and had no industrial tradition. There was no substantial demand for steel within a two-hundred-kilometre radius and Gioia Tauro was situated in a high-risk earthquake zone. None of these arguments mattered. They were outweighed by the needs of the local Christian Democratic and Socialist Party bosses for public money to renew their sources of patronage and thus their power.

After the 1973 oil crisis the demand for steel in Europe dropped sharply. But work continued on the infrastructure of the project which had become one of the most expensive skeletons in the country. The nearby industrial zone lies vacant. Oto Breda, the arms manufacturer, built a plant in the 1980s to produce a new Nato missile. By the time the plant had been finished, the missile had been superseded. Later projects to build a power station were first thwarted by the local environmental lobby and then by the involvement of the local Mafia, the 'Ndrangheta, who were angry that they weren't getting their cut of the business. Gioia Tauro has one of the highest rates of infiltration by organised crime, with around sixty 'Ndrangheta families operating in the area. In 1990 magistrates froze all construction contracts on suspicion that the business had gone to front companies of the 'Ndrangheta. In January 1993 thirty-nine people were arrested on corruption charges in connection with the power station, including the chairman of ENEL, the Italian state electricity company.

Today an artificial port is linked to the neighbouring town of Gioia Tauro by a country road that turns into a dirt track, a cruel irony when you consider that so many deserted parts of the region, which never even had the dimmest hope of industrialisation, are endowed with a three-lane autostrada. First you come across an abandoned village of workers' huts, made with corrugated iron. Then you see a trawler beached on a sandy dune, rusting into oblivion. From the dune you get a spectacular view of five kilometres of virgin quayside. In the distance three large blue cranes stand idle. To their right a vast container park. It's completely empty but for one burnt-out petrol truck stranded right in the middle. The salty wind whistles across the industrial plain. The only human activity is two urchins driving their flock of sheep across the building site of the steel mill, now covered by a threadbare carpet of grass. A lone fisherman, sitting on a yellow mooring post, lazily flicks his rod into the still and serene waters of what should have been Europe's biggest container port. So far the billions of dollars sunk into the project have only produced a handful of arrest warrants and a lot of disillusionment amongst the local population.

The empty building site stands in lurid contrast to the ramshackle town of Gioia Tauro, a name which means 'Jewel of Taurus', inappropriate in 1994 but, I suspect, not in 500 BC. Although the town started its urban life as an ancient Greek settlement, it bears an alarming resemblance to a South African township. Most of the labour in the nearby orange plantations is provided by black African immigrants from Ghana or Senegal. You will not find any immigrants in the few local bars, restaurants or in the Benetton clothes shop on the main road. At dusk, when they have returned from the plantation, the workers huddle around small camp-fires on the side of the road. They live in abandoned cottages or makeshift huts. Despite their squalid existence these are the only people in Gioia Tauro actually doing any work. They get paid 50,000 lire a day, about £22, much less than an Italian worker could ask for.

The male population of Gioia Tauro still pins its fading hopes to the container port. 'Five thousand jobs, one-quarter of the local population, that's what they promised us when they came to chop down the orange trees in 1965.' Giancarlo Calucci, a local journalist, told me that the project was only temporarily on hold. 'Once they have sorted out all this political mess,' he continued, 'they'll carry on working. They've got to.' What Giancarlo didn't want to admit to himself was that the only reason for building a container port in Gioia Tauro, hundreds of miles from any industrial or commercial centre, was political. Once the political system that produced the building site had imploded, the project too was doomed.

4

Couch Confessions
of an
Ancien Régime

Until he was sacked on 22 April 1992, Dr Piero Rocchini rejoiced in the title of Health Consultant for Clinical Psychology to the Italian Chamber of Deputies. Dr Rocchini, who is in his forties and has a dense beard and glasses with thick lenses, worked for ten years on the medical staff that ensured that Italy's parliamentarians were in the best shape to represent the needs and wishes of the people who had elected them. The medical and psychological care was free of charge, a service provided by the taxpayer. Having listened to the fears, dreams and desires of over 200 deputies who had regularly sought the solace of his couch in his practice behind the Colosseum, Piero Rocchini became deeply anxious. What he found was a parliament on the edge of a nervous breakdown: tired deputies unable to carry out their duties because they kept waking up at night in a cold sweat, an increasing number of persecution complexes, identity crises, cyclic depression, nervous rashes and chain-smoking. Tranquillisers had become the most popular item sold over the counter at the parliament's own in-house chemist.

Dr Rocchini has never revealed the names of his honourable clients. But in April 1992 he wrote of their collection of symptoms in an article. He wanted to warn the Italians about the mental state of their elected assembly. Unfortunately this was seen as an act of gross indiscretion which incurred the wrath of his patients and led to his dismissal. The position was never filled again. With more time on his hands the doctor then turned his mind to a book: *Le Nevrosi del Potere* (*The Neurosis of Power*). It was published and the launch party was held in a hotel next to parliament.

Many of the guests were Rocchini's patients. In fact most of the deputies have remained on the doctor's register, unable to sever the strong emotional bond that they had established over the years with their confessor. Out of power and in disgrace, many seek his advice these days about how to deal with the stresses of unemployment. With one-third of the outgoing parliament in 1994 under investigation for everything from bribery to links with the Mafia, only a handful of Rocchini's patients were re-elected.

In 1992, just as the old party-political regime was collapsing, the doctor was dealing with different stresses. His surgery always got overcrowded during election campaigns. In the weeks before the spring elections of 1992, which have gone down in Italian history as the calamitous '5 Aprile', the parliamentary shrink was in greater demand than ever. The deputies' anxieties were justified: the Christian Democrats and the Socialists, the parties that had exercised an almost divine right to rule for decades, suffered their worst ever haemorrhage of votes. According to Dr Rocchini's diagnosis, this reflected the breakdown of communications between the politicians and the people they represented.

While the umbilical cord between the electors and the elected was being severed, another emotional tie was getting stronger and stronger. The patients' energies were concentrated to an unhealthy degree on the relationship with their party. This gave rise to what Dr Rocchini called the *Partito Mamma Syndrom*, the 'Party Mum Syndrome'. The party had become the ersatz Mother, or in the doctor's words, 'a perverse place of refuge, a kind of political womb, which allows the deputy to play out his private fantasies'. Devotion to the party was so great that it stifled any other affiliations or affections. The deputy was unable to conduct normal relations with his family, his friends and most importantly his voters. This politically induced Oedipus complex was seen by the opponents of Italy's *partitocrazia* as one reason why the all-powerful parties had become so corrupt and lost touch with that part of the electorate that merely voted for them, but that didn't owe its job, bribe or other material benefits to a party.

The party wasn't just Mamma. She was also an increasingly fickle mistress, thanks to an electoral law that was passed in

1991. This produced the so-called 'Single Preference Syndrome', perhaps the only time in the history of psychology that an electoral law has created a neurosis. The law abolished the system whereby voters were allowed to list four preferred candidates from one party. Now they could list only one. The struggle to be *numero uno* led to furious bouts of jealousy, infighting, intrigue and back-stabbing between those deputies who were nurtured, as it were, by the same Mamma. In a survey conducted by the Centre for Socio-Psychological Studies amongst 250 politicians from five Italian cities, it emerged that the interviewees feared their own parties more than the opposition.

But by far the most serious psychological disorder, afflicting the Italian parliament was the so-called *Di Pietro Syndrom*. Dr Rocchini named it after Antonio Di Pietro, the Milan magistrate who has led the judicial crusade against corruption. When the extent of corruption was first uncovered and Antonio Di Pietro started issuing the famous *avvisi di garanzia*, warrants that notify a subject that he or she is under criminal investigation and may soon be taken into preventive police custody, Dr Rocchini's work-load also increased exponentially. His couch became crowded with parliamentarians fearing disgrace.

In spring 1992 the Socialist Sergio Moroni resorted to suicide as the only way out of his humiliation. Under parliament's immunity law protecting deputies from arrest – unless waived by a majority vote in the assembly – he was in no danger of going to jail. But he had been issued with a warrant. His was the first in a long line of suicides, provoked by the stresses of the corruption scandal. After Onorevole Moroni's death a collective nightmare began to keep parliament awake. 'My patients started having recurring dreams,' Dr Rocchini said. 'They're locked in a house at night. There's a loud knock on the door. The door is suddenly flung open and a policeman is waiting outside with a pair of handcuffs. In another common nightmare my patients dream that they are being led in handcuffs from an expensive restaurant filled with their family and friends.' The dreams were remarkably lifelike and, it seemed, prophetic. Perhaps they were inspired by a guilt complex, whose origins may be explained by the findings of another survey conducted by the Centre for Socio-Psychological

Studies. Asked why they wanted to go into politics in the first place, thirty-eight per cent of the politicians said they did so in pursuit of power and public office, thirty-four per cent admitted they were in it just for the money and only sixteen per cent said they became politicians because they believed in the ideological principles represented by their parties. A remarkable display of honesty for a group one-third of whose members were under indictment.

By 1992, the year in which Dr Rocchini's couch was fully booked, Italy's regime had degenerated into a smouldering decadence. The psychiatrist's couch had become the symbolic deathbed of the *partitocrazia*. It was easy to forget the fact that Italy had prospered under that system. Whether because or in spite of the *partitocrazia* – to this day people can't really make up their minds – Italy emerged from Fascism and civil war to become a stable democracy and one of the seven wealthiest nations in the world. The system under which it achieved this was one of the most bizarre acts of political acrobatics in modern history. Like the Tower of Pisa that leans more and more every year but never seems to fall, Italy's 'democratic regime' defied almost every rule in the handbook of democracy. Between 1945 and 1992 the country had fifty-two governments, creating the impression of permanent chaos among those who haven't understood the genius of the system. In fact the chaos masked a rigid continuity that verged on rigor mortis. Every government was dominated by one party: the Christian Democrats. This was one of many paradoxes. Another was that Italy's election results seldom changed despite a consistently high turn-out and a lively political debate. For millions of Italians voting became a regular ritual, as ceremonial and meaningless as going to Midnight Mass on Christmas Eve. A two per cent swing in results for or against the Socialists or Christian Democrats was considered a political earthquake. But however violent the tremors, the tectonic plates of Italy's coalition governments barely shifted. Political scientists have explained this rigidity in two ways: firstly Italian voters used to see their votes less as a means of political change which enabled them to throw out a government they didn't like, than as a statement of creed. Many Italians adopted a political party for life, just as the party often adopted them for life too. The livelihoods of millions of voters depended on the patronage of one party or another. The town of Crotone in Calabria was a case in point. The town's only large-scale employer was the local sulphur factory. The factory was run by a Christian Democrat who had been placed there by the party. The party was seen as the local benefactor and most of the factory's employees and their families voted for the Christian Democrats.

The system was quasi-feudal. The ruling parties carved up the country's bloated public sector from the steel industry to the railways as if they were private fiefdoms. This culture of patronage created its own vocabulary of political abuse, as peculiarly Italian as it was untranslatable. One of the key concepts was *sottogoverno*, literally 'undergovernment'. This was the alternative power structure which had been nurtured by the parties to provide them with patronage and votes. Although it was set up by the governing parties, it undermined the influence of government itself. The executive was less important than the parties. The purpose of government was not so much to legislate as to preserve the fiefdoms set up by the parties and to ensure that the spoils were shared out fairly. *Sottogoverno* was created by *lottizzazione*, or 'parcelling out'. This was the widespread practice of giving jobs to the boys, even if the boys weren't particularly qualified. Perhaps the most bizarre word in the warped vocabulary of Italian power was *trasformismo*, or 'transformism'. The term was coined after Italian unification in the 1860s and describes the traditional acquiescence of the opposition to the party of government. It stems from the instinctive fear of conflict and the preference for compromise which has become a ground rule of Italian politics. This was another Italian paradox. Despite the fact that the ideological fault-line of the Cold War ran right through Italian society, with Catholic Conservatives in government and the biggest Communist Party in the West in perpetual opposition, the two had reached a *modus operandi* soon after 1948, when the Christian Democrats swept the elections and established themselves as the ruling party. In the late 1970s the Communists stopped being a genuine party of opposition and became a minority shareholder in the system of patronage. Italy was thus deprived of an alternation between government and opposition. When the electorate did change in 1992, they threw out the whole regime.

The extraordinary continuity of Italian post-war politics is best exemplified by a man who was a founding member of the Christian Democratic Party in 1942 and took up his first full cabinet post in 1957. He served his last term as President of the Council of Ministers in 1992, the last Christian Democrat to do so before the party was disbanded and reborn as the Popular Party. Giulio Andreotti had helped to write Italy's 1946 Constitution, he sat in thirty out of fifty-three post-war cabinets, he was Prime Minister seven times, including once at the time of the murder of another Christian Democrat Prime Minister, Aldo Moro, by Red Brigade terrorists in 1978. He was also a devout Catholic, went to Mass every morning at seven and once wrote a book entitled *Popes I Have Known*. There were four! This close association with God and his highest representatives on earth, however, did not protect Andreotti from what the Italians call *odore di mafia*, the smell of the Mafia. At the time of completing this book, Andreotti was preparing to go on trial for alleged collusion with the Mafia, a fact which earnt him the dubious honour of being perhaps the only statesman in the world commonly referred to as 'Beelzebub' in the press. Before losing his parliamentary immunity from prosecution in 1993 he had already fought off twenty-six separate parliamentary inquiries into a variety of peccadillos concerning the abuse of power and corruption. He has always been suspected of forming a pact with the Devil, and once upon a time was even mildly flattered by these whispers. 'I have been blamed for every possible disaster in Italian history,' he once lamented, 'with the possible exception of the Punic Wars [264–241 BC]. And that's because I was too young at the time.'

Andreotti has survived every other European statesman of his time. His longevity used to impress Italians, who saw in him the incarnation of a quality that they have always highly valued: *furbo*, or cunning. He proved to be a masterful negotiator during all night sessions of the European Community and more than a match to someone like Margaret Thatcher. He was also a rounded personality with diverse interests. Gifted with an elegant but simple Italian, he wrote a weekly newspaper column and several biographies. But none of their plots could compete in intricacy and suspense the real plot of Andreotti's life.

The 'Old Fox' was also a quintessential Roman. One could imagine him as the wise and cunning senator in ancient Rome, wearing a large ring filled with white powder, or as a cardinal at the Vatican, the *éminence gris*, behind a weak pope. The more power Andreotti possessed, the more discreetly he wielded it. His other nickname was *zio*, or uncle. Until recently Andreotti used to conduct an avuncular morning ritual that seemed more like a scene from *The Godfather*. At the crack of dawn he gathered a group of his closest advisers and friends in his bathroom to discuss world affairs, party politics or just gossip. While the others sat on stools or the edge of the bath, Andreotti himself would lean back in a reclining chair and be shaved by his favourite Roman barber. Once the conclave was over he would go to Mass in his local church in Rome's Via Giulia. Andreotti was a peculiarly Roman mixture of Machiavelli and incense. Half of his schoolmates have become bishops or cardinals. He became the high priest of the *partitocrazia*.

Now shrivelled by illness and abandoned by his party and friends, he still stalks the upper chamber as one of seven life senators. A gaunt and ghostly figure with an increasingly hunched back, he has become the death mask of the old regime. Some of the charges against him seem literally unbelievable. Andreotti is currently under investigation for allegedly ordering the murder in 1979 of Mino Pecorelli, an investigative journalist and blackmailer who claimed that Andreotti had allowed his friend and colleague Aldo Moro to be killed by the Red Brigades. According to one theory – and there are many – Moro had opened the way for the Italian Communist Party to participate in government, a fact that enraged the United States.

If the Mafia turncoat Baldassare Di Maggio is to be believed, Andreotti not only let himself be manipulated by organised crime, he also allowed himself to be kissed by its bosses. Di Maggio told judges how he had personally witnessed a meeting between Andreotti and the boss of all the bosses, Toto Riina – currently in jail – in Palermo in 1988. At that meeting Riina is alleged to have kissed Andreotti on the right cheek, an avuncular but highly symbolic Mafia gesture, which establishes the superiority of the kisser over the kissed. The former Prime Minister has rejected these charges as ludicrous and part of a plot to ruin him. When I interviewed him in his office, filled with thousands of pages of evidence that he hopes will prove his innocence, 'the uncle' – who was wearing slippers and a cardigan – dismissed Di Maggio as a 'poor old fellow', who had been forced to lie in order to stay in the state's witness protection programme.

Even if they are completely groundless, Andreotti is partly responsible for the allegations. Massimo Franco, his biographer and a personal friend, told me that 'Andreotti consciously nurtured the mystique around him by promoting a sense of ambiguity about everything he did. He has become the victim of his own ambiguity.' Part of this mystique is in an archive, kept in a cellar somewhere in Rome, where all the dark secrets and shady names of the First Republic have been stored by the former Vatican archivist. Rome is full of journalists, newspaper readers and politicians in awe of Andreotti's personal archive, crammed full of potential incriminations. Of course the archive may not exist outside the minds of most Italians. Perhaps that was the intention? The implied threat, which Andreotti has never spelt out himself but which others have made on his behalf, is that some of these secrets will become public should the former Prime Minister be put on trial. The archive has become like the secret Italian state library of dirt and a Delphic oracle: a universal key to understanding the mysterious bombs, kidnappings and murders of illustrious persons that scar Italian history and that have never been fully explained. It is thus part of the rich undercurrent of mysteries and conspiracies that flows through Italian politics and that expresses a common obsession with hidden truths. The Italians even have a word for this: *dietrologia*, literally 'behindology'.

The elder statesman embodied the shape of post-war Italian government. Power was a mysterious and mercurial commodity that was founded on patronage and the ability to manipulate factions within one's party. Andreotti was the master juggler, supple, subtle and highly astute. He wove together the different factions within his party with great skill, making them dependent on each other and him. There was little room for moral high-

47

mindedness. Since Andreotti's power-base within the Christian Democratic Party was both his native Rome and Sicily, where many members of his faction came from, it is highly unlikely that he could have avoided dealing with the Mafia. They controlled his electoral fiefdom and its votes. Cosa Nostra on the other hand would not have delivered millions of votes without demanding some payment in return. The only proof to underpin this, and it is a tenuous one at that, was the murder of Salvo Lima by the Mafia two years ago. Lima was shot outside his home in the elegant Palermo seaside suburb of Mondello. At the time he was a Christian Democratic member of the European parliament and an intimate friend of Giulio Andreotti, who has always defended his reputation. Lima was widely thought to be the man responsible for delivering the Sicilian vote. In return he bought the laxity of certain judges towards mafiosi who had been caught, and secured their release on appeal. When he failed to deliver a raft of trial annulments and favourable appeals after the Maxi trial of 1987, in which hundreds of mafiosi were sentenced simultaneously, he was killed. He was unable to keep his part of the deal because in 1990 his party no longer had the power over the judiciary that it once enjoyed.

Andreotti exercised power through nudges and winks. The biggest price that he would probably have had to pay for the Mafia's votes and cooperation was to leave the organisation alone. The secret of his power was not that he tried to impose his will on everyone around him, but that he left them to their own resources. In that too, he embodied the old regime. One of the biggest crimes of the old political élite was that they didn't govern. They allowed malignancy to spread in the interests of preserving power within their own party. 'Power only tires those who do not possess it,' the sibylline Andreotti once said, when asked how he had managed to stay at the helm for so many decades. The reason is that his type of power demanded the minimum exertion. It was power without responsibility.

To understand how he came to be the master practitioner in such a warped system one has to return to the making of Italy after the collapse of Fascism. Don Giulio, was brought into politics by his mentor and Italy's greatest post-war leader, Alcide De

Gasperi. In the 1930s and early 1940s De Gasperi was the chief archivist of the Vatican Library in Rome. One of his assistants was Andreotti, a young devout Catholic who was as studious as he was reclusive. De Gasperi would speak to God and Andreotti to the priest. A Roman by birth, Andreotti had a humble upbringing. His father, an elementary school teacher, died when Giulio was only two. He was brought up in religious schools and had his first personal encounter with a pope at the age of eight when he crashed an audience that Pope Pius XI was giving for a Belgian delegation. As a student Andreotti became a member of the Catholic Graduate's Association together with Aldo Moro, the former Prime Minister killed by the Red Brigades in 1978. Both were recruited by De Gasperi into the Christian Democratic Party soon after it had been founded in Milan in September 1942.

The party itself was not new but recycled. Its ancestor was the Popular Party, a mass Catholic party founded in 1911 and modelled on the German Zentrums Partei. The Popular Party had been killed off in 1926 by internal divisions, by Fascist repression – Mussolini banned all opposition parties in 1926 – and by the fact that the Vatican, the party's main source of influence and inspiration, was coming to terms with the Duce. Three years later this resulted in the Lateran Treaties that gave the Catholic Church massive financial compensation for the properties it had lost during Italian unification in the previous century and established the Vatican City as an independent state.

Alcide De Gasperi, who had been the last General Secretary of the Popular Party, was motivated first by anti-Fascism – he had been imprisoned by the Fascists in 1927 – and then by anti-Communism. Once Fascism collapsed in most of Italy in 1943, De Gasperi considered the battle between Communism and Christianity the principle struggle of his lifetime. He saw it as a war between two visions: the broad social solidarity of the Catholic Church on one side and the domination of one class by another, as interpreted by Marxism, on the other. De Gasperi wanted to turn the Christian Democrats into a Catholic party of the masses, appealing to capitalists and landowners as much as to workers and peasants. He managed to achieve this thanks to a lot of help from two quarters: the Vatican and the Allies who occupied Italy at the end of the Second World War.

Pope Pius XII, who was elected in 1939, ideally wanted to see Italy become a Franco-style dictatorship, undemocratic and very Catholic. When he realised that this was impossible he started casting around for political support elsewhere. Gradually and somewhat begrudgingly he adopted the Christian Democrats as the Church's party. He helped it in several crucial ways. In 1944 after the liberation of Rome by the Allies the Vatican instructed priests to speak out in favour of the Christian Democrats, and encouraged Catholic groups like Catholic Action or the Coldiretti, a peasant's association, to give their allegiance to the fledgling Christian Democratic Party. Within weeks the party was handed the support of millions of Italian Catholics and their grass-roots organisations on a platter. Much of this support came from rural and urban working-class associations. The fact that they backed the Catholic right as opposed to the left undermined the Communist Party's hold on large swathes of the working population, especially in the staunchly Catholic Veneto region, Lazio, the Campania and much of the south. This too was part of the *trasformismo* instinct, the ability to create a consensus amongst people or groups who in other countries would have battled each other. The Christian Democrats not only championed socially progressive issues like land reform and the rights of factory workers, they also appealed to the traditional instincts of Italy's family culture with a 'mission to restore the family to health and morality' after the devastation and uprooting of the war. This campaign was aimed above all at women and it later reaped its dividends in the 1946 elections, the first in Italian history in which women were allowed to vote. Significantly the Communist Party also tried – far less convincingly – to become the champion of a wholesome family life. But it did more to expose the Communists to ridicule. Father Lombardi, known as 'God's microphone', made his broadcasting career by pointing up the differences between the Communists' family policy and Marxist belief that the family should be abolished.

If the Vatican gave the Christian Democrats moral help, the Allies, in particular the Americans, provided invaluable material assistance. As the British historian Paul Ginsborg has described in his excellent book on post-war Italy, Washington played a crucial role in ensuring that the foundations of modern Italy were built on Christian Democracy. As early as June 1945 Joseph Drew, the then acting Secretary of State, had written: 'Our objective is to strengthen Italy economically and politically so that the truly democratic elements of the country can withstand the forces that threaten to sweep them into a new totalitarianism.' For totalitarianism read Communism. Acting through the United Nations Rehabilitation and Relief Administration in 1946, Washington was already providing the majority of imports into Italy. Furthermore the committee that ran the UNRRA in Italy was headed by the American chief of mission and by a close associate of De Gasperi who was also the brother of the future Pope Paul VI. The brunt of American intervention in Italy's internal affairs, however, came to be felt after 1947. There were two reasons for this. Firstly the Christian Democrats and De Gasperi were rapidly losing support amongst the electorate. The rate of inflation had risen to an alarming fifty per cent in the first six months of 1947; and in February the Peace Treaty was finally signed. It was a massive blow to De Gasperi's prestige: Italy lost all her colonies including those acquired before the First World War; the country had to pay reparations worth 360 million dollars to Russia, Greece, Albania and Ethiopia amongst others; the Istrian peninsula went to Yugoslavia and the city of Trieste was not to remain Italian but became a so-called free territory under international supervision. Regional elections in Sicily showed that the damage to the Christian Democrats was severe, and national elections were due in 1948. Meanwhile the Americans had formulated the Truman Doctrine. The Cold War had begun. Everything needed to be mobilised to ensure a victory of the right. And it was.

In the first three months of 1948 the United States dedicated 176 million dollars in interim aid to Italy, while the American embassy and the Christian Democrat authorities made sure that this injection of money received the most intense publicity. The arrival of every hundredth ship bearing food, clothes and medicines was celebrated in a variety of ports from Genoa to Reggio Calabria. The goods were then loaded onto special 'friendship trains', often accompanied by the American ambassador. If clarification were still needed, George Marshall declared on 20 March 1948 that the plan that bore his name would stop immediately for Italy if the Communists won the elections. Meanwhile the Western Allies managed to remove the worst clause of the infamous Peace Treaty, by promising the Italians months before the elections that Trieste was after all to be Italian.

Hollywood was also enlisted in the election campaign. Film stars recorded messages denouncing the Communists. Over a million letters were sent by Italian immigrants to family members in the 'old country', urging them to vote anti-Communist, i.e. Christian Democrat. And in a cosmetic but effective gesture the US fleet in the Mediterranean reinforced its presence around Italy. American warships anchored off the coast of Naples, just in case the wrong party was elected.

The Vatican weighed in behind the Americans. On 29 March 1948 Pius XII told the Romans that 'the solemn hour of their Christian conscience had sounded'. The episcopate warned that 'it was a mortal sin to vote for lists and candidates who do not give sufficient assurances of respecting the rights of God, the Church and mankind', in other words the Communists. Local parish priests echoed the message from the pulpit, virtually threatening deviants with excommunication. The Christian Democrats waged a crude campaign, exaggerating the threat of Communism and fuelling the fears it produced. One poster showed a giant Stalin trampling on the 'wedding cake', the white marble monstrosity in the centre of Rome that was built as a monument to Victor Emmanuel II and Italian unification. The party also enlisted the help of the stomach. 'Don't think,' one poster proclaimed, 'that you'll be able to flavour your pasta with the speeches of Togliatti [leader of the Communist Party]. All intelligent people will vote for De Gasperi because he has obtained free from the Americas the flour for your spaghetti and the sauce you put on it.' The culinary propaganda paid off. The Christian Democrats received 48.5 per cent of the vote and 305 out of 574 seats in the chamber of deputies, an absolute majority.

Although the Christian Democrats were never again to repeat such stunning results, the elections of 1948 and the help provided by the Vatican and the United States established them as the party of government for the next four decades. Equally important to the future shape of Italy was the behaviour of the Communists. Essentially this was one of acquiescence towards their electoral enemies, the Christian Democrats. The Communists never managed to capitalise on the fact that they dominated the anti-Fascist Resistance Movement and the several hundred thousand Italians who took part in it. Under the leadership of Palmiro Togliatti, they abandoned working-class militancy and started the transformation from a revolutionary movement to a mass party. The decision was made, much to the dismay of the more eager and dogmatic comrades, at a meeting in Salerno in 1944. It became known as *svolta di Salerno*, the turning point of Salerno, and set the party on a course of cooperation rather than confrontation. Like future leaders of the Communist Party, Togliatti was hamstrung by the Western Allies, whose troops were still based in northern Italy as late as 1947, and by the hold of the Catholic Church over the Italians. The Communist 'Church' simply couldn't compete, a fact which Togliatti admitted when he arrived in Rome in 1944. 'We the Communist Party have declared, and I repeat this declaration here in Rome, the capital of the Catholic world, that we respect the traditional faith of the majority of Italian people.' Meanwhile Togliatti was convinced that the Christian Democrats, who had managed to capture the support of a significant part of the working class, were committed to social reform. This turned out to be a mistake, but the fact that the Communist leadership was fooled had as much to do with their own delusions as with De Gasperi's ability to exploit them. Even after Stalin had called the Italian Communists to heel in the first Comintern in 1947, Togliatti, who had been Minister of Justice under De Gasperi, refused to adopt the path of militancy and chose to fight the Christian Democrats on their own terms, namely at the ballot box. As we have seen, the playing field was far from level.

From then on the Italian Communist Party was torn apart by the need to preserve its left-wing identity and the desire to become accepted as a mainstream party of government. It became a masterpiece of ambiguity. Others called it institutionalised schizophrenia. As it moved from ideology to pragmatism, the only way to preserve the unity of the party was through some masterful intellectual juggling. In this the party leadership was helped by Italy's chief philosopher, Antonio Gramsci. One of the founders of the party and its secretary from 1924 to 1926, Gramsci had been imprisoned by the Fascists until his death in 1937. While in prison he jotted down his thoughts on literature, philosophy, history and the party. The writings, published as the *Prison Notebook*, were often so muddled and disjointed that they produced a veritable cottage industry of interpretation. Some chose to see the *Notebook* as a celebration of Stalinism, others as an affirmation of a watered-down Socialism. In any case, Gramsci was dissected and borrowed to underpin whichever line the party's leadership chose to paper over the cracks. For its friends the party's stance was a constructive ambiguity, for its enemies a policy of *doppiezza*, or duplicity. The party, it was claimed, was engaged in a duplicitous double game of seducing the voters with the respectable mask of a constitutional party, only to reveal the hidden face of Soviet-style Communism once in power. Historians are still divided over whether this accusation was fair or not. The fact is, however, that the Communist Party was always mistrusted, in the words of its own official historian Paolo Spriano, 'as a Trojan horse in the bourgeois citadel'. This mistrust was so deep that it emerged during the elections of 1994 and deprived the successors to Italy's Communist Party of an election victory which they had assumed would be theirs after four decades in the wings. Last year the policy of cooperation, begun in 1944, was finally supposed to come to fruition. It was thwarted by Silvio Berlusconi, a media tycoon who had only entered politics two months before the elections and who revived atavistic and misplaced fears about a Communist takeover.

The most important political contribution to post-war Italy made by the Communists was the *modus operandi* that they had established with the ruling Christian Democrats and their allies. It reached its most sophisticated form in the 1970s. Using the 'grand coalition' that had been set up in West Germany between the Social and Christian Democrats as a model, the Communist Party leader Enrico Berlinguer announced the policy of 'historic compromise'. Although not part of the governing coalition, the Communist Party would vote with the government on key issues of foreign and domestic policy. For the first time since 1947 the Christian Democrats began to reintegrate the Communists into the governing system. The reconciliation was engineered by, amongst others, Giulio Andreotti, Prime Minister – for the third time already – in 1976. In return for their indirect support in parliament, the Communists were given some sizeable crumbs of power, including the presidency of the chamber of deputies and the chairmanship of seven parliamentary committees. Behind the scenes party leaders hammered out common policy programmes which were then presented to the parties as a *fait accompli*. In the obtuse language of Italian politics the parties had established the so-called 'constitutional arch', the cooperation of all those parties in parliament who had taken part in the drafting of the Italian Constitution in 1946. This comfortable arrangement would have continued to flourish had it not been for the unjust-ified fears of the White House that the Christian Democrats were opening the doors of government to the Communists. The kidnap and murder of Aldo Moro by the Red Brigades finally pulled the rug from under the Communists' feet and the government's strategy. Pressurized by discontent amongst the rank and file of workers, the Communist Party abandoned support of the govern-ment in 1979 and forced new elections. But even this was only a temporary phenomenon. The Communist Party never turned its back fully on the policy of acquiescence set out three decades earlier. Instead of taking power at a national level, it proved to be a very effective force of local and regional government.

Unlike the Fascists, the Communists really did make the trains and buses run on time. Bologna, a stunningly beautiful city with Europe's oldest university, is the capital of Italy's traditional red belt. The city is a shining example of municipal efficiency. The streets are spotless, the transport system works, there is even a housing policy for gay couples, in a country that barely recognises the existence of homosexuality. Bologna, called *la Grassa*, or 'the Fat One', by Italians because of its obsession with food, is not so much a Socialist Workers' paradise but a monument to bourgeois good living and civic values. In many parts of central Italy like

Umbria and Tuscany where the Communists have always run local administration, the party is seen not exactly as the ideological heir of Marx but rather, the opponent of clerical misrule. Before the unification of Italy these areas were part of the Papal States and as such they were notorious for their bad administration, poverty, neglect and high taxation.

The backscratching between those in power and those in opposition expressed a deep desire for consensus after the trauma of Mussolini's dictatorship. It was further consolidated by an electoral system of pure proportional representation that allowed no party to gain an absolute majority in parliament and that kept the four-party coalition in power until 1993. Italy became a democracy deprived of the balancing act of government and opposition taking turns. This is what finally inspired the electoral reform of 1992, when 38 million Italians more than eighty-five percent of the electorate, opted for a British-style majority 'winner takes all' voting system. The irony was that this system had been tried at the beginning of the century and had been rejected because it was blamed for giving too much power to local party bosses, who ran their constituencies like Mafia fiefdoms. Even after the 1993 referendum, legistlation took care not to scrap the old system entirely. Twenty-five per cent of parliamentary seats were still elected by proportionl representation and brittle government by coalition was doomed to continue. The instinct for compromise and consensus prevailed.

Since the unification of Italy, the country's history has been signposted with different incarnations of the same phenomenon. Under Count Cavour, the first Prime Minister of a unified Italy, it was the *connubio*. Then it became the 'transformation of parties' under Depretis, the 'national government' under Fascism, the 'conciliation' between the Church and Mussolini in the late 1920s, the 'centre-left' coalition between the Socialists and the Christian Democrats in the 1960s, the 'historic compromise' between the ruling coalition and the Communists in 1973, Aldo Moro's famously twisted 'converging parallels' and 'national solidarity' in 1976, and the *partito trasversale*, or 'cross-over party', of the 1980s. The leitmotif was compromise and cohabitation.

I came across one rather amusing example of this phenomenon

last year, during the conference season of political parties. It was a Sunday morning and I had set off to the outskirts of Rome to report on the congress of the neo-Fascist Movimento Sociale Italiano. The party, which for years had hovered uneasily in the twilight zone of Italian politics, was in the process of changing its name to the more clubbable-sounding Alleanza Nazionale, or National Alliance. The congress was taking place in a huge hotel turned conference centre. As I walked into the lobby of the Hotel Ergife I was perturbed to find a riot of red flags, badges of Marx and Lenin, a banner with the face of Che Guevara. I knew the neo-Fascists were trying to change their spots, but wasn't this going a bit far? When I asked an official what was going on, he told me that I had landed – unbeknown to me – at the national conference of the orthodox Communist Party, Communist Refoundation. 'I'm looking for the neo-Fascists!' I said, somewhat irritated and convinced that I had written down the wrong location. 'Oh, you mean the blackshirts,' said the official. 'They're over here, come with me.' We descended into the bowels of the hotel, walked through cellars, darkened corridors and dank passages to emerge ten minutes later in a room decked with pictures of Mussolini and crowded with young men wearing bomber jackets, black armbands and all sporting extremely short haircuts. We had crossed from one end of the political spectrum to the other without leaving the building. I can't think of any other country where parties representing the two political extremes could stage congresses at the same hotel.

The lack of alternation between the perpetual parties of government and a toothless opposition had several consequences. The first and most obvious one was an extraordinary degree of continuity. Italy may have had fifty-three post-war governments, but until recently every one of them was dominated by the Christian Democrats and their allies. The cabinets were like a game of musical chairs where no one ever removed the chairs. Giulio Andreotti and his seven Prime Ministerships was not the exception. Amintore Fanfani, who served three times as President of the Senate and twice as secretary of the Christian Democratic Party, formed his first government in 1954 when Eisenhower was President of the United States. He formed his last in 1982. Emilio

Colombo entered the cabinet for the first time in 1955 and left it for the last time in 1992. Amintore Fanfani, Aldo Moro and Mariano Rumor had each served as Prime Minister five times. One study showed that between 1946 and 1976, 1331 ministerial and subcabinet positions were held by no more than 152 politicians. The only other governments that illustrated such a high degree of continuity were those of President Babanguida of Malawi, who was ousted at the age of ninety-two. The only modern statesman who has outgoverned Giulio Andreotti is Fidel Castro, and that's probably because the Cuban leader was a late starter by comparison.

This exclusive club of ministers was not reappointed over and over again because of their exceptional qualities but because they represented certain political factions. Factionalism became the dominant characteristic of the Christian Democratic Party, this amoeba-like alliance of shifting interest groups. In a classic example of Italian *sistematizazione*, or systematisation – a favourite word, especially in Italy's distinctly unsystematic south – the appointment of junior ministers and undersecretaries of state was worked out through a mathematical calculus known as the Cencelli Manual. Massimo Cencelli was a cabinet official who administered and established the criteria by which certain factions would receive certain posts according to their strength. For instance the Christian Democrats' Dorotei faction, named after the Santa Dorotea monastery in Rome where the founding members of the group first met, were almost always given the interior and public works ministries. Another rule was that a minister who leaves a cabinet post during the lifetime of a government has to be replaced by another minister from the same faction, whether he is qualified or not.

If the moderate conservative character of the Christian Democrats was determined by its war leader, De Gasperi, then the structure of the party as an alliance of factions, sometimes at war, sometimes at peace with each other, was the legacy of his successor, Amintore Fanfani. In his attempt to loosen the ties between the party and the Vatican and to turn the Christian Democrats into an independent party controlled neither by the Church nor by big business, Fanfani did what Mussolini had done before him: he 'colonised' the state's numerous industries and banks and turned them into reservoirs of political patronage. In 1956 Fanfani set up the Orwellian-sounding Ministry of State Participation to consolidate the party's control over the public sector economy, which was expanding rapidly during Italy's economic miracle of the 1950s. By the end of the 1980s the state controlled eighty per cent of the country's banking, more than a quarter of its industrial employment and half its fixed investment.

These vast public corporations, described by the Swiss journalist Theodor Wiener as 'a byzantine archipelago of some 45,000 companies', became the main sources of patronage. Theoretically they were independent. Some were even commercial and had private stockholders. But in reality the public corporations were controlled by the political parties like fiefdoms belonging to different factions. They included not only the state's banks and large industrial firms like the Ilva steel factories but also television and radio, theatres, museums and universities. Through the public corporations the political parties, first the Christian Democrats but then also their coalition partners and the Communist opposition, reached every corner of society. This was the 'party state' apparatus. The difference between Italy and East Germany was that it was in the hands of several parties and not just one.

The system of patronage can be illustrated by looking at IRI, the Institute for Industrial Reconstruction. IRI was set up in 1933 by the Fascists. Before its gradual privatisation in 1992 it was the largest state holding company in Europe. Its realm was vast, an impenetrable forest of 600 holding companies which controlled the country's iron and steel production, most of its shipbuilding, telecommunications and electronics industry, much of its engineering, road and motorway construction, city planning, the national airline Alitalia, national broadcasting and most of the shares in Italy's three large banks. In many sectors sound economics were replaced by pure Machiavelli. As the party literally 'colonised' large areas of the state economy, this encouraged the formation of factions competing or in many cases warring to secure their chunk of patronage. Four large chemical groups were set up in the 1960s and 1970s, each allied to a specific faction. Italy's map of motorways still reflects the country's political factions. A stretch of the motorway near Avellino in the Campania is called the 'De Mita', because this was the home region and power base of Ciriaco De Mita, the former Christian Democrat Prime Minister. The Arezzo stretch of the A1 between Florence and Rome is known as 'the Fanfani'; the superstrada from Rome to Latina as 'the Andreotti'.

Only a few parts of IRI such as the Banca Commerciale Italiano escaped the stranglehold of the parties. The rest became dominions of *lottizazione*, the system of jobs for the boys. In return for their jobs the boys were then expected to deliver votes during the elections. Many public corporations became giant electoral factories, serving their party-political patrons. The bond of patronage trickled right down to the lowest level. For instance, until four years ago the administrators, doctors, nurses and even patients at Palermo's Civic Hospital could be 'expected' to vote *en masse* for the Christian Democrat deputy Salvo Lima, who was killed by the Mafia in 1992. The deputy and former mayor of Palermo, who was also the representative of Giulio Andreotti's faction in Sicily, could thus count on something like 8000 votes from the hospital alone. This was possible because the head of the hospital, appointed naturally by the Christian Democrat authorities in Palermo, was Lima's brother. With millions of people employed in the state sector and millions more dependent on their salaries, it's not difficult to imagine the number of votes that were determined not by ideology, persuasion or habit but by money and patronage. Although many companies managed to do well despite being under the thumbs of the parties, in other cases the quality of the product or service suffered. It only takes a stint in an Italian state hospital to discover this. Since the basic services in so many hospitals are deplorable, most Italian families become nurses in residence when one of their members is taken ill. Go to any ward in Rome's San Giacomo Hospital for instance, a crumbling terracotta palazzo that takes all the romance out of crumbling terracotta palazzi, and you will find family members fussing over the patients. They bring in food, drink and clean sheets. They often administer the medicines. They do most of the nursing, partly because they are suspicious of anyone who is not 'family', partly because the available care isn't good enough.

The distrust of the Italian health system doesn't just apply to ordinary citizens. When Pope John Paul II was shot in St Peter's Square in 1982 the ambulance preferred to fight its way through Rome's rush-hour traffic to the private Gemelli clinic at the other end of the city rather than to take the Supreme Pontiff to the aptly named Santo Spirito Hospital behind the Vatican. The Pope's advisers obviously thought he stood a better chance of surviving stuck in an ambulance than stuck in a state hospital. If more proof were needed of the damage of *lottizazione* and *sottogoverno* to public services, I would advise a trip by Alitalia. The inefficiency, surliness and running costs have grounded it somewhere at the bottom of the ladder of good airlines not far above Aeroflot, according to a 1993 survey in the *Economist* magazine last year.

The public corporations weren't just carved up to renew the patronage of the governing parties, they were also bequeathed to the opposition as a price for their acquiescence. Thus the Communists were given control of the railways and much of the public arts. Again the results were not always favourable. Perhaps the best example of how the parties have devoured the state sector is RAI, the national television and radio network. Until last year RAI 1 was still in the hands of the Christian Democrats, RAI 2 belonged to the Socialists and RAI 3 to the Communists, which was then renamed as the Democratic Party of the Left. One consequence was a discernible political bias in the news reporting on each channel, especially in the hours devoted to the patron party and to the mundane declarations of its leadership, which were reported punctiliously. Until recently the three parties tried to exclude a number of other political movements, seen as a threat to the cosy but corrupt status quo, from their coverage. Lilli Gruber, a feisty and attractive newscaster on RAI 1, who leans into the camera like a flirtatious barmaid and who led the newsroom rebellion against the old editorial *nomenklatura*, told me how she had been ordered not to include news about the Northern League, despite or perhaps because of the fact that the League was fast becoming the most popular protest movement in Italy. Understandably Umberto Bossi, the cantankerous leader of the Northern League, demanded his own television station, in the absence of fair reporting from the state channels. Even today RAI television news often sounds more like political gossip sheets than a national information service. Newscasters still tend to refer to political figures by their surname without bothering to remind viewers of the person's position or title. The bulletins buzz with jargon picked up in the lobby bars. Miss two days of news gossip in the ever unfolding saga of Italian politics, and it's like leaving the country during a long-running television soap. You return feeling completely lost and bewildered by the drama of the headlines. Closer inspection will reveal that very little has really changed.

The other consequence of appointing news editors because they represent the right faction rather than the right qualifications is simply that the quality of much of the broadcasting on RAI is sloppy and substandard. News footage tends to look as shaky and out of focus as a holiday video. The reports are thin on facts but dense on comment, and despite its generous state subsidies and licence fees RAI has produced little television drama or documentary material of any lasting value. This may now change as the leadership of all three RAI channels has been taken out of the hands of the parties that once controlled it. Indeed in the case of RAI 1 and 2, the parties no longer exist, or they have been renamed. Nevertheless it will be more difficult to remove the dead wood of middle management in RAI accumulated over years of *lottizazione*.

Another victim of one of the more absurd examples of *lottizazione* is Rome's hapless opera house. In 1991 a new director was appointed. Giancarlo Cresci had been a television producer but his main qualification for the job as opera director was that he belonged to the Christian Democrats and was a close friend of Rome's mayor. In less than two years Cresci managed to turn a 300,000-dollar annual profit into a 50-million-dollar debt. It was mismanagement on a truly operatic scale. Cresci tried to improve the reputation of Rome's lacklustre opera house by throwing money at it. He dressed the ushers in original eighteenth-century brocade uniforms, made them learn English in private lessons that cost thirty dollars a head per hour. He decked the lobbies in Persian rugs, commissioned one of Italy's most famous architects to build a canopy over the main entrance. He paid exorbitant fees to singers, including 15,000 dollars to the Spanish tenor José Carreras for a single performance. He hired private planes to fly in violinists. For an ill-fated production of *Aida* he recruited the services of several monkeys and camels at 3000 dollars a piece per night. The camels became incontinent at the brassy sound of fanfares. When the new city administration was elected in November 1993, Cresci was sacked. The opera house, one of the oldest in Europe, was almost closed down. Bailiffs confiscated several rows of front stalls. The hire charge for the seats had not been paid in months. To recoup some of the losses the number of productions was slashed and the budget was halved. On my only visit to the Rome opera house I was amused to find that the ushers in livery had been replaced by traffic wardens, parading the rows of seats as if they were looking for parking offenders.

If Giulio Andreotti, the elder statesman, embodied the subtle nature of power of the old regime, then another Prime Minister personified both its successes and self-inflicted failure. Bettino Craxi has fallen further than perhaps any other politician in Italy. After rising through the Socialist ranks, Craxi became the party's leader in 1976 at the age of forty-three. For sixteen years he ruled the party like a personal fiefdom until he was ousted at a raucous party congress in 1993, disgraced by corruption charges and abandoned by those who had for years treated him like a prince. Craxi transformed the nature of the Italian Socialist Party, the PSI. He stopped any flirtation with the Communists and established the principle that the ignominy of government was preferable to the nobility of opposition. From then on the Socialists attracted voters who were looking for an alternative to the Communists and the Christian Democrats. A master tactician, Craxi played one party off against the other and finally became the indispensable kingmaker of governments, able to topple an administration at a whim. His price was to occupy an increasing number of *poltrone*, or 'armchairs', of power for his party. Although the PSI received no more than an average fourteen per cent of the vote at the height of its popularity, it ended up holding almost forty per cent of key government and administrative positions.

While Andreotti wove a subtle web of power, Craxi imposed

his will on the party like a feudal overlord. He strengthened his own position in the party, which up to then had been a mercurial alliance of factions, selecting and ejecting leaders with alarming regularity. In 1981 Craxi changed the party's constitution. From now on the party secretary would no longer be elected by the central committee but by the congress, made up of 200 local party representatives, 100 parliamentary deputies and 100 Socialist celebrities, intellectuals, veterans, actors, singers and other luminaries who were selected by Craxi himself.

The last remaining scraps of Socialist ideology were buried in the unabashed pursuit of power. Occasionally the party still paid lip-service to the Socialist belief in distributing the wealth created by others, but in reality it started to redistribute an ever larger quantity of money to itself. The party's new pragmatism had become a self-fulfilling prophecy. Dwarfed by the Communist Party, the Italian Socialists had always found it difficult to convince others of their ideological integrity. Antonio Gramsci, the Communist philosopher, called the PSI a 'Barnum's Circus . . . which never takes anything seriously'. In 1920 Lenin wrote a damning letter to the Italian Socialists: 'You seem to yourselves so terribly revolutionary . . . but in reality you are frightened.' It was Fillipo Turati, the man who founded the PSI as Italy's first mass party in Genoa in 1892, who said: 'What a beautiful thing Socialism would be if there were no Socialists.' His remark turned out to be prophetic. Since most of the genuine Italian Socialists could be found in the Communist Party, the PSI has always suffered from an identity crisis. The party swung periodically like a pendulum from extremism to moderation, losing credibility every time. But in the 1980s the Socialists and Craxi were to Italy what the Conservatives and Thatcher were to Britain: the upwardly mobile and motivated by the pursuit of wealth and happiness, a hedonistic escape from the doldrums of the 1970s.

Craxi became Prime Minister in 1983. His rule, hailed as one of the most effective in post-war Italy, lasted four years, longer than any other government before or since. As he pointed out to me during an interview: 'The history of modern Italy, which is Europe's youngest country but one of its oldest civilisations, has always been fraught with instability since unification in the 1860s.

There are only two periods of stable rule in more than a hundred years. One was the authoritarian episode of Fascism, and the other was my prime ministership.' Most other politicians would have shied away from such a comparison. But not Bettino Craxi.

On the surface the economic successes of his four-year rule were remarkable. The Milan stock exchange, the only one in Italy, increased its capitalisation fourfold. Inflation came down, growth rates increased from 0.85 per cent in 1982 to 2.5 per cent in 1984. In January 1987 Italy experienced the so-called *sorpasso*, when, according to figures of the OECD, its gross national product (5998 billion dollars) overtook that of Britain (5474 billion dollars). Italy moved from sixth to fifth place on the G7 ladder of world economic powers – after the United States, Japan, Germany and France. Italian newspapers started referring to their country as *il quinto potere economico mondiale*, the fifth global economic power. Italy had finally become richer than the country whose soldiers had helped liberate it from Fascism. Not surprisingly the *sorpasso* produced an unprecedented degree of self-congratulation and national pride. Much of it was justified.

'Made in Italy' became a coveted hallmark of style and quality. By the end of the 1980s Italy's export boom had transformed the lifestyle of Northern Europe. From Sunderland to Stuttgart people were paying a small fortune to buy extra-virgin olive oil, tomatoes dried by the Calabrian sun, and Armani. But like in Britain, Italy's economic growth ultimately depended on the United States and the reflation of the American economy *à la* Reaganomics. Economists now believe that Craxi rode the wave of economic growth created by someone else and used the euphoria of the day to over-expand and ultimately lay the foundations of his own demise. According to most of the testimonies that have emerged so far in the *tangentopoli* scandal, the mid-1980s saw the exchange of bribes for contracts flourish unfettered. As the power of the parties, especially the Socialists, swelled, so did their demand for money to oil the wheels of patronage. The collection of *tangente* for public works contracts turned into systematic extortion. One consequence was a renewed building boom. The other was a mushrooming debt. By 1989 Italy had the highest budget deficit in the European Community. While the government was preaching the virtues of closer European integration and the Maastricht Treaty it was laying the foundations for its own exclusion from Europe's first division. By the time the treaty was signed in Maastricht in December 1991, Italy failed to meet all of the seven economic requirements set out in the document. This was the legacy of Bettino Craxi's prime ministership.

The grandees of the Christian Democratic Party wore their power like the gold-embroidered humility of the princes in the Vatican. They were remote and aloof. In deference to their creed they maintained a degree of restraint. The Socialists of Bettino Craxi on the other hand soaked themselves with abandon in the luxurious bubble bath of power. The party leadership became notorious for jetting from one Socialist International congress to the next in a fleet of chartered planes with scores of family members, hangers-on and *portaborse* or 'bag-carriers', in tow. In a kiss-and-tell book about the most lurid days of Socialist hedonism, the actress Sandra Milo described virtual orgies in the roof garden of the Raphael Hotel, Craxi's traditional residence in Rome. Meanwhile the collection of *tangente*, which were used to finance the party campaigns became increasingly crude. Silvano Larini, a close aide of Craxi's, told the judges that he regularly stacked bundles of billions of lire in cash in Craxi's own office at party headquarters.

As Craxi's power grew in the party so did the influence of his family. His portly son Bobo became the head of the Socialist Party in Milan, at the age of twenty-eight, before resigning because of an investigation into illegal party funding. Craxi's brother-in-law Paolo Pilliteri was mayor of Milan twice, before being investigated for corruption.

At the height of his power Craxi enjoyed a personality cult, unusual for Western Europe. At the Milan party conference in 1989, delegates were greeted at the door by a sign inviting 'Comrades' to 'Wait here if you want to pose for a photograph with Party Leader Craxi.' While Craxi's family preened itself on stage, the conference sang 'Long live the Red Carnation'. Meanwhile the head of the family was meeting his close friend, the media tycoon Silvio Berlusconi, in his camper van. The conference programme reassured delegates that the beautiful hostesses hired by the party for the occasion were chosen for their good looks and their height, which, as the leaflet informed, 'oscillates between 168 and 173 centimetres'. The Socialist journal *Mondo Operaio* celebrated the purveyor of tall women as 'a politician with eclectic human and cultural interests, avid in his research as well as his imagination, lucid in thought and tenacious in deed'. He was referred to in the party press as 'the impresario'. Even *Time* magazine hailed him as 'Maestro' on its front cover. As the tall and bulky Craxi became increasingly puffed up with power, admiration gradually turned to ridicule. Giorgio Forattini, the well-known cartoonist of the *Repubblica* newspaper, always depicted him as the 'Duce' figure in jackboots and uniform, accentuating Craxi's jowls and assertively fleshy lips. His first name, Bettino, was changed to Benito, as in Mussolini. The pretensions of the former Prime Minister were proportional to the wrath he later incurred from the public. No politician was more loathed at the height of the corruption scandal. Craxi and his cronies no longer dared to show their faces in public. Waiters refused to serve them at Maiella, their favourite restaurant behind the Piazza Navona in Rome. The night that parliament voted not to lift his immunity from prosecution and caused an uproar in the chamber, Craxi walked out of his Rome residence, the Hotel Raphael, into a hail of coins and verbal abuse. When convicted thieves were paraded through the streets of medieval Rome, throwing coins was the one way the public expressed disgust. Shortly afterwards Craxi was ousted as the leader of the party he had dominated like a feudal retinue for sixteen years.

Before his downfall Craxi rarely gave interviews, especially to foreign journalists. I was thus pleasantly surprised to hear from his office that he would be prepared to see me and my colleague David Willey at the Hotel Raphael in September 1993. He clearly had time on his hands. The Raphael is a medium-sized hotel tucked behind Piazza Navona in a dark street. It is completely covered in ivy which gives it a rather forbidding and mysterious air. For fear of bombs there were no cars parked in the front of it, apart from one police van, filled with bored carabinieri, and the two armoured cars that Mr Craxi and his bodyguards still used until he fled the country in the summer of 1994. The lobby was decorated with carved wooden statues and precious antiques. Sitting on his own amongst the artefacts, slouched into a sofa in front of a coffee table groaning with empty glasses, coffee cups and overflowing ashtrays, was the former Prime Minister. He looked at home in the lobby and seemed to treat it like his own living room. His bodyguards and a brace of hangers-on, including a very large man in a shiny grey suit, pigtail and sunglasses, occupied another part of the foyer.

Craxi wasn't wearing a jacket. His tie was undone and hung lazily around his neck, like a noose. His shirt was creeping out of his trousers, which threatened to slide down his bottom. The former Prime Minister had lost weight. Were these the withdrawal symptoms of power, or just the self-neglect of a man who was no longer in the public eye? Craxi, who was extremely friendly, beckoned us to take a seat and offered us coffee. He wasn't so much sitting as lying on the sofa, smoking one cigarette after another. I watched with fascination as the tip of ash grew longer and longer, and finally dropped onto his shirt, on his trousers, on my trousers, in the orange juice, on the floor, on my bag. Craxi didn't seem to mind. The front of his shirt was covered with ash stains. When the ashtray was too full, you could hear the sizzle of the cigarette ends as they were stubbed out in the dark sludge left at the bottom of a coffee cup. The Maestro was defensive. 'I have been in politics for twenty-two years. I was elected seven times to the chamber of deputies, three times to the European parliament. I was Prime Minister for four years. And I have never had a brush with the law. No one has ever proven, or will ever prove that I have deviated for one second from the path of legality. I have never, I repeat *never*, been bought by anyone.'

There was a brief silence. Then Bettino Craxi took us on a guided tour of his conspiracy theories. 'There are so many liars, so many hypocrites today. Just think of the big industrialists, who have always financed our political system and now pretend to be victims and saints. They are such terrible liars, I call them extra-terrestrial.' Craxi shook with laughter, spilling ash everywhere. His voice rose and fell in a mesmerising melody. 'Of course, power corrupts,' he admitted. 'In Italy there has never been a genuine alternation of power, a certain degree of degeneration is bound to have occurred. The Communists are the worst,' he suddenly said. 'They behave like goody-two shoes, but they were *the* extraterrestrial *per se*'. I was trying to imagine the leader of the former Communist Party in a spacesuit. What did he mean? 'They were paid by Moscow,' he thrashed on, 'controlled by the KGB. Stooges. Spies. The lot.' Ash was flicked off and landed somewhere near my right shoe.

Did he have any evidence to prove this? I asked. 'Evidence! Evidence! Mountains of it. All will be revealed in good time.' Why not now? 'The time is not ripe. Not just yet.' The air was thick with dark threats. Like Andreotti, Craxi has been around for a long time. He knows or pretends to know everything about everyone. He will probably never go on trial, let alone to jail. The man who a year before was still able to make or break governments had already received his worst punishment. He had been stripped of his power. His court had vanished. For Craxi, personal enrichment was much less important than the influence inherent in extracting a *tangente* from the business community.

A week before the interview, removal men had taken the last pieces of furniture out of the Socialist Party headquarters in the Via del Corso. The party that is alleged to have stolen tens of billions of lire was now bankrupt with debts of over 180 million dollars. The Socialists could no longer afford to pay the rent. The landlord had them evicted. So who, I asked, paid Signor Craxi's bills at the Raphael? 'I still have many friends, many more than you think. Friends in the Middle East. They pay the hotel. They have also given me a plane for my travels. I spend a lot of time in the Middle East.'

I asked him what he did all day. He told me he gave advice, a lot of advice. 'Many people still come to see me, you know. And I write. I am currently writing reports to the judges to clarify my situation . . . and the situation of others. I have started on my memoirs. I am writing a book called *Tunisian Thoughts*. These are things that have occurred to me while I was in Hammamet. I am also writing a novel.' Is that all? I asked. 'No,' said Craxi, 'I am also thinking of rewriting a number of books by little-known

Italian authors from the last century. Wonderful books. Everyone should read them, but they are written in an Italian that few understand.' It was a picture of unruffled confidence, serenity in the face of adversity and, some would say, of Olympian arrogance. It marked the end of the interview and Craxi accompanied us outside. Did he dare show his face in public? my colleague asked him. 'Of course. But yesterday I was walking from my car to the hotel, when two boys came up to me and called me a thief.' What did you do? we asked. 'I punched them,' he replied.

Like Bettino Craxi, most of the patients that used to frequent the couch of Dr Rocchini, Italy's parliamentary shrink, are now unemployed, voted out of power by an electorate bent on vengeance. Some, like Craxi, are brooding in exile and trying to avoid the courts. Others have discovered new vocations. Gerardo Bianco the former floor leader of the ruling Christian Democratic Party and a respected Latin scholar, is writing a book about the animals in Virgil. Gianni Prandini, a former Public Works Minister, is learning Spanish and helping his wife, who is an insurance broker. Claudio Martelli, the former Justice Minister, has enrolled as a mature student in an economics course in London. He attends classes whenever he doesn't need to attend other people's trials in Italy. Others are learning how to paint or play the piano. One former Liberal has taken up deep-sea diving. Some are hatching new plots or have been recycled as 'new' politicians for one of the new parties like Silvio Berlusconi's Forza Italia. The people who ran Italy two years ago, and who represented five decades of rigid political continuity, are suddenly nowhere to be seen. They have been toppled by their own excesses. They destroyed the source of their own power: the party. In Dr Rocchini's words: 'They killed Mamma.'

After five decades it was perhaps to be expected that a political system in which the parties in power never swapped places with those in opposition was to become stale and corrupt. But when the Italians got rid of the old ruling class and its *partitocrazia* many of them had forgotten that the system had virtually been imposed on them by the Vatican and the Americans, whose paramount desire was to keep Italian Communism at bay. Considering the potential for conflict in a society that had just come out of one civil war and now found itself on the fault-line between East and West, it was a stroke of genius to let the Italian Communists share power without ever formally handing over the reins of government to them. Not only did the Italians avoid internal conflict, their country also became a stable democracy and one of the richest nations of the world.

In 1992 it was fashionable in Italy to blame the lack of political accountability and of healthy political alternation between government and opposition on the electoral system of pure proportional representation. Mario Segni, the reform politician and renegade Christian Democrat, led a successful movement to change Italy's electoral system. The movement culminated in a referendum in April 1993 which was meant to give Italy a British-style voting system, where all the deputies are elected in single-member constituencies or electoral colleges. The candidate with the largest number of votes would win. The party or parties with the largest number of seats in parliament would form the ruling majority. It was a nice idea. But then Italy intervened. It took months to hammer out the new law in parliament. The final result was a typically Italian fudge. Seventy-five per cent of the seats were now to be elected in single-member constituencies and twenty-five per cent according to the old proportional system. The minimum threshold to get into parliament was a five per cent share of the vote. Thanks to this small window of opportunity many parties still thought they had a chance of getting into parliament on their own, instead of merging with others. In the 1994 elections sixteen parties fielded candidates, producing a dizzying array of emblems and candidates. The result was more unstable government under Prime Minister Berlusconi and a ruling coalition more brittle and fractious than most of its predecessors. Another bout of reform became inevitable. Those who saw electoral reform as the panacea for Italy's problems had clearly forgotten the fact that the British-style voting system had been tried at the beginning of the century. It was scrapped in 1919 because it gave too much power to the victorious party and turned the successful candidates into Mafia bosses in their own constituencies.

The reason why Italy has never been able to adopt the Anglo-

Saxon system is that Italy is neither Britain nor America. The Italians are ill at ease when too much power is concentrated in the hands of too few. The tribes that make up Italian society, be they political parties or powerful families, distrust each other too much and have too little faith in the institutions of the state. Power therefore has to be shared. This is the real reason for the *trasformismo* between opposition and government or for what Aldo Moro elliptically and absurdly called the 'converging parallels' between the Christian Democrats and the Communists. This is also why the Italians began to chip away at the power of Prime Minister Berlusconi. His wealth and influence had impressed them during the election campaign. But the voters were angered by his apparent attempts to silence the troublesome judiciary and to control the state media when he already enjoyed a monopoly of commercial television. Berlusconi threatened to become too powerful. On the other hand he had also promised to be the 'Man of Destiny' which the Italians have yearned for since Machiavelli wrote *The Prince*: a charismatic figure who could unite Italy and restore the glories of the old Roman Empire. History had encouraged the Italians to dream of such a man. Bitter experience, especially in the form of Mussolini, had taught them to distrust him. As Silvio Berlusconi has shown, this remains the conundrum of modern Italy.

One of the reasons why this riddle cannot be solved is that one hundred and twenty years after its creation Italy is still a country in the making. The 'First Republic', as the Italians now like to call the period between 1945 and 1992, provided stability at the price of corruption. Its collapse has left an institutional vacuum and an alarming degree of confusion. It's as if Italy had been sent back to the drawing board once again, just as it had been in 1918 after the First World War, under Mussolini and after the Duce's histrionic experiment to 'make Italy' had suffered its miserable failure. As an elegant lady with excellent English once put it to me at a diplomatic dinner in the breathing space left between the veal cutlets and the lemon sorbet: 'All this upheaval is nothing but a renewed attempt to turn us Italians into proper citizens. The trouble is you can't create Italy without the citizens and you can't create the citizens without Italy. Until we've solved that one, we remain nothing more than the world's best-dressed and best-fed tribesmen and women.'

5

Jacobin Judges

L ocated between the wild mountains of Abruzzi and the fertile plains of Puglia, Molise is one of Italy's poorest and smallest regions. The village of Montenero di Bisaccia is typical of the area. It clings defensively to the side of a mountain and has only a few asphalt roads. Fierce winds blow dust and rubbish through the maze of squat farm houses. In the summer, the earth is bone dry and cracked like the skin of an old man; in winter, rain turns dust and earth into rivers of mud and sludge. The majority of Montenero's inhabitants are over the age of fifty. The younger ones have either left the village to work in the Fiat factory near Campobasso, the regional capital, or they have moved to another part of Italy. But for the cars, mopeds, the Dalek sounds coming from the fruit machines in the Bar Centrale and the unavoidable rash of cement construction, Montenero di Bisaccia has changed little since 1933, the year that Giovannino Palma, one of the village's farmers, took his flock of sheep, his son and his favourite horse, Regina, to the neighbouring town of Cannita for the monthly fair.

At the fair everyone admired Giovannino's horse and made offers to buy it, but Giovannino only wanted to sell his sheep and refused. That night, while the farmer and his son were sleeping in a barn, thieves came and stole the horse. Giovannino was distraught. The horse had been his most precious possession. The following night the farmer dreamt that the horse had been taken to the village of Sannicandro. At dawn he set off and in a fenced paddock outside the village he discovered twenty horses. One of them was his own horse, Regina. Giovannino went to the

74

local carabinieri, told them that he had discovered his stolen horse and asked them for permission to take it back. The carabinieri refused, saying that Giovannino didn't have enough evidence to claim the horse. The farmer sought the advice of lawyers. They told him to secure the return of his horse through the courts. Giovannino Palma waited two years for his case to go to court. He had waited in vain. Fed up with lawyers, the sluggish court and the creaking machinery of justice, he decided to take matters into his own hands. He returned to Sannicandro and discovered his horse in the same paddock. Giovannino was about to open the gate and grab Regina when three men appeared, armed with shovels and pickaxes. They called him a horse thief and threatened him with the weapons. Giovannino refused to back off and explained why he had come. The men stood firm. Finally Giovannino took out a picture of the Madonna of Montenero, which he had kept concealed in his shirt, and showed it to the three men. At the sight of the Madonna, they dropped their weapons immediately and ran away. Giovannino opened the gate, took his horse and rode back to his village.

On hearing the news, almost the entire village gathered in the main square and a photographer was summoned from the neighbouring town to commemorate the occasion. Once a picture had been taken the villagers, Giovannino, his wife, whose nickname was 'Pazienza' because of her long-suffering nature, and the children all went to church for a thanksgiving Mass. They took the horse with them. The photograph was pinned next to the Madonna. Later in the year Regina had two foals.

The most extraordinary aspect of this story is the man who tells it. Antonio Di Pietro is the hero of Italy's 'sweet revolution' and the grandson of Giovannino Palma. Palma and the horse are part of the living legend that has been woven around this investigating magistrate whose crusade against corruption has toppled the country's political élite. According to one biography, the story of the horse explains 'his resilience, his thirst for justice and truth, his disdain for the sluggishness of Italian law' and so on. The points are listed one to ten. Antonio Di Pietro is proud of his peasant origins. He still looks like one of the villagers in the yellowed black and white photograph taken at his parents' wedding fifty years before. He is stocky, has a kind round face with two small but intelligent eyes set far apart, his hands are large and he speaks with the slightly stilted and clipped accent of his home region. His language, even in court, seems refreshingly blunt compared with the usual grandiloquence of Italy's profession.

Like millions of other Italians who have emigrated to the wealthy north, Di Pietro frequently returns to Montenero. Most of his wider family still live there. When he and his bodyguards arrive in their armoured motorcade they are greeted by graffiti that can now be seen all over Italy: *Grazie Di Pietro*. Indeed, Antonio Di Pietro is worshipped more than any film, rock or football star. His face adorns T-shirts, plates and coffee mugs. He has inspired films, novels and even a musical. A ten-foot effigy of him has been paraded through the streets of Italian cities during Carnival. When Di Pietro came to Rome for the first time after the eruption of the corruption scandal, women rushed into the street to kiss and hug him. He was showered with carnations. The number of students enlisting in university law courses has shot up, not because a degree in jurisprudence is a useful qualification for the civil service – the traditional reason – but because Di Pietro has launched a thousand trainee magistrates, yearning to follow their hero's footsteps. Had Di Pietro stood for parliament as thirty magistrates did in 1994 he would have been elected with a resounding majority. Many Italians wanted him to become Prime Minister. The media tycoon Silvio Berlusconi tried to cash in on his popularity by asking him to become Justice or Interior Minister. Di Pietro turned him down, saying he had more work to do in cleaning up politics. Thus, a country that was notorious for flouting the law at every level worshipped an enforcer of the law. Italy has once again started a trend. In France and Spain anti-corruption judges had been holding the political class to account. In all these countries the legal system is based on the Napoleonic Code and its tradition of magistrates as politicised but unelected civil servants. In Italy the judiciary had evolved from the instrument of law and order into the battering ram of political change. This was unique in a modern democracy.

Yet Di Pietro's fans were not applauding his punctilious application of the law but rather his political role. Di Pietro, the son of a humble peasant, had become a Jacobin hero, a Robespierre who had taken on the arrogant *Palazzo*, the Italian establishment and brought it crashing down. He and his team of *Mani Pulite* judges spearheaded the investigations into the systematic exchange of bribes for contracts. Their weapons were pieces of paper, the so-called *avvisi di garanzia*, warrants that notify a person that he or she is under criminal investigation. At the height of the corruption scandal, one of these *avvisi* was issued to a powerful politician or an industrialist almost every day. Every time the delivery became a spectacle, often broadcast live on television. Paolo Cirino Pomicino, a Christian Democrat, former Minister of Public Works, and party boss of Naples, received his *avviso* in Naples. It was delivered in an armoured police van. Many others were first leaked to the press before reaching their recipient. Scores of ministers resigned upon receiving them. The tycoon Raul Gardini, once the superstar of Italian big business, shot himself in the head only hours before he was due to receive his.

Italy's élite was presumed guilty, as it always had been. The end of the Cold War had finally removed the excuse for the perpetual re-election of the Christian Democrats and their allies as the protectors against the Red Peril, the budget deficit had become big enough to threaten Italy's standing in Europe and the parties ran out of money to buy votes. While Antonio Di Pietro and his colleagues issued warrants, the Italian electorate voted their former leaders and their parties out of power. Judges and voters both egged each other on without a single verdict of guilty having been issued. The Christian Democrats and Socialists began to implode at the ballot box before the first *tangentopoli* trial had even started. Whether the defendants were guilty or not, justice, as it always had been, was a powerful political tool.

Antonio Di Pietro's team and their suave boss Francesco Saverio Borelli worked in Milan's Palace of Justice, or Palazzo Di Giustizia, a granite monstrosity built at the time of Mussolini. The word justice is sculpted in large uncompromisingly square letters on the front façade, and, like most other 'palaces of justice' in Italy, the size of the building doesn't, or at least didn't until recently, necessarily reflect the amount of justice that emanates from it. Now, guarded by carabinieri and shown every night on Italian television from every possible angle, the palace has become a fortress of justice. The giant halls with square marble columns and cold neon lighting echo to the din of litigation produced by hundreds of judges, lawyers, clerks, secretaries, policemen, bodyguards and desperate citizens milling around, feeding the factory of 'justice'. While trials are in session on one floor, jurors are lunching in isolation on the next, interrogations are being conducted on another. Everything takes place under one roof. Antonio Di Pietro and his pool work on the fourth floor, guarded by carabinieri with machine-guns and clusters of bodyguards in civilian clothing, watched by scores of cameramen and journalists, waiting for scraps of news.

With his stocky build and jowly face Di Pietro looks more like a private detective from a Raymond Chandler thriller than an Italian magistrate. This is not entirely surprising. Before becoming a magistrate he was an ordinary policeman. Before that he was a *Gastarbeiter*, or guest worker, in a West German factory. Di Pietro interrogates his suspects with the streetwise psychology of a cop on the beat and with the legalistic logic of a magistrate. Roberto Mongini, a Christian Democrat financier and 'collector' or bribes for the Milan Malpensa airport project, has described how Di Pietro made him sweat during their 'talks'. The magistrate apparently squeezed confessions out of his subjects with a mixture of tough no-nonsense questions and menacing patience. With theatrical timing he would take off his watch and slowly dismantle and reassemble it like a watchmaker. The effect was unnerving. Mongini and hundreds of others confessed. If they didn't, a spell in prison could easily be arranged under the magistrates' sweeping powers of arrest to facilitate such a confession. The issue of preventive custody is currently part of a heated political debate in Italy.

Before becoming a subject of public worship Antonio Di Pietro spent ten years collating the evidence that would allow him to pounce in February 1992. Using a computer, a revolutionary tool in Italy's archaic legal system, Di Pietro was able to piece together the picture of *tangentopoli* like a puzzle. By sifting through company and party accounts, he discovered the systematic exchange of bribes for contracts. He and his colleagues were helped by the political climate. The parties were already losing some of their power in 1990. Dissent grew in their ranks. More and more information leaked out. One of the unanswered questions of *tangentopoli* is how the judiciary suddenly discovered the wealth of information that allowed them to charge thousands of politicians and businessmen. Several judges have told me that Di Pietro the computer whiz-kid had collated the incriminating evidence well before the scandal erupted but was unable to proceed because he was being blocked by the parties, who then still controlled a large part of the judiciary. According to another theory the information about *tangentopoli* was leaked to the Milan judges by the Italian secret services, acting on behalf of the Christian Democratic Party. The Milan Socialists under Bettino Craxi had become too greedy and the Christian Democrats wanted to teach them a lesson. The secret services provided Di Pietro with the incriminating software. If this was indeed the motive it soon backfired, as the corruption scandal spread from the Socialists to the Christian Democrats and from Milan to Rome. Whatever the trigger for *tangentopoli*, the *partitocrazia* was losing power and disloyalty within its ranks produced a growing number of 'confessors'. Meanwhile businessmen were flocking to Di Pietro in droves to confess that they had paid bribes. The recession had made it more and more difficult for them to pay the illegal tithe. Di Pietro's computer has become part of the living legend. The cover of *Time* magazine showed him sitting next to his electronic tool, holding a floppy disk, presumably stuffed with evidence. The loyal Dr Watson to Di Pietro's Sherlock Holmes, the computer is often assembled next to the prosecutor in court, like some daunting oracle that contains the secret of *tangentopoli*.

The trial of Sergio Cusani, a Neapolitan nobleman and financier who was sentenced to eight years in jail and ordered to pay 91 million dollars in damages last year, illustrated the high drama of Italian justice. The 'Processo Cusani' was the first major trial in the corruption scandal. The roll-call of witnesses read like a *Who's Who* of Italian government. The defendant was found guilty of falsifying company balance sheets, misappropriating funds and violating the laws that regulate the financing of political parties. The forty-five-year-old financier was held responsible for defrauding the Ferruzzi Montedison industrial empire of 91 million dollars, and passing 14 million dollars of that money to politicians like Bettino Craxi, the former Socialist Prime Minister. The Ferruzzi business empire was allowed to sell its stake in Enimont, a chemical joint venture with ENI two years before, back to the state at vastly inflated prices. It was allowed to do this despite the fact that Enimont had been a catastrophic failure. The price paid by Ferruzzi was a *supertangente* of almost 100 million dollars, which was used to buy the acquiescence of the political leadership for what was essentially a bad deal. The case was a textbook illustration of all the fraudulence and waste of *tangentopoli*. It gave the Italian public a first-hand insight into the maze of corruption that had flourished at the highest level of business and politics. Apart from showing long extracts of the trial on the nightly television news, RAI 3 used to screen the 'best of Cusani' twice a week. The programme regularly attracted audiences of over twelve million viewers, eclipsing even the most popular soap operas. It was compulsive, riveting viewing.

The trial's casting was perfect and the script of this modern morality play could have been written by Bertolt Brecht. Antonio Di Pietro, who had worked his way up from street cop to magistrate, stretched Cusani, the haughty nobleman from Naples, on the rack of justice. As the trial progressed, Cusani looked increasingly haggard and increasingly noble. Wearing elegant dark suits he sat bolt upright in the defendant's chair, with his legs crossed, a tragic figure of dignity. His long thin neck was tailor-made for the guillotine. Cusani's lawyer, Giuliano Spazzali, looked like the devil's advocate, ordered from central casting. He had a grey goatee, startlingly alert eyes and demonic eyebrows that curled up at the end. His voice was shrill, his comments sharp. The Chief Judge, Giuseppe Tarantola, had the languid and slightly bored air of a supreme arbiter who had spent a lifetime witnessing the sleazy side of human nature. One of the key witnesses in the trial was the former chief executive of the Ferruzzi empire, Carlo Sama, who had married into the Fernizi family. Smooth and handsome, he was the Master Seducer of *tangentopoli*. Every week

Sama's revelation masked in a boyish smile would spell the kiss of death for another politician. Sama told the court that the Communist Party, which had always claimed it was squeaky clean, had received 600,000 dollars in bribes. Even the Northern League, which was once alone in occupying the moral high ground of Italian politics and had thrived on its reputation as an honest party of protest, was implicated. Sama told the court that the party's treasurer had received 200,000 dollars. According to Sama, financial journalists were also paid off, to conceal the truth. It was a sorry picture of almost universal corruption and corruptibility.

Di Pietro played his epic part with consummate skill. His unshaven, dishevelled look gave him the appearance of a working-class hero in a revolutionary people's court. Wearing the long black gown of a state prosecutor, he flapped his arms as if they were the wings of a bird of prey. Under the gown he often wore little more than a white vest which gradually rolled over his fleshy paunch as he became more and more agitated. In contemplative moments, Di Pietro would rub his stubbly chin on the court microphone as if it were an electric razor. It was a refreshingly raw and uncouth performance. Di Pietro mocked, cajoled, teased and insulted his victims. He accused Cusani of being a liar, a thief and a 'triple traitor'. But often he also joked with him. The performances were always unpredictable. The courtroom frequently erupted in laughter, leaving some to wonder just how serious the trial was and whether, if found guilty, the defendant would actually have to face the consequences of his actions.

Di Pietro's finest performance was his interrogation of Arnaldo Forlani, the former leader of the Christian Democratic Party. For-lani embodied the Christian Democratic Party's mixture of raw power, paternalism and Catholic devotion. Over the years his po-faced expression under a halo of grey hair had become a rigid mask of aloofness. In court the mask was shattered. Forlani was only a witness to the prosecution but he was treated like a defend-ant and he behaved like one. He was literally mesmerised by Di Pietro, unable to utter anything but barely audible denials. He said that his sum knowledge of *tangentopoli* had come from the newspapers. He blamed any deviation from the law on Severino

Citaristi, a Christian Democrat parliamentarian who orchestrated the collection of bribes for his party. As Forlani stumbled through the hearing white foam appeared in the corners of his mouth. The secretion of fear. The scene was shown again and again on television. This was the ritual humiliation of the old élite.

Sergio Cusani's punishment was harsh. The prosecution had only asked for a seven-year sentence. The judges gave him eight and ordered him to repay almost one hundred million dollars. In his emotional final testimony Cusani accepted personal responsibility but said that he didn't want to become the sole scapegoat for an entire system of corruption. Cusani had already spent five months in custody before being charged. Ironically he may never go to jail again, now that he has been found guilty. The case will inevitably go through two appeal stages, which may last up to seven years. A different judge in a more lenient political climate may well annul the sentence.

Just as Antonio Di Pietro's grandfather tired of waiting for a decision from the courts about his stolen horse, many Italians regard the law not as a guarantee for justice in society, but as an intrusion by the hostile state into the private lives of citizens. The law is either flouted or feared. The Italian judicial system has done little to reassure citizens that this is not the case. The country's creaking machinery of justice is notoriously slow and like so much else in this country a victim of good intentions, ruined by inadequate application. The Italian Constitution guarantees three trial stages as a means of achieving maximum fairness. But the human and financial resources are so inadequate that the average length of a trial from its first appearance in court to the final verdict is ten years. Some cases take longer: a disagreement over fishing rights off the island of Sardinia went to trial in 1858 and was settled in 1981. A dispute over the will of Don Carmelo Parisis, the Duke of Leucadi and Casakecchio, began in Messina in 1914 and was concluded in 1980, and then only because the property in dispute had become a ruin and the banknotes had lost most of their value. The family decided there was no point in pursuing the case. There are more serious examples. In 1969 a bomb in Milan's Piazza Fontana killed sixteen people and injured ninety. The trial, in which three extreme right-wing terrorists were charged with murder, began in Rome in 1972. It was later transferred first to Milan and then to Catanzaro in Calabria. There it didn't resume until 1974, only to be postponed until 1977. A verdict of guilty was reached in 1979, but the case was appealed. A second verdict was reached in 1982, only to be quashed by a higher court. In 1985 the trial was closed without verdict. Last year a Milan judge tried to get it opened again. The case continues. The bombing of an Italian airliner over the Sicilian island of Ustica in 1979, in which eighty-one people were killed, hasn't even reached the trial stage yet, because the investigations have been blocked consistently at a higher level. Witnesses have died in mysterious circumstances, vital evidence has been lost or shredded.

The Italian judicial system frequently does its best to fuel Italy's cottage industry of conspiracy theories and suspected plots. But frequently injustice is the result of a mundane but debilitating lack of resources. Italy spends less than most other European countries on its judicial system. The court administration tends to be crude and understaffed. The filing systems are inadequate. There is a lack of computers, court stenographers and office space. The judges are often badly allocated, with too few in the lower courts and too many at the appeal level. The geographic distribution of judges dates back to 1941 and is today woefully out of sync with the country's population shifts. There is a glut of judges in provincial capitals, especially in the south, but a shortage in big northern cities like Milan and Turin.

Because the machinery of justice creaks so slowly only about five per cent of cases get from the preliminary investigation to the trial stage. Despite this, the total backlog of cases in the three branches of the judiciary – administrative, civil and penal – is more than three million! And although the judiciary may be slow to bring trials to court, they are quick when it comes to arrests. Thanks to powers which stem from the authoritarian days of Fascism and were renewed at the time of the terrorist scare in the 1970s, it is very easy for Italian judges to issue arrest warrants, and very difficult for those arrested to get bail. More than half of Italy's bloated prison population of over 50,000 inmates is still awaiting trial. They are being held under 'preventive' or 'precautionary' arrest. The precaution is against a suspect fleeing the country, destroying the evidence or committing another crime. A person can theoretically be held for up to three years and three months without being charged. Although the recommended time is considerably shorter, even a six-month spell in jail is a terrible punishment for someone who turns out to be completely innocent. Meanwhile many genuine criminals are allowed to go free because their cases never make it to court.

Perhaps the most notorious case of pre-trial imprisonment took place after the wave of extreme left-wing terrorist attacks. In 1979 the police arrested twenty well-known Marxist intellectuals, suspected of links to the Red Brigades and involvement in the murder of the former Prime Minister Aldo Moro. Toni Negri, a professor from Padua University, spent four years in jail without being tried. He was released not because the authorities had decided they had no case against him but because the Italian Radical Party, outraged by his treatment, made him a parliamentary candidate. Negri was elected and thus automatically received parliamentary immunity from prosecution and arrest. Parliament subsequently voted to lift his immunity. Professor Negri didn't wait for the outcome of the vote and fled the country. A few years later he was sentenced in absentia to thirty years in jail. In another case, a well-known television presenter called Enzo Tortora was arrested on the hearsay of a Mafia killer who had accused him of being a drug dealer. Tortora spent several years in prison before being released. He was never charged.

The 1989 judicial reform limited the 'recommended' period of 'preventive custody' to just over a year, and the *tangentopoli* saga has rekindled the debate. Over 2000 suspects have been held without being charged or tried. Many have been kept in custody in order to extract confessions. The government of Prime Minister Berlusconi was particularly strong in describing this as an unacceptable practice. The judges responded that without custody no one would have confessed, the extent of corruption would not have been discovered, the much-heralded change would not have come about.

The *tangentopoli* saga has obscured the fact that Italy's judicial system is in a dreadful mess. The absence of *habeas corpus* and a decent bail system has produced some appalling travesties of justice. Even before the corruption scandal about half the Italian prison population – 27,000 prisoners – were awaiting trial. Prison authorities do not distinguish between suspects and convicts. On one visit to Rome's notorious and inappropriately named Regina Coeli – Queen of the Heavens – jail I found *tangentopoli* suspects and convicted drug dealers sharing the same overcrowded cell. The prison had been built for 500 inmates. It was now home to three times as many. One of the causes of this overloading, 'preventive custody', has been condemned periodically by international human and civil rights organisations like Amnesty International. In August 1994 Prime Minister Silvio Berlusconi tried to get the law scrapped by decree. But behind the pleas for *habeas corpus* the judiciary and the majority of the public suspected an attempt by the media tycoon to help some of his own friends like Bettino Craxi and his brother Paolo, who was facing an arrest warrant for bribery.

Although 'preventive custody' is one of the oldest and most fiercely debated ills of the Italian judicial system, it was scarcely touched by the much vaunted 1989 legal reform known as the *Nuovo Codice di Procedura Penalel*. This reform was above all designed to limit the sweeping powers of the *pubblico ministero*, the public prosecutor. For instance, the reform has scrapped the old provision of secret investigation. A suspect might not have been told what the charges against him were until his first day in court. This made it very difficult for the defence to prepare their case. The ambiguous verdict of 'annulling the case because of insufficient evidence', which helped hundreds of mafiosi to get off the hook, has also been abolished. A verdict now has to be either guilty or not guilty. Today public prosecutors also need the permission of a judge to issue an arrest warrant.

On a visit to Milan's San Vittore jail, the premier prison of *tangentopoli*, I wasn't allowed to interview illustrious prisoners. But I was introduced to William Mamone, a long-term resident who was serving ten years for armed robbery. Mamone came from Calabria. He was called William in honour of an American pilot who had rescued his father during the Second World War.

William emigrated to America where he became a rock music producer and then a cocaine dealer. Later that year he was due to be extradited to the United States. William was allegedly caught in a shop in Los Angeles with a sub-machine-gun.

William Mamone was one of those prisoners that make jail a homely kind of place. Having been to two other prisons he was a connoisseur of coolers. He was kind, witty, articulate and well dressed. He grew basil and marjoram on his window-sill. The leaves crept up the bars like a pergola. He knew fifty different pasta sauces and cooked them in the tiny loo of his cell, which he had converted with the help of a Bunsen burner into a makeshift kitchen. He edited the *San Vittore Journal*, the glossy in-house monthly which featured gossip, legal advice, political commentary, features on 'life outside' and a special set of horoscopes tailor-made for the readers (*Sagittarius*: Your sign is in the ascendant. Bail may be coming up for renewal)! But above all, William Mamone was one of the few prisoners who talked to the people he called 'the white-collar criminals', the illustrious arrestees of *tangentopoli*. 'I saw many of them cry,' he told me. 'Imagine the humiliation of suddenly being carted out of a restaurant or from your nice home and being taken here. Most of them carry on wearing their suits for a day or two. They can't quite believe that they are here. They think they'll be let out the next day. When it dawns on them that they may have as much as six months or more inside, they start wearing more casual clothes. I saw one guy sitting on his own. He was a very well-known businessman. I can't tell you the name. Anyway he was sobbing. I asked him what was wrong. He said that his son had been attacked and teased at school because of his father. The arrest was all over the newspapers.' William believed that it was unfair that most of those arrested were businessmen and not politicians. The latter only lost their parliamentary immunity from prosecution and arrest in spring 1994. 'Businessmen make money. They create jobs. Most of them should be let out. I would much rather see someone like Bettino Craxi or Giulio Andreotti here. I could teach them how to cook.'

Tangentopoli has shown that in Italy there is no such thing as one unified judiciary, but over 8000 individual magistrates, prosecutors and judges. Some of them are left wing, some right wing, some independent. The politicisation of the Italian judiciary is partly historical. Most of the senior judges in the immediate post-war era were inherited from Fascism. Consequently the younger generation became radicalised in the 1960s and 1970s as a reaction to their deeply conservative superiors. For some like the jurist Federico Mancini, the courts became a weapon in the class struggle. 'All laws,' Mancini wrote, 'should be interpreted with this yardstick: partisanship is a virtue and neutrality a misconception or a fraud; so is independence; a judiciary cloaking itself with these sham values is a servant of power . . . judges must defend the oppressed, the downtrodden, and cooperate with the labour movement.' Yet, if some judges were *pretori d'assalto*, intent on battling the Establishment, others were only too happy to serve it. Corado Carnevale, a senior Appeal Court judge, was known as 'the quasher' because he released legions of mafiosi on the grounds that there was insufficient evidence against them. Two years ago Carnevale went into early retirement. Since then more than twenty judges, including Carnevale, have been investigated. Some have even been arrested for allegedly collaborating with the Sicilian Mafia or the Neapolitan Camorra.

Although Italian judges are far more politicised than their counterparts in England or Germany they are not elected, like, say, an American district attorney. They cannot be held accountable for their political leanings, despite the fact that these leanings often interfere in the process of justice. According to the Napoleonic Code, judges or examining magistrates have to pass a tough public examination like senior civil servants. If they're successful they are appointed for life and enjoy sweeping powers. Some suffer from delusions of grandeur. One magistrate closed down Silvio Berlusconi's three national television networks for a week on a technicality. Another ordered a raid on his headquarters days before elections that brought Berlusconi to power. The magistrate from the Calabrian town of Palmi was looking into the links between politics, Masons and mafiosi and wanted a list of all the candidates of the media tycoon's Forza Italia Party. She could also have called the Interior Ministry's information department. In both cases Berlusconi suspected a left-wing plot to countermine him.

But Italian magistrates don't always need plots in order to exercise their powers. Another magistrate issued an arrest warrant for Yasser Arafat.

Theoretically the judges are servants of the state whose political independence is enshrined in the Constitution and guaranteed by the judiciary's governing bodies, the Superior Judicial Council and the Constitutional Court. But as usual, politics intervenes. The Constitutional Court, which was set up in 1956 and has the power to overturn legislation deemed unconstitutional, consists of fifteen members, who serve nine-year terms. The five appointments decided by parliament have traditionally been the most partisan. Historically, according to an unwritten agreement, two of the nominees went to the Christian Democrats, and one each to the Communists, the Socialists and lay parties like the Republicans. The President had five nominees, which were also open to partisan influence. In the case of the five appointments made by the judiciary itself, the political leanings were perhaps less difficult to trace but no less real. Now that the Christian Democrats and the Socialists have ceased to exist or become irrelevant, it will be interesting to see how the country's highest judicial posts will be carved up in the future, or whether the appointments will be left entirely to the judiciary. So far, at least, the Italian judicial system has always mirrored the country's rigid political pluralism. Within this amorphous body there was a balance between right and left, but this didn't help the individual left-wing suspect investigated by a right-wing magistrate or vice versa.

Perhaps the most bizarre aspect of the Italian judicial system is the large number of laws that have been inherited from Fascism and which fill the statute books in total contradiction to the spirit of Italy's very liberal Constitution. One-third of laws are still thought to be of Fascist vintage. The 1931 Codice Rocco, which was named after Mussolini's Justice Minister Alfredo Rocco and formed the basis of the repressive legal code under Fascism, has never been scrapped in full. Only individual laws, like the death penalty and certain aspects of censorship, have been repealed. The most notorious one still in force is the old-fashioned-sounding *vilipendio*, or vilification.

Theoretically a person showing contempt or disrespect towards state institutions, the national flag, the armed forces, the Italian nation, religion, the president and the pope can be sent to prison for several years. In 1980 the editor of the satirical weekly *Male* was sentenced to two and a half years in jail for making fun of Pope John Paul II. By remarkable coincidence His Holiness was speaking to the Rome press corp at the same time about the need to guarantee freedom of speech in modern societies. The most recent and most absurd example of *vilipendio* took place in 1992 when Rome's favourite madman was charged with vilifying the President of the Republic, Francesco Cossiga. A forty-five-year-old doctor of jurisprudence who lives with his mother, the 'ballerino di Piazza Barberini' has invented what he calls the 'universal theory of five dimensions', a key to unlock the mysteries of the universe. He wears a bizarre headdress that consists of a baseball cap fitted with thin metal spokes. His identity and kidney donor card dangle from the spokes. The ballerino prances and pirouettes around the Bernini fountain in the middle of the square every day, preaching his 'theory' to pedestrians, tourists, pigeons and passing cars. He spits and spices his delivery with insults against the president, the prime minister of the day and a certain Professor Feinstein, about whom he is particularly vitriolic. Although charges were brought against the man, when his insanity was proved beyond any reasonable doubt – it took five minutes – they were dropped.

The problem is that the old Fascist laws on the statute books could be used by a future government. If so, such a government could theoretically find a law for every repressive measure in the complex and contradictory quilt of Italian justice. Therefore genuine reform in Italy must involve a complete redrafting of the legal code by parliament, a redefinition of the rights of the judiciary and an insurance against any political interference. In fact all these provisions already exist on paper. The rub is – as ever – in the application. The only way to shrug off the contradictions of the legal system is to start again from scratch, and this may be impossible. In Italy the preferred method of change involves the grafting of new layers of legislation onto the old rather than a fresh beginning. Italy is, after all, a palimpsest of all the cultures and civilisations that have flourished on the peninsula. Where else can you see so many medieval churches built into Roman temples, redesigned by the Renaissance, spoilt by the Baroque, repainted at the time of the Risorgimento, surrounded by Fascist lamp-posts and restored with late-twentieth-century technology? The seam of continuity runs through this chaotic but profoundly conservative country. It is one of its greatest strengths and weaknesses.

For me the most striking monument to the good intentions and inadequate application of the law in Italy is the Palace of Justice in Naples. If Milan's Palazzo di Giustizia looks inspired by the film director Fritz Lang, the Naples palace hails from Dante's *Inferno* and the works of Samuel Beckett. The building is a sixteenth-century palazzo with the sturdy, angled walls of a dank and sinister fortress. Situated next to Spaccanapoli, one of the city's most crime-infested streets, it is guarded round the clock by soldiers.

It was there that I met Rafaele Marino and Antonio Mancuso, two leading anti-Mafia magistrates largely responsible for uncovering the links between the Neapolitan Camorra and the city's Christian Democratic grandees. The judges were fighting three battles, they told me: one against the corrupt political leadership of the city, the other against corrupt judges and the third against overcrowding. Six magistrates and two secretaries shared one small office with three desks. The cupboards and cabinets were groaning with files. Court records dating back to the 1970s were piled up to the ceiling, leaning over precariously. Because of government cuts there was only one computer between six. The court stenographers had gone on strike because they hadn't been paid for two months. Many judges were forced to write their dispositions by hand. Others were crouching in the corridors, working on laptop computers, wearing their flowing court robes.

'We are lucky,' said Judge Mancuso. 'Most of our colleagues work either from home or in portable cabins which have been put up in the courtyard behind the kitchen.' There was in fact a brand-new, spacious, fully equipped courthouse only half a mile away in the Centro Direzionale, an ugly cluster of skyscrapers in the derelict 'Manhattan' of Naples. The court building had been ready for three years, though in 1992 the Camorra burnt part of it down in an arson attack and it had to be repaired. The judiciary still can't move in until a legal dispute with a neighbouring skyscraper has been cleared up concerning the laying of electricity lines. Faced with this nightmare of surreal pettiness, the death threats from the Camorra and the stresses of a *vita blindata*, or 'armoured life', of bodyguards and bulletproof cars, I was amazed to find Judges Mancuso and Marino in such good humour. 'We could charge every one of the politicians that we are investigating today, right now,' they told me. 'But if it came to a trial we wouldn't have the resources to bring them to court. In Naples the administration of justice is on the verge of collapse. What's more, we have to deal with all these.' Judge Marino picked up a pile of papers and dropped them onto his desk with a thud. 'Hundreds of cases involving petty crimes, such as cigarette smuggling. We are deluged.' It was very sad to think that Italy's 'sweet revolution' would flounder because of a mundane but crippling lack of resources.

Many Italian magistrates and judges clearly deserve their status as heroes, or in some cases martyrs. Giovanni Falcone, his wife, who was also a magistrate, and their five bodyguards were killed by a massive car bomb near Palermo airport in May 1992. Two months later Paolo Borsellino and his bodyguards were killed by a car bomb in the centre of the city outside the house of his mother, whom he had just been to visit. These murders, more brazen than any before, galvanised the anti-Mafia struggle in Sicily. They helped to break the infamous *omertà*, the blanket of silence under which the Mafia managed to kill, rob and extort with impunity for over a century. They also fuelled support for grass-roots movements like Leoluca Orlando's La Rete Party, which attacked the Mafia not just as a band of organised criminals but as an affront against civilised society and as a cancer thriving on complacency. Today the tree outside Falcone's house in Palermo has become an anti-Mafia shrine. The trunk is studded with hundreds of messages of gratitude and homage.

In Milan Antonio Di Pietro and his team have launched an unprecedented crusade against corruption. They forced an arrogant and bloated political élite to recognise what is written in every Italian courtroom: *La legge é uguale per tutti*. 'Everyone is equal before the law.' They proved to the Italians just how wasteful, corrupt and damaging the old system had been. But they would also fool themselves if they thought they could have acted to the same extent without the help of the electorate. Their fight against politics was in itself political. The electorate had become a jury of 40 million people. By voting against the old parties, the Italian people issued a collective verdict of guilty before any trial had even taken place. This gave Di Pietro and his colleagues the courage to bring politicians like Craxi and Forlani to court. As Di Pietro himself declared at the beginning of the Cusani trial: '*We* are the people. Not the parties.'

There are shades of Robespierre in this statement which would probably make any British barrister or American attorney cringe with embarrassment, or, for that matter, blush with envy. Indeed, at a conference on *tangentopoli* at the European University at Fiesole in the hills above Florence, a round table of academics were warning about the dangers of a 'Republic of the Magistrates'. At a time when the old parliament had still not been dissolved, and the honesty of the president had been called into question by a scandal in the deviant secret service, they pointed out that the only institution of state that was still functioning properly was the judges. Unfortunately, everyone agreed, the judges were too divided to form one homogeneous body. Politics should not be left to them.

As one episode from the Cusani trial illustrated, the law is still feared as a means of repression and not respected as a guarantee of liberty for every citizen. On 4 January a businessman called Domenico D'Addario sat in the witness chair in one of the cold granite and marble courtrooms in Milan's Palazzo di Giustizia. Dressed in his black robe, Antonio Di Pietro began the questioning. 'Who are you?' he asked. 'I'm Domenico D'Addario,' said the witness. Di Pietro asked him what he was doing in court. 'I thought you would know that. I'm here to give evidence, I presume.' 'No, no,' said the prosecutor. 'We wanted Amadeo D'Addario, not Domenico. You've got nothing to do with this trial.' (Laughter from the courtroom.) 'Does that mean that I can .go?' (More laughter.) The court had accidentally approached the wrong D'Addario, a distant relation of the man they wanted to question. What was astonishing was that the wrong D'Addario had actually turned up in court, without even bothering to inquire what he could possibly have witnessed. He had just assumed that he was guilty of something.

6

The State Versus the Citizens

Italy, as anyone who has lived here will realise, is *not* a lawless society. From the formal greetings to the social ritual of the *passeggiata*, the life of the average Italian is defined by a set of rules as complex and intricate as those of a secret monastic sect. But these are rules and not laws, and the Italians have become very adept at making the distinction. Rules are observed. Laws are imposed by the state and are therefore automatically regarded with suspicion. Historically the state has always been either distrusted or feared by the Italians. Under the Spanish Bourbon monarchy the state was a foreign power. According to the popular myth the state under the Popes in central Italy was nothing but an excuse to collect high taxes, administer as little as possible and use God for moral blackmail. Mussolini and the Fascists worshipped the state as a universal remedy. Under them it invaded the lives of citizens more than ever before, and suppressed those who didn't worship it. In the post-war republic the state was abused by the parties who carved it up for political patronage. Its reputation was further tarnished by the fact that the state's highest representatives from senior civil servants to former prime ministers stole from its own coffers. Prime Minister Berlusconi became widely despised for looking like a tycoon who wanted to incorporate the state into his business empire. Meanwhile, with deplorable public services from the transport system to health care only a small majority of Italians actually feel they are getting something in return for their contributions. Who can blame them for trying to dodge their taxes? The relationship between citizen and state in Italy is clearly in urgent need of repair.

Nowhere is this more obvious than in the realm of taxation. Which tax? one might well ask. The income tax? The car tax? The tax on your driving licence? The tax on your car purchase? Was that a used car or a new car? The tax on your refrigerator, your television, your first home, your second home, your boat, your helicopter, your pet, your fur coat, your marriage licence? Separate taxes exist for all of these and many more. Luigi Enaudi, Italy's most eminent post-war economist, calculated that if every tax in the Italian law book were collected the state would earn 115 per cent of the nation's entire income and wealth. As it happens, the state collects only a fraction of the tax it is owed. Italy's tax policy owes more to Samuel Beckett than to Franz Kafka. It verges on the absurd. Take the story of the ISI tax imposed in the summer of 1992.

August is the hottest month. In Rome the cobbled streets flicker under an intense heat. They are deserted but for groups of sweaty tourists shuffling like forced labourers in search of the handful of bars and restaurants that have remained open. Debilitated and delirious they are easy prey for the few street vendors and souvenir sharks who sell tempting bottles of mineral water and flaccid Coca Cola at exorbitant prices. You hardly ever see the few Romans who have not escaped to the sea or the mountains. They spend all day indoors behind closed shutters that keep the sun out and the flies in. Many of them only venture out before dawn. In August 1992 they did so not because this was the coolest time of the day, but because they wanted to be at the top of the queue which formed every day at sunrise outside the *catastro*, the municipal land registry office. This was the ISI queue. The ISI, or *Imposta Staordinaria sugli immobili*, was Italy's new property tax, agreed by parliament at the beginning of August, due for collection by 31 September. It was one of the desperate measures drawn up by the government of Prime Minister Giuliano Amato, who, in the wake of new EC targets, had the unenviable task of whittling Italy's monstrous budget deficit down to an acceptable European level.

The new property tax was straightforward enough. Property owners had to pay 0.2 per cent a year on the value of their home, above the figure of 50 million lire. The collection of the tax was, however, not so straightforward. You had to fill in a form which you could get only at one of the few designated land registry offices. You had to pick up the form in person. That is, four forms were available. But to join the queue for the form you needed a special ticket, without which you had no right to be in the queue. A police van was posted outside several offices in Rome after there had been angry scuffles. Forms had run out soon after the office had opened, and the office had opened three hours late. A crowd of thousands of diligent, law-abiding citizens had forgone their God-given right to be at the beach to head back to the steaming capital on the sweltering autostrada, all to pay a new tax. Understandably the crowds were seething. In Milan a minor riot ensued when the computer system broke down at the municipal land registry office and three world-weary officials had to process the forms of over 2000 applicants by hand at a snail's pace.

But the forms which had caused all the unhappiness were only preliminary ones. They merely enabled you to fill in another form, that is if you had found the right documents to back up the information about your property required in the first form. If you were cunning, patient and above all lucky enough to have filled out all the right pieces of paper and get them approved, you could then pay your tax. But failure to do so would have resulted in prosecution. As the commentator in the newspaper *La Repubblica* put it: 'I don't think there is another country north of the Antarctic where people get up before sunrise just to hand their money over to the state, and what's more at a time when they should be on vacation.' A SUMMER OF SHAME, thundered the *Corriere della Sera*. A cartoon showed a confused citizen, scratching his head in front of a tangle of corridors, revolving doors and staircases that seemed to lead up and down at the same time. In the end, of course, the Italian government did what it so often does with such taxes: it decided to scrap it. It was, the government realised, unenforceable – just like the dog/pet tax of the previous summer, which involved stamping the hind leg of the dog upon receipt of the tax, or the fur-coat tax, which saw thousands of Italian women turning up at the tax office to register their dead mink, rabbit or sable. Unperturbed, however, in 1993 the authorities, quite desperate to collect taxes more efficiently, drew up the ultimate tax. Called 740, it was a new income tax form. And it was so complicated to fill in that special programmes were broadcast on television to show people how to do it. Accountants who specialised in tax forms were in great demand. Form 740 became a universal topic of conversation, more feverishly debated than the football or *tangentopoli*.

The state has become ingenious at torturing the citizens. But the citizen has become equally adept at evading the state. Tax dodging is perhaps the most famous Italian national sport. It is a complex subject that says as much about the way the individual regards the state as it does about how Italians regard each other. The Finance Ministry has calculated that two-thirds of the budget deficit – around £850 billion – could be paid off in one go if the government were able to collect all the taxes due to them. The main culprits here are the so-called *autonomi*, the self-employed workers that include everything from farmers to architects and accountants: everyone whose income doesn't get taxed at source. SECIT, the tax inspection unit of the Finance Ministry, estimated in 1990 that the average annual income of all self-employed workers – around eight million Italians – was 8.6 million lire, just under $6500, judging from their own tax assessment. The figure was clearly absurd. This is about one-third of the average income of someone who gets their tax deducted at source, the so-called *dipendenti*. According to these calculations a dentist is likely to earn half as much as a worker who stuffs turkeys, or welds car parts at a factory. Unlikely! According to the financial newspapers *Il Sole 24 Ore* the worst tax dodgers are economists and statisticians, followed closely by furriers, accountants and stockbrokers. Those who dodged least in this category were doctors, who only failed to declare on average 20.5 per cent of their annual income. Because the self-employed are so modest in their tax returns about the amount of money they earn, the state has decided to tap their wealth in other ways. When the government announced a tax on second homes, yachts, helicopters and luxury cars, this didn't just send a ripple of anxiety through the ranks of the superrich but worried millions of Italians.

It delighted millions more. Italy is not a class-ridden society in the British sense. Social values, airs and graces do not percolate down the pyramid from an outdated landed aristocracy. Nor does Italy see class as purely a matter of wealth. What counts in Italy is which part of the country you come from and whether you pay taxes, dodge taxes or abuse the state in other ways. The social hierarchy thus consists of three principal layers: the tax-dodging *autonomi* at the top; the tax-paying but free-loading *statale*, or privileged state employee, in the middle; and on the bottom rung the largest group, the *dipendenti*, dependent workers, taxed at source but enjoying none of the benefits of the group above them. What dilutes these divisions is the fact that members of all three often belong to the same family.

The tax dodging of the self-employed is sneered at by those who get taxed at source. But even here there are important distinctions. The income of the *statale* may be taxed automatically, but he has other means of abusing the state that he works for. Take, for example, the civil servant. In Italy the civil service exists to *be* served rather than to serve. With over two million civil servants Italy has one of the world's most bloated bureaucracies. The category 'civil service' is very broad: it includes everyone from the undersecretary of state at the Interior Ministry to the man who cleans his executive loo and the porter who doffs his cap to him in the morning. To become a civil servant at even the lowest level, you have to pass a *concorso*, or a public exam. If the Ministry of Cultural Goods wants three new loo cleaners it can't just stick an advertisement in the newspaper, it has to set up a national *concorso* and wait for literally thousands to apply. The *concorso* is meant to ensure that the job isn't given to a friend or the friend of a friend. In theory it is very fair. In practice it is not. The complex and highly subtle machinery of bribes, friendships and favours means that the person best qualified to clean the loos in the Ministry of Cultural Goods does not necessarily get the job. But the reason why so many people apply in the first place is that the job is like gold dust, a meal ticket for life, a firm foothold on the greasy pole, a position with status and power.

First of all, the *statale* receives an extraordinary number of privileges denied to all *non-statali*. He or she only works from 8 a.m. until 2 p.m., gets discounts on public transport and can retire after fifteen years of service on a full pension. If you had started your career as a loo cleaner in the Ministry of Cultural Goods at the tender age of eighteen you could then retire on ninety per cent of your salary at the ripe old age of thirty-three. Millions of 'baby pensioners' did, before the law was changed in 1993. Of course their salaries were not very big, perhaps two million lire a month (about £800) and taxed at source. But that is not the point. The majority of *statali* have at least two or three jobs. After lunch they work in their father's trattoria, in their mother's shoe shop or they run their own olive oil export business. Before 2 p.m. many use the phones at the ministry to set up the 'afternoon economy'. The *statali* are resented by everyone who is not a *statale*. The self-employed think they are lazy, forgetting the fact that most *statali* become *autonomi* after two o'clock in the afternoon. Jealousy has no doubt fuelled the myth machine. In one case there was a policewoman in Turin who was discovered working in a brothel during a police-raid by her colleagues. She was wearing her uniform as an added 'disciplinary' attraction.

Absenteeism and fake sick leave have become endemic in the civil service. In Rome a judge ordered all hospitals to examine thousands of claims for sick leave amongst staff. Miraculously they always fell ill *en masse* before or after a holiday period. The *dolce vita* of the *statale* has definitely been soured by draconian reforms in the public service. Baby pensions have been outlawed, other state pensions have been frozen or cut, the number of 'invalid' pensions which had produced an army of two million perfectly healthy invalids – all that was needed to become 'invalid' was a certificate from a 'friendly' doctor – have been cut. Today the applications for such pensions are scrutinised more rigorously.

The government has also invented a whole array of surveillance measures to make sure that the *statale* actually works for the state when he's in the office. Staff at the Ministry of Cultural Goods, Italy's awkwardly named cultural ministry, have been given new electronic identity cards with which they have to clock in for work every morning. A computer gives an automatic read-out of the number of absent or sick days. The Minister of Public Affairs, a lugubrious professor who has made it his life's task to pull the

Italian civil service out of the dark ages, introduced the so-called 'Cappuccino Law'. This draconian piece of legislation, applicable only to *statali* has banned the ritual mid-morning cappuccino break. The reason was that the ten-minute constitutional often merged seamlessly with lunch.

The differences between the three categories *autonomi*, *statali* and *dipendenti* are further underlined by their political affiliations. The *dipendenti* form the rank and file of what is now the Democratic Party of the Left and in some working-class areas like Turin they support the old-style Communist Party. In the rich regions of northern Italy many of the self-employed have flocked to the Northern League and Forza Italia. The League especially is the political voice of the hard-working, tax-dodging *autonomo* who resents the little he contributes to the national exchequer being squandered by a corrupt government in Rome. Since the civil service has traditionally been dominated by Italians from the south, it is not surprising that many *statali*, afraid of losing their privileges and their job in times of recession, have flocked to the neo-Fascist National Alliance, the party of white-collar paranoia in the poor south. Furthermore the existence of a bloated civil service depends on the survival of a strong, united Italian state. The latter is a central plank of neo-Fascist thinking. It dates back to the time of Mussolini. Although the Duce wanted to reduce the civil service in size to purge it of its non-Fascist members, he ended up doubling it. The dictator realised that one way of keeping the legions of over-educated and under-employed students from southern Italy quiet was to recruit them into the bureaucracy. The practice was continued during the post-war democracy.

Despite their mutual animosity all three groups – *autonomi*, *statali* and *dipendenti* – need each other much more than they think. The *statale* who belongs to the neo-Fascist party justifies his anger by pointing at the *autonomo* who votes for the Northern League. He in turn exonerates his own tax dodging by pointing at the excesses of the *statali* from southern Italy. The *dipendente* needs both in order to hoist the red union flag on the moral high ground. In November 1994 over half a million demonstrators, waving red flags and protesting against the proposed pensions cuts of Prime Minister Berlusconi's budget, crowded into the Circus Maximus, the oval-shaped basin chosen by the film-makers of *Ben Hur* to stage a chariot race. The one line that the crowd repeated over and over again was: 'We are the Italy that works and pays taxes', proving that although the Italians define themselves by their family, their region, their political affiliation, they also do so by their relationship with the state.

That relationship is fraught with rivalries, jealousies and distrust, which have been made worse by the *partitocrazia* of the last five decades. Until the relationship can be mended there is probably little hope of real reform in Italy. Italian society will continue to lack a social contract based on individual citizens who see the rule of law as a guarantee for equal opportunities and rights and neither abhor the state as a threat nor worship it as an end in itself. What is required is nothing short of a collective change of mentality that allows people to put more trust in the state and less in all the alternatives that have sprouted in its place from the political party, to the Masonic lodge, to the Mafia and to the most important building block of Italian society – the family. Ousting one ruling class and replacing it with another is not enough. What's needed is fundamental constitutional reform that creates a benevolent federalist state, which takes into account the country's regional differences, simplifies the tax laws and recreates a sense of civic responsibility. It's a delicate and perhaps even impossible balancing act. For now such reform is hindered by the most popular mutual protection society in Italy: *la famiglia*. The family fills the gaps left by the state in the most mundane but important ways. This institution, which has survived despite the distractions of modern consumer society and a dramatic decline in the birth rate, is both Italy's greatest strength and its greatest weakness.

7

Family Values

O ur escort, a local newspaper photographer, told us to bring cakes 'as a sign of respect'. The Trimbolis of Plati were not known for their afternoon hospitality, especially when it came to entertaining foreign journalists. They had always regarded outsiders with suspicion. If they took an interest it was more because of your value as a potential commodity. The Trimbolis are one of Calabria's notorious kidnapping clans. In October 1992 Francesco Trimboli, the seventy-year-old head of the family, was in jail, accused of masterminding the kidnap of Cesare Casella, a teenager from Pavia in the north of Italy who had been abducted in 1988. The boy was hidden in a cave for a year and a half before the authorities managed to find him. They were only spurred into action when his mother chained herself to the railings of the courthouse in nearby Locri in protest against the police's inactivity. In the case of Casella no ransom had been paid.

Francesco Trimboli's sons, Domenico and Paolo, were also behind bars. They had been members of the local Christian Democrat Party and had sat on the town council, when Plati still had a town council. In 1991 the entire assembly, including the Trimboli brothers, was thrown into jail, accused of corruption and 'Mafia-type activities'. Being a town elder of Plati also meant belonging to one of the most feared crime syndicates on the Italian peninsula. The authorities had impounded thirty million dollars of assets belonging to the Trimboli family and another famous local clan, or *cosca*, the Barbaros. These were some of the revenues from years of toil and devotion in the family industries for which Plati in particular and Calabria in general have become famous: drugs, arms and kidnapping.

That left Bruno Trimboli, the nephew, to entertain us. It was he who had invited me and Charles Richards, a friend and colleague, to visit Plati. The cakes, as it turned out, were not such a great idea. Bruno Trimboli, whose pale blue eyes stared at us through the cracks of his dry tanned skin, was not impressed by our beautifully wrapped box of cream puffs. 'There was really no need to bring them,' he declared solemnly, leaving us in some doubt whether he was being politely humble, angered because we had felt the need to buy his hospitality with a gift or just unhappy about our choice of cake.

The Trimboli family lived in a street which had been dubbed Via Bolgetti. This was the local pronunciation of Paul Getty. In 1973 the Getty oil dynasty unwillingly became the biggest single benefactor that Plati and the surrounding villages have ever had. The Getty family paid 730,000 dollars in ransom to the kidnap gangs who had abducted their son Paul Getty Junior and held him in the dense forests and craggy hills of the Aspromonte for six months. The kidnappers hurried along the ransom by sending the priest of the Getty family a part of the boy's right ear. It was as an expression of their impatience, entirely rooted in local tradition. Before the gangs of the Aspromonte kidnapped humans they used to steal sheep. It was usual to send a sheep's ear to the owner as a kind of calling card and as a reminder that payment was expected. With every week that went by another part of the sheep was cut off and despatched. We sat in the kitchen, newly equipped with all mod cons of modern kitchen technology. Bruno's three daughters milled around the kitchen table. The eldest, who was cross-eyed and wore a pink lacy dress and a pony-tail, made the tea and coffee. It was a picture of domestic bliss tinged with rural kitsch.

We asked Bruno about the members of his family who had been incarcerated. He was adamant that no Trimboli had ever been involved in kidnapping or any other crime. 'The real criminals are those people in Rome,' he snorted, crossing his arms ceremoniously. 'They are the ones who steal!' Mr Trimboli was on a roll. 'Look at us here in Plati. They have just abandoned us.

Let us rot. All they send us are soldiers and carabinieri.' His local dialect was so strong that our friend the photographer had to translate what he was saying into ordinary Italian. Trimboli's lament was a common refrain in Plati, which we had also heard in one of the bars and near the abandoned town hall, where the carabinieri stand guard in bulletproof vests and armed with machine-guns.

Successive governments in Rome and in the administrative capital of Calabria, Catanzaro had indeed done little to help Plati. The Justice Ministry had effectively declared Plati a no-go area. Since the town council had been dissolved, a state administrator, appointed by Rome, travelled to Plati twice a week. He stayed for a few hours, was briefed by the local carabinieri commander and occasionally listened to complaints from local shopkeepers about inadequate electricity and water supplies. Plati frequently found itself cut from the Calabrian power net. The authorities said the entire town had neglected to pay its bills.

The legacy of neglect and mutual antagonism between the national authorities and Plati went back a long way. A landslide had washed away part of the town in 1953, killing eighteen. Nothing was done to repair the damage and secure the mountain face looming above the town. In 1973 another landslide devastated the same area. Luckily no one was killed. The authorities built a canal to divert the flow of the water. But the civil engineer in charge got it wrong. The water continues to erode the mountain-side and the only thing that fills the canal is a reeking flow of tins, bottles, rotting food, broken furniture and discarded washing machines, dumped there by the locals. It was hard to believe that this was as much a part of Italy as the prosperous towns of Alba in Piedmont, Todi in Umbria or Bergamo in Lombardy, all brimming with civic responsibility, neighbourhood watch schemes and legally acquired wealth. Like so many other villages and towns in the Aspromonte, Plati was effectively at war with the rest of Italy. The Trimboli family were as typical a local product as the thistles growing on the bare mountainside.

Why, we asked Bruno Trimboli in his squeaky-clean kitchen, had he not got together with his neighbours to clean up the mess, repair the roads, do some of the things that the authorities had neglected for years? 'It's got nothing to do with me,' came the blunt reply. As a local Calabrian saying goes: 'If your neighbour's house is on fire, pour water on your own!' Not all of Plati's woes could be blamed on the government. The town had become ungovernable. In the 1980s two mayors were gunned down in the street by a rival Mafia clan. In 1992 only 400 souls out of a population of 3800 took part in the municipal elections, well short of the quorum necessary to elect a new town council. The only party that fielded a candidate was the neo-Fascists. The burghers of Plati lived in fear of each other. Even if they had wanted to, they were unable to improve their lives. The traditional solution had been to emigrate. In 1881, when Italy had its first population census, Plati counted more than twice as many souls as today. Since then most of the inhabitants have emigrated to northern Italy, Australia, Argentina or the United States.

But emigration is no longer an option. Today the town is a ghostly ruin. The city hall is boarded up, the door to the school padlocked. The wall next to it has been painted with a giant mural depicting a rural scene with farmers, cows, olive trees and carabinieri firing machine-guns. The town, like much of Calabria, is run by the families that make up the 'Ndrangheta, the Calabrian version of the Mafia, which has recently inherited much of the expertise and trade of its Sicilian tutor, currently fighting off the Italian authorities as never before. The 'Ndrangheta may in fact turn out to be less vulnerable to internal strife, betrayal and therefore the wrath of the police thanks to its tight structure. The organisation is based on families, loosely cooperating with each other. It does not have an organisational pyramid like the Mafia's cupola which acts like a council of elders recruited from different families and regions. Pino Arlacchi, Italy's foremost expert on the sociology of organised crime and himself a Calabrian, believes that the 'Ndrangheta is far more ruthless and powerful than the Mafia, helped by the backwardness of Calabrian society and by the structure of the family. The Trimbolis would certainly qualify for what one sociologist has called 'amoral familism'. But they also share some of the values that have made the Italian family such a strong unit: they stick together, share resources, live under one roof and see themselves, in the words of the late Luigi Barzini, the veteran spokesman of the Italian soul, as 'the first source of power in Italy and the stronghold in a hostile land'.

The negative side of Italian family values has obsessed academics for a long time. In the 1950s Italian sociologists discovered the phenomenon of *familismo* to explain a whole array of society's ills from organised crime to dumping rubbish in your neighbour's garden. The American sociologist Edward Banfield denounced 'the amoral familism' of the peasants he had studied at Chiaramonte in the poor region of Basilicata. For him the backwardness of Chiaramonte was due to the 'inability of villagers to act together for their common good, or indeed for any good transcending the immediate, material interests of the nuclear family'. The conclusion was that the family had become the biggest obstacle to turning Italy into a unified, modern country with law-abiding citizens. It was the family that absorbed the resourcefulness, intelligence, cunning and energy of the ordinary Italian which would otherwise have been invested in the *patria*, the institutions, democracy, and law and order. Even Mussolini was aware that the family was a hindrance in realising the project of a unified, uniform, obedient Fascist state. He tried to overcome the problem by becoming the Father of the Nation, by turning Italy into one giant family of which he was the self-declared paterfamilias.

Prime Minister Berlusconi has tried the same, by different means of course. When he launched his 1995 austerity budget he talked about 'good housekeeping for the Italian family'. By the 'Italian family' he meant the whole country. It was an appeal for national solidarity that didn't work, partly because the members of the 'Italian family' suspected that Berlusconi had the interests of his own family and family business empire at heart. For instance, in the budget he encouraged Italians to move from state to private pensions, as a means of slashing Italy's vast pensions bill. But could this also have had something to do with the fact that Berlusconi owned three of Italy's biggest insurance companies, offering private pensions? Berlusconi, is after all, the quintessential Italian family man. His brother Paolo works for the family firm. His eldest sons sit on the company board. His children are all shareholders. And his distrust of the world outside his family and the small coterie of executives who run his company, his political party and much of his government is so intense that Berlusconi has even built a family tomb in his fortress-like villa outside Milan. The Italian family remains, at every level of society, a tightly knit, sometimes paranoid, social unit.

Its solidarity, which is partly voluntary and partly enforced by the negligence of the state, becomes apparent in a number of important ways. The first is the sharing of resources. Most young Italians live with their parents because the state can't provide them with a cheap apartment. A recent survey showed that almost no Italian men or women under the age of twenty-five lived away from their parental home. Even when they get married Italian couples often stay with their parents until they can afford to find a flat of their own. The advantages are that you get your shirts ironed by mother, your meals prepared, your baby looked after by a trusted sitter, free use of the phone, the car and the garage. The disadvantage is that there is no privacy. Millions of Italians have lost their virginity or conceived their first child in the back of a Fiat Uno or some other small car that calls for acrobatic nimbleness. From dusk till dawn car parks, motorway slip-roads and badly-lit lanes on the outskirts of towns are full of stationary but shaking cars. A tell-tale sign that something more serious than a kiss is taking place is the newspaper pasted on the windows for privacy. When the serial killer, known as 'the Florence Monster' stalked the Tuscan countryside for a decade in search of mating couples, this did not put a stop to the practice of car-park sex; it merely encouraged scores of vehicles to huddle together for safety.

Italian couples would of course prefer to live in a separate apartment from their parents but not necessarily under a separate roof. My girlfriend and I live in a typical family palazzo in the historic centre of Rome. The building is almost exclusively inhabited by the Pediconi family that built it in the seventeenth century. The palazzo is still divided on a hierarchical basis. Francesco the porter lives on the ground floor with his surly girlfriend, the cars and mopeds. The octogenarian widow of the head of the family lives on the first floor, the *piano nobile*. She and a handful of Filipino maids rattle around in a vast flat with frescoed ceilings and rococo furniture. The flat above is inhabited by the brother of the deceased *capo di famiglia*. It is slightly less ornate and a little smaller. The next floor is occupied by the eldest son and heir. The two apartments above him are lived in by his younger brothers. The back of the building is reserved for a few vagrant spinster aunts, cousins and a sad looking professor of mathematics, a distant and destitute relative who doffs his hat at everyone. The lower your rank in the family, the higher up you live and the lower your ceilings. We live in the top flat. Compared to the four floors below, our ceilings are squat and beamed. One of the conditions of moving in was that we would not insist on etching our own names into the brass plate by the front door. Hence visitors are confused by the fact that almost every one of the twelve surnames listed is a Pediconi. Modern apartment blocks, also called 'palazzi', make it more difficult for families to live together under one roof. Hence many Italian families share a second house by the sea, in the mountains or in the village of their origin. In the southern province of Puglia the family stronghold becomes a fortress. The traditional Puglian *masserias* is a kind of walled, windowless complex in which all the members of the family live with their livestock like a beleaguered clan, cut off from the outside world.

Family resources are shared in other ways. One reason why the Italians have one of the highest savings ratios in the world – in some areas as much as twenty-five per cent – is that the average family spends much less money than its British or American counterpart on housing. Mortgages are almost unheard of. Banks are reluctant to take them on. Nevertheless the housing market is booming. The reason is that the family clubs together to build a home for the next generation. Parents tend to buy or build their children a house. Often it is understood that they will occupy one floor when they have retired. In rural areas houses are often built by the families themselves. The hills of Umbria and Lazio are dotted with small building sites, teeming with members of the clan who have come up for the weekend to help lay bricks or tile roofs.

By saving money on housing the Italians are free to spend it elsewhere. The Italians spend twice as much as the European average on clothing, about 3000 dollars a year each. In Italy the fur coat isn't just a rare and much-maligned luxury item, it is the great social equaliser. More Italian women have real fur coats than women of any other nationality. Walk down the Corso in Rome or even down a lesser street in any small town in the weeks before Christmas and you will be surrounded by minks, racoons and foxes. Cars, too, are a national obsession and Italians are inordinately proud of their vehicles, even if so many of them are tiny and bruised by reckless driving. They own more cars per capita than the French, the British or the Dutch and slightly fewer than the Swiss and the Americans. As one would expect from a country blessed with a sumptuous and varied cuisine, a lot of money also goes on food and restaurants. Italy has one establishment per 257 of the population, Britain one per 451 and France one per 795. Anyone who has been to Italy knows the Sunday ritual of whole families going out for a lavish lunch with children, babies and grandparents in tow, making a lot of noise and occupying the full attention of the handful of waiters.

The key to Italian family unity is the umbilical cord between the children, especially the son, and their mamma. This is never fully severed at birth. It applies to the most unlikely situations. While the CNN television network was showing American para-troopers heroically clambering ashore on the beach at Mogadishu to launch 'Operation Restore Hope' in 1993, RAI showed Italian soldiers bidding farewell to their mothers at the airport. Mother and soldier were both crying into each other's arms. Men bristling with machine-guns, bayonets and pistols were screaming '*Mamma!*' No one was embarrassed. The mamma even occupies a central role in Italian political science. The Christian Democratic Party was commonly referred to as the *partito Mamma*, the Mommy party. Most Italians, even sober-sounding newsreaders, do not talk about *la madre* the mother but about *la mamma*: mommy. Imagine a news bulletin in Britain talking about the Queen Mum or the tragic death of President Clinton's mommy. Italian sociology has invented an 'ism' to describe the phenom-enon: *mammismo*. The children, usually sons who suffer from it are called *mammoni*. With a whole generation of single children currently coming of age, Italy is in danger of being swamped by selfish brats.

If the mother–child relationship provides the emotional glue of the family, economic interests provide the financial glue. Italian families are run like businesses with parents, grandparents, aunts, uncles and children all contributing to the family kitty. Family members are not only willing to bail each other out, it is expected of them. It's perhaps not surprising then that Italian private businesses tend to be run by families. Ninety per cent of all private enterprises in Italy are family companies. This applies to the trattoria – where mother is stuck in the kitchen, father does the accounts and the children rush back from school to wait at table – as well as the very large conglomerate. Berlusconi's Fininvest empire was a family business until Silvio Berlusconi became Prime Minister. The company wasn't even listed on the stockmarket. The carmaker Fiat is a public company but the Agnelli family is the majority shareholder. Most of the rag trade companies from Stefanel to Missoni are family firms. In 1993 I went to see one of the best-known and most successful families: the Benettons of Treviso near Venice.

Today Benetton is the world's largest buyer of wool. Its colourful, well-made clothes are worn all over the world. Its controversial poster campaign, depicting a patient dying of Aids or a newly born baby splattered in blood and placenta, is celebrated or despised. The company has become a leading sponsor of sports events. Its Formula One racing team is one of the best in the world. When other Italian companies were making losses and the whole of Europe was embraced by recession, Benetton's sales increased by ten per cent. Its global success is reflected in the understated self-confidence of the corporate headquarters near Treviso. The firm is situated amongst lush fruit orchards and vineyards. Benetton makes its own wine. The company canteen serves lettuces and tomatoes from the Benetton vegetable garden. The two thousand or so employees at the main plant, where the clothes are designed and the fabrics coloured, don't work in a single block but in a corporate village built around an artificial lake and ponds. The roofs are made of steel coated with a liquid metal that changes colour with the fluctuating outside temperature. When I arrived in the chilly morning the roofs of Benetton were purple. When I left in afternoon sun they had turned strawberry red. Underneath the village is an artificial shopping street displaying the various Benetton shops on offer. Benetton sells its clothes by selling franchises to retailers who undertake to abide by a strict set of rules. The shops are furnished by Benetton. The sales staff are taught in the Benetton school. All the clothes on sale are Benetton. But the shop is privately owned by the retailer. This way the company tries to guarantee a unity of product and sales philosophy. It ensures that its products are sold but it is unburdened by the overheads and rental costs of running a high street shop. The same principle is used for production. Although the clothes are designed, coloured and packaged at company headquarters, the stitching, weaving and sewing are farmed out to small family firms in the area.

Despite this level of sophistication and a corporate culture that can look like the mysterious rites of a religious sect, Benetton is still run like the small family firm, which began making woolly sweaters in the 1950s. The family remains the core of the business. While most of the employees sit in the psychedelic corporate village, the members of the family preside over production, sales and marketing in a sixteenth-century Palladian villa in the heart of the grounds. The offices are located in the former stables and outhouses built around a courtyard. Luciano Benetton, the chairman of the company, has his spacious frescoed offices in one corner Giorgio, his brother and deputy chairman, is on the other side of the courtyard. The third brother, who deals with marketing, works on the *piano nobile* overlooking the courtyard. His office is next to his sister Giuliana's, who designs the clothes. The Benetton siblings can be seen flitting across the courtyard to discuss the latest deal, corporate strategy or design. They all meet for lunch in a common dining room.

'There is nothing incestuous about our company,' Luciano Benetton told me. 'We are a typical Italian family business. We stick together. Decisions are made quickly. There are the occasional disagreements but we don't quarrel too much.' It would be difficult to imagine a successful business being run by a family fraught with sibling rivalries. Italy is not so much a homogeneous country as an archipelago of families. Some of them are Benettons. Others include Trimbolis.

Both are above all pragmatic and practical. Nepotism is not regarded as an evil but as a necessity. The fact that Bettino Craxi put his son Bobo in charge of the Socialist Party in Milan and promoted his brother-in-law Paolo Pilliteri as the city's mayor hardly raised eyebrows, until the family became discredited in the corruption scandal. Before becoming Prime Minister, Silvio Berlusconi not only divided the ownership of his empire up between the family, he also put his closest friends in top management posts. In 1994 Italy was run by a kitchen cabinet made up of the tycoon's closest advisers. Very little has changed since Pius VI made his nephew Charles Borromeo a cardinal at the age of twenty-two and gave him an annual salary of 50,000 scudi. However, in all the above cases nepotism only blessed those who were worthy of it. A relative who is an oaf would never be put into a position of power. His stupidity might jeopardise the family. It would be an unpragmatic choice.

The miracle of the Italian family is that it has survived the onslaught of modern technology, promiscuity and mobility. Although the great majority of Italians still get married in church the number of marriages has declined from just over 440,000 celebrated in 1947 to just over 300,000 in 1992. Since divorce was legalised after the 1974 referendum the divorce rate has also increased. However, in Italy only eight per cent of marriages failed in 1991 compared to one in three in France or Britain. This does not mean that Italian couples are necessarily happier. What it does mean is that marital infidelity isn't always a reason to break up a family. A mistress, and increasingly a lover, have as little shock value in Italy today as they did three centuries ago. The pursuit of extra-marital peccadilloes is frequently seen as a matter apart from marriage itself, which is regarded as a contract for life. Four out of five Italians who do get divorced decide to remarry, a far greater proportion than in America or Britain. Only nine per cent of broken marriages end in the courts, as opposed to thirty-nine per cent in Britain. Despite the increase in divorce, the family is a durable concept in what is essentially a very conservative society.

One of the most significant changes is that the Italian family has shrunk. Considering their love of children it may surprise the reader to find out that Italy has the lowest birth rate in the world. According to UNICEF figures, the average American family produces 2.1 children, the average British and French family 1.8. The average German, Luxembourgeois, Danish, Dutch or Hong Kong family has 1.5. But Italy, with 1.3, tops the list. The average African woman has 7 children. For the Vatican it's a cruel irony that Italy, the most established home of Catholicism, heeds the Church's call to procreate even less than any other industrialised nation. The Church blames the birth rate, which is much lower in the north than in the poorer south, on artificial contraception and on the excessive wealth of a consumer society more keen on holidays in Bali than on bambini. But this is only part of the truth. The Italians are as fond of children as they ever have been.

Another reason why Italians have so few babies is that they can't afford to have more and maintain them in the style and comfort to which they have grown accustomed. Spoiling a child is an expensive business. Toddlers in Armani jumpsuits, babies swaddled in cashmere being chauffered around in designer prams are testimony to the fact that the Italians spend twice as much as any other nation on children's clothes. A childbirth is still a reason for great, albeit increasingly rare, festivities. The day a bambino or bambina is born, his or her birth is announced by a rosette pinned to the front door or the façade of the building. Blue for girls and pink for boys. British or American families look mortified when their baby starts to scream or squeal in a restaurant or a museum. The Italians crowd around your pram, cuddle your baby, hold its hand or tickle its feet. Whether rich or poor, the bambino is king.

Yet the idyllic picture of the Italian family, albeit reduced, is being shattered more and more. Judging from the thousands of calls that congest the lines of Telefono Rosa, a helpline set up in 1990, Italian husbands abuse their wives. In 1993 almost eighty per cent of those who rang up were wives beaten or put under psychological pressure by their husbands. There were few registered cases of sexual abuse. But eighty-two per cent of those who committed the abuse were sober when they did so. Child abuse also appears to be on the rise, although nowhere near the levels of Britain or America. Italy registers 1000 teenage suicides a year.

This figure is steadily rising, a fact which psychologists blame on the alienation of modern society and on the loneliness of only children brought up by parents who both work. In October 1994 there was a particularly sad example. Marco Bollini, a twelve-year-old boy from Padua, hanged himself in the cellar of his parents' house. The suicide took place a week after an eight-year-old American boy called Nicholas Green had been killed by highway robbers who had shot up his parents' hired car in Calabria. The parents donated the boy's vital organs to six Italian children waiting for organ transplants. Because Italy has very few organ donors the children would almost certainly have died if the Greens hadn't displayed such goodwill. Italy was aggrieved about the death of the young American and so shamed by the generosity of his parents that the country went into paroxysms of guilt. The number of organ donors shot up. Marco Bollini seized the opportunity. In his suicide note he wrote that he no longer wanted to live, that his life had become worthless, but that he would like someone else to live with the help of his heart, liver and kidneys.

The Italian family has come under siege. But it is holding out better than in most other industrialised societies. It is Italy's secret shock absorber in times of social upheaval. It makes a lot of money and saves enough. It provides welfare, housing and care where the state doesn't. Go into any Roman, Neapolitan or Milanese hospital and you'll find the corridors and wards congested with family members bearing food, drink, clean sheets and sometimes even medicines. If families don't trust the state on such important matters as health care, it's easy to understand why they don't see much point in paying taxes. The negligence of the state has encouraged the family to think of itself as besieged. This mentality has in turn prevented the state from encouraging civic values. With few exceptions the community still tends to be a narrow circle based around the clan. The Mafia are Italian family values taken to an extreme. An example: in 1993 Toto Riina, the head of the Mafia who had been captured by the police after twenty-three years in hiding, was confronted for the first time with one of his principal accusers, the famous Mafia turncoat Tommaso Buscetta. Buscetta, who lives in the United States under a witness protection programme with a new nose, a new face and a new name, was flown to Rome specifically for this meeting in the courtroom at the capital's high-security Rebibbio jail. Buscetta sat in front of the judge, surrounded by bodyguards, so that Riina and the public could not see his new face. The boss of all the bosses was led inside. He sat on a stool and promptly declared that he would neither talk to Buscetta nor listen to him. Riina was clearly in a huff, crossed his arms in a defiant gesture and spent the next hour staring at the ceiling. He had every reason for doing so. Riina and Buscetta were arch-enemies. Riina was responsible for killing thirty members of Buscetta's family. Buscetta's testimony enabled the Sicilian judges like Giovanni Falcone to understand the mentality, hierarchy and operation of Cosa Nostra for the first time. It contributed to Riina's downfall. In short, the two men loathed each other. It was quite understandable that the boss of all the bosses, who would probably remain in jail for the rest of his life, refused to converse with the Mafia's supergrass, who was a free man. But no one expected the reason that Riina gave for his silence. 'I refuse to exchange any words with this man,' said Riina in a haughty voice, pointing at Buscetta, 'because this man was unfaithful to his wife. He has slept with too many women.' Toto Riina . . . ever the family man. His family values have little to do with romance and a lot with pragmatism. One of the vows that the Mafia makes its new recruits swear by is 'never to sleep with another mafiosi's wife or girlfriend'. Infidelity leads to jealousies. Jealousy leads to family feuds, violence and cracks within the organisation. By sleeping with scores of Mafia wives Buscetta was personally responsible for fuelling one of the most violent Mafia wars of the century.

British or American conservatives lamenting the decline of the family and the extinction of family values in modern society would do well to remember the testimony given by Toto Riina, boss of all the Mafia bosses, in the bunker-like courtroom of Palermo's grim Ucciardone jail last year. The diminutive Signor Riina, known to his friends as 'U Curtu', the Short One, and to his enemies as 'La Belva', the Beast, was listening patiently and courteously to the murder charges against him. Then the man who had already been found guilty of several murders and was being tried for dozens more, the man who used to dissolve his enemies in acid, killed women, judges and policemen, who ran the most vicious and sophisticated crime syndicate in the world, controlled the drugs traffic from Bangkok to Bolivia and the arms traffic from Yugoslavia to Yemen, this man who can be no taller than five foot one, has four children and a loyal wife, stood up before the panel of judges, shrugged his shoulders and said: 'But Your Honour. Look at me! I'm just a family man.'

8

Mafia: Myth and Malice

On 14 November 1994 Pope John Paul II sat on a gilt throne outside a petrol station in the suburbs of the Sicilian city of Catania and celebrated an outdoor Mass, attended by thousands of people. Those who didn't find standing room in the street, crowded onto the balconies and rooftops. Bishops and cardinals in their ceremonial robes sat in the front row, surrounded by dozens of bodyguards with earpieces. It was a surreal clash between the splendour of the papal court and the grey misery of a working-class district in Sicily. This was the Pope's third visit to Sicily. John Paul II was the first Pontiff to go to the island for six centuries. Karol Wojtyla, who had lived under the smothering embrace of Polish Communism, had come to tell the Mafia to convert and the Sicilians to stand up against organised crime. The seventy-four-year-old Pope, grimacing with pain from a hip replacement operation he had undergone earlier in the year, was angry. 'It is the duty of every one of you,' he told the congregation, waving his silver-tipped cane, 'to speak out against the arrogant minority that oppresses and intimidates. Silence is a form of complicity.'

The morning after the Pope's call for rebellion against the Mafia, Father Gino Saccetti woke up in his house in the district of Termini Imerese outside Palermo. When he went out to buy a newspaper he discovered a calf's head nailed to his front door just beneath the brass name-plate. There was a note too. 'If you're not careful,' it read, 'you'll end up like this one day.' The priest, an outspoken campaigner against the Mafia, was one of the many foot-soldiers who had taken the Pope's defiant message against organised crime to the local pulpit. The priest, the police, the newspapers and the public all assumed that the calf's head had been sent by the Mafia. 'Cosa Nostra at war with the Church,' thundered a headline in the *Giornale di Sicilia*.

The bloodied head had been a timely message, coinciding with the Pope's visit, but it had not been the first. Several priests had received threatening phone calls demanding they tame their sermons or face the consequences. But the most dramatic strike against the Church took place in October 1993. Father Giuseppe Puglisi, another ordinary priest who had spoken out against organised crime, was shot in the back of the head as he walked home one night from the community centre in his parish in Palermo. The assumption – that Cosa Nostra was behind it – was confirmed by a Mafia turncoat a year later. He told investigators that the organisation wanted to send a strong warning signal to the religious community by killing the priest. This was the first time that the Mafia had assassinated a member of the clergy because he was preaching against it. It was an indication of Cosa Nostra's desperation. The Mafia, which Judge Giovanni Falcone once described 'as enjoying the same strict unity of faith and command as an established religion', was afraid of losing the battle against the Catholic Church, a battle over the minds of ordinary Sicilians. The organisation had always thrived on a potent mixture of myth and malice to intimidate and suppress the people of Sicily. That mixture was now being exorcised.

The Vatican's stand against the Mafia was new. Previous popes had tolerated the Mafia with their silence. The rank and file, apart from a small group of Jesuits, took their cue from the Vatican and generally upheld the silence. The 'M' word was hardly ever mentioned. It was a pragmatic decision, dictated by political expediency. Until 1992 Sicily had always been ruled by the Christian Democrats, the Vatican's and – as some priests would have you believe – God's chosen party. They guaranteed that Italy, the country with the largest Communist Party in the West, didn't fall into the hands of the Red Peril. Securing votes in Sicily meant conniving with the Mafia. It was a pact with the Devil that was unfortunate but unavoidable. The end, after all, justifies the means. Just as they had done when the American troops liberating Italy in 1944 let thousands of mafiosi who had been imprisoned by Mussolini out of jail, appointed them as mayors and gave them more authority and guns than they could have dreamt of. The aim was to defeat Fascism and close the door to Communism. This was achieved at the price of establishing the Mafia as a power in Sicily that would rival the Italian state and force the ruling parties into a shameful legacy of compromise. But by 1993 things had changed. The Christian Democrats were no longer in power, Communism had been defeated, the Mafia was on the run. Many of its bosses had been imprisoned. Eight hundred Mafia turncoats, known as *pentiti* or 'repentant ones', were helping the police in return for the state's protection or because they wanted to settle old scores. In Palermo a mayor was elected on an openly anti-Mafia ticket. All these events were linked. The battle against Cosa Nostra on a military, political and psychological level was essentially the consequence of political upheaval at the centre in Rome.

The Mafia wasn't just at war with the Italian state. In many ways it had replaced the state, a process which began almost as soon as modern Italy was born. The etymological origins of the word 'Mafia' are obscure but most agree that it first appeared in the 1860s, when the Bourbon dynasty fell and when Sicily was subjected to the upheavals of Italian unification. The Mafia was a product of feudal Sicilian society. As the author Giuseppe di Lampedusa described in his classic novel about the persistent feudalism of Sicily, *The Leopard*, the role of the mafiosi was to guard the vast *latifondi* of absentee landlords who lounged in the opulence of their Palermo palaces. Gradually the Mafia became an alternative authority thriving on the neglect of government and of the ruling class. The mafiosi suppressed labour unrest on the estates of their landowners, but they also protected the peasants and stole from their employers. The Mafia became the intermediary between the *palazzo* and the *piazza* in a fragmented society, loyal only to itself, motivated solely by the pursuit of power and profit. In that sense little has changed. The modern mafiosi still looked after the *latifondi* of their landlords. The *latifondisti* of the 1980s didn't cultivate cereals or vines but votes. They were the Christian Democrat and Socialist politicians in

Rome. Their *latifondi* were vast electoral estates, whose regular harvests yielded the deputies and parliamentary majorities that enabled them to stay in power.

In its rather technical usage the term 'Mafia' means organised crime, dealing in drugs, arms, extortion, prostitution or pornography. Moscow, Warsaw and Belgrade now have a Mafia, apparently inspired if not instructed by their mentors in Sicily. Giovanni Falcone was the first Italian magistrate who tried to defeat the organisation by understanding it from within. To him the Mafia was 'nothing but the expression of a need for order, for control by the state'. He wrote: 'I believe it is the lack of a sense of state, of state as an interior value, which is the root cause of the distortions of the Sicilian soul: the dichotomy between society and state, the consequent over-reliance on family and on clan.' According to Giovanni Drago, a Mafia super-killer who later turned informer, this desire for order was taken to absurd lengths. Drago told investigators in a detailed confession amounting to 500 pages how he cleaned up Cosa Nostra's own backyard. 'The police were so incompetent at stamping out petty crime,' he told investigators, 'that we had to do it ourselves. I personally killed several known pickpockets and rapists.' A person might get dissolved in a bath of acid by the Mafia, but he wouldn't get mugged.

The yearning for order is reflected in the way that the crime syndicate is organised along the lines of a parallel feudal state. The Mafia has a strict hierarchy, based on four levels. It is headed by the so-called *commisione* or *cupola*, a regional Sicilian council of ten members, ruled by the *capo di tutti capi*, the head of all the family heads. The next layer consists of regional representatives from six Sicilian provinces. Each of these chairs a regional council which is made of five district bosses who are chosen from the local heads of the Mafia families. The heads in turn appoint a so-called *capo decina*, a leader of a group of ten Mafia 'soldiers'. The organisation is strictly hierarchical to overcome internal strife – not always successfully. It is also fragmented at the lower levels for security reasons. The members of one *decina* are not told who are the members of another *decina*. The identity of regional bosses is also supposed to be kept a secret.

The Mafia is rich in ritual, some of which, like the initiation ceremony, has been heavily inspired by Catholicism. Once a new 'Man of Honour' has been chosen by the head of family after months of careful observation, he is anointed by an elaborate initiation ceremony. In the presence of at least two witnesses the new recruit has to swear to seven commandments. While he swears to one oath after another his finger is pricked with a rose thorn. The blood is trickled over an image of the Madonna which is then burnt once the oaths have been made. Membership of Cosa Nostra is for life. The only way out is to die or get killed. There is no early retirement. The rituals are a way of sanctifying the organisation's practical need for secrecy and loyalty. The first step in defeating the Mafia was to realise this. The second was to penetrate the society and battle it from within. This is where the *pentiti* came in. Giovanni Falcone realised their value and gained most of his intelligence about the Mafia from Tommaso Buscetta, the most prominent *pentito* who repented in the mid-1980s. The *pentiti* have become the Italian state's most effective weapon against organised crime. And although this weapon is fundamentally flawed because its effectiveness depends on the reliability of each individual *pentito* it has yielded some important results.

In the small Sicilian town of San Giuseppe Iato three carabinieri stand guard outside an empty house. The shutters are closed. It's the only house in the street with empty washing lines. On the door there is a notice: *No Seventh-day Adventists, please.* But the inhabitants of number 17 Via Roma now fear a visitor who offers deliverance of a different sort: the Mafia. The owner of the house, Baldassare Di Maggio, no longer lives here. The Italian police gave him and ten members of his family a new home, a new name and 'Baldu', as his friends called him, also a new face. Di Maggio was a lapsed mafioso who had broken his vow of silence, and told the police where they could find the man they had been hunting for twenty-three years: Salvatore 'Toto' Riina. For ten years Di Maggio had been his driver. When police captured him last October he feared that Riina would have him and his family killed to prevent them from breaking their silence. Di Maggio's chances of staying alive were better under the state's new witness protection programme than at the mercy of the Mafia in or outside prison. If the authorities find out that a *pentito* has been lying they and their family are immediately taken out of the witness protection programme and delivered to the mercy of freedom without bodyguards. As an incentive for telling the truth it seems to have worked, so far at least.

Di Maggio turned out to be reliable. On the morning of 15 January fifteen policemen took up positions near a busy round-about on the outskirts of Palermo. When a black Lancia drove past the Agip petrol station, two officers stopped the car and asked to see the papers of the man inside. The last photograph of Toto Riina was taken twenty years ago. The stocky peasant features in the black and white photograph seemed to fit. The man sitting next to the driver was arrested. There was no shoot-out. In fact Riina and his driver didn't even carry guns. Their car wasn't the black stretch limo of Mafia movies with tinted windows and a minibar. It was an ordinary family car, a with a small plastic Madonna dangling from the rear-view mirror. At first the boss of all the bosses protested that he was an ordinary farmer on his way to the supermarket to do some shopping. He was probably telling the truth. Later, however, he congratulated the carabinieri for having made such a big catch. The most wanted man in Italy was a stickler for etiquette and treated his jailers as warmly as an old, long-lost uncle. When Riina's number two, 'Nitto' Santa-paola, the boss of Cosa Nostra in eastern Sicily, was arrested six months later he behaved in the same way. Police stormed the bunker in which he and his wife had been hiding under an olive grove. There was a Bible, a crucifix and a pistol on the bedside table. When the officers broke down the door, brandishing machine-guns, Santapaola was still lying in bed. He made no attempt to grab the gun. Instead he sat up, greeted his captors and congratulated them on a job well done. As one of the carabin-ieri later told a newspaper reporter: 'It was so easy, it was creepy. Sometimes I wish he had tried to shoot.' The mafiosi have been eerily dignified in defeat, especially when there was no chance of escape.

After his arrest the police discovered that Riina had been living right under their noses for ten years. The man for whom they had combed the mountains of Colombia and for whom generations of sniffer dogs had nosed through the remote caves of Sicily, had lived in what an estate agent might call 'a moderately well appointed garden condominium', near the centre of Palermo, next to one of the city's busiest roundabouts.

How was it possible that the authorities didn't know about his presence? The question still hasn't been answered in a satisfactory way, but according to numerous conspiracy theories the Italian government was only too well aware of the Riina family home. It just wasn't prepared to do anything about it for fear of upsetting the Mafia on whose electoral cooperation it relied in Sicily. If this was the case the Riina family certainly obliged their protectors by keeping a relatively low profile. The Riinas' bungalow was spacious without being ostentatious. The swimming pool was small, surrounded by mushroom-shaped garden lamps and the obligatory Hollywood swing. The house, more suited to a dentist than to the head of an international crime syndicate, couldn't have been more ordinary. Rather like some of the corrupt politicians who used to rule Italy, the heads of Cosa Nostra have always cherished the power to extract money more than the money itself. The only indication that something may have been amiss about the garden condominium was the reluctance of the neighbours to acknowledge the existence of the Riina family, whom they had been living next to for so many years. The cult of *omertà*, the code of silence which has protected mafiosi and their crimes for over a century, lives on in many quarters, not least of course in Corleone, Riina's hometown.

Dominated by an unseemly cone-shaped rock that protrudes from the centre of town and is home to a small monastery, Corleone looks like a stage set for a Mafia film. The small stone houses are dark and look more like dwellings in a Welsh mining village. The average age of the Corleonesi seems to be seventy and older. With almost the entire population sitting on stools in front of their houses or on their balconies gazing at life in the street or at each other, the town must have invented neighbourhood watch. Nothing escapes anyone. The Sicilians appreciate the subtle approach, so I asked a group of old men who sat on a bench near Riina's family home, a cramped, narrow three-storey house with an illuminated Madonna above the door, whether they had heard of the following list of names: John Major? 'Oh, yes,' they nodded. Hillary Clinton? 'But of course!' O.J. Simpson? 'Hmm, yes,' they said after a little delay. Toto Riina? '. . . Who?' came the chorus of feigned ignorance. 'Toto Riina!' I repeated the question, 'your former neighbour'. 'Never heard of him!' said the wrinkled masters of the deadpan reply. Their lack of cooperation probably had as much to do with *omertà* as with the feeling of annoyance at coming across yet another foreigner who asked about the Mafia. The more one enquires about the Mafia in Sicily the more one begins to doubt one's own sanity, even today.

An air of disbelief also surrounds the diminutive, almost goon-like figure of Toto Riina, for years the most wanted man in Italy. 'Toto' is short for Salvatore. His other nicknames are 'La Belva' – the Beast – or 'U Curtu' – the Short One – depending on your relationship with him. Toto had been tried in absentia for five murders before he was caught and for another ten after his arrest. An alleged master in the art of liquidation, one of 'the Beast's' specialities was to dissolve his victims in acid. This extinguished any evidence of the crime. The Mafia calls this method *la lupara bianca* – literally the white shotgun – in deference to Cosa Nostra's traditional weapon. During the Mafia wars of the late 1970s and early 1980s that brought Toto and his Corleonesi clan to power, Riina allegedly ordered the death of women, flouting one of the oldest Mafia sacraments. When it was known that Tommaso Buscetta had become a turncoat, investigators believe that Riina had three women in his family killed immediately: Buscetta's mother, aunt and sister. 'The Beast' was clearly a very unpleasant man. I was thus surprised to find him personally rather charming when I met him briefly in 1993 three months after his arrest. Riina was in a cage in the courtroom of Rome's high-security Rebibbio jail, on the outskirts of the city, a God-forsaken place somewhere between a motorway bypass and a shanty town for Northern African immigrants. We had been invited to listen to a preliminary hearing in one of the many murder trials facing Riina. Both sides of the large subterranean courtroom were lined with cages. The hall was filled with journalists waiting for the judge and jury to arrive. The stifling heat and the flickering of indecisive neon lights filled the room with a soporific air. I was half asleep when I turned round and saw 'the Beast' sitting on a stool in the last cell. He was completely alone. Two carabinieri officers stood in front of the cell. The room was suddenly filled with an atmosphere of near hysteria as journalists and cameramen rushed towards the cage and surveyed 'the Beast' inside. Riina, who had extraordinary composure, was wearing an immaculate cashmere jacket and a smart casual open-neck shirt. His thin grey hair had been combed carefully. His tiny blue eyes twinkled brightly. Toto looked like the respectable owner of a hairdressing salon or perhaps the chief cashier at the local post office. I simply could not imagine this man controlling the most vicious and complex syndicate in the world, manipulating the Italian stockmarket, conferring with his Colombian counterparts from Medellín, or dissolving an enemy in acid, all of which he stood accused of having done. When Toto Riina stood before the judge on his first hearing, he said with sad ironic eyes: 'But sir, I am just a simple peasant!' One was inclined to agree with him, despite the evidence.

Standing on the other side of the bars to Riina and looking into the lively eyes of this man whose appearance so belied his reputation and his criminal record, one was somewhat lost for words. I was about to ask him a question when the reporter next to me, a voluptuous blonde, from RAI, butted in with the very issue that was on my mind. 'Did you, Signor Riina,' she asked, 'kiss the former Prime Minister Giulio Andreotti on the cheek?' 'The Beast' looked at the questioner, smiled, placed both his hands on the bars flanking his face and gently pushing his head forward as far as he could, he hissed: '*Sei bella!*' ('You're beautiful!') '*Come ti chiami?*' ('What's your name?') The reporter was speechless. The mixture of myth and malice was still having its effect, even on a hardened TV reporter.

In 1994 the Italian government was beating its drum over the wave of arrests. Every week another prominent mafioso ended up behind bars or decided to 'repent'. The Mafia threatened to burst Italy's already overcrowded jails. In two years the Italian authorities arrested over 4000 Mafia suspects, more than Mussolini's notorious Mafia basher Prefetto Mori had done in the 1930s. Without the *pentiti* the government would have remained impotent in the battle against organised crime. But the willingness of the *pentiti* to come forward was above all due to new legislation giving more state protection to informers. This was a political fact which reflected the new will of the parties in Rome to fight organised crime. The Men of Honour may not be aware of it, but their demise also started with the collapse of the Berlin Wall and the consequences for Italy's four-party regime. The end of the Christian Democrats and their allies as the dominant force in Italian politics meant that the Mafia had lost its principal political protectors in Rome. The business relationship between Palermo and Rome which had been based on an exchange of votes in return for tolerance was beginning to disintegrate. The Mafia was no longer able to deliver enough votes to stem the electoral haemorrhage of the parties. The Christian Democrats and their allies were no longer in a position to deliver favours. One incident illustrated this change more than any other.

On 12 March 1992 a silver-haired gentleman in a dark blue pinstripe suit left his spacious villa in Mondello, Palermo's elegant seaside suburb, and got into his car. Salvatore Lima, Salvo to his friends, was a Christian Democrat member of the European parliament in Strasbourg at the time. He had held many illustrious offices. He was mayor of Palermo in 1987. He was a long-standing member of the Italian parliament. Most importantly, indeed most fatally, he was Prime Minister Giulio Andreotti's nuncios on the island of Sicily. He was the proconsul who ensured that the 'Old Fox' would receive a sufficient number of votes from Sicily to ensure his power and the influence of his *corrente* (literally, current) or faction within the amorphous Christian Democratic Party. As he got into his unarmoured car – since Salvo Lima's protection came from the Mafia itself, there was no need, or so he thought, for bulletproof metal casing – two men approached on a moped and started spraying him with bullets. One shot hit Lima in the shoulder, another in the left arm. The honourable member for Sicily in the European parliament got out of the car and crawled down the street, which was wet thanks to the morning drizzle. The two men drove slowly after him on their moped and fired another volley of shots.

Lima's murder, a Mafia turncoat later explained to the police, was a signal of disapproval. The the ruling council of the Mafia, was disappointed that Lima was unable to get a number of court convictions quashed for mafiosi who had appeared in the famous Maxi trial of 1987. Whether Lima had lost his clout with the judges, or whether Andreotti had ruled against the 'adjustment', or whether it was the fact that the Christian Democrats had already lost their once divine right to rule, something in the chain of command between politics and organised crime had collapsed. By killing Lima in March, a month before Italy's 1992 general elections, the Men of Honour had entered the election campaign with a bloody reminder that their interests after all these years of vote buying and ballot stuffing could not be ignored. But Andreotti and his party could not reverse the tide of history. The seventime former Prime Minister defended his murdered friend. 'In all the years I knew Salvo Lima in the party from 1968 onwards I never had any firm reason to believe, never in fact had a single idea, that Lima led a double life or that he served the interests of the Mafia . . . Quite the contrary!' According to Andreotti, Lima first and foremost served the interests of Rome. This was indeed the case!

Lima was the link between the *palazzo* in Rome and the Mafia. After his death investigators followed the trail of blood directly to Giulio Andreotti. In the summer of 1994 Andreotti was charged by magistrates in Sicily with actually being a member of the Mafia. Part of the evidence on which the charges are based comes from Baldassare Di Maggio, the same informer who had turned in Toto Riina. What he told the investigators was that the relationship between the Christian Democrats and the Mafia had been sealed, like so many other political relationships in Italy, with a kiss on the cheeks. According to Di Maggio, Andreotti was kissed by Toto Riina during a meeting which allegedly took place in 1987, while Andreotti was on a visit to Palermo. The *baccio di mafia* is more than just a peck on the cheek. It is a highly symbolic gesture indicating the power of the kisser over the kissed. Andreotti had vociferously denied that the meeting let alone the kiss ever took place. He said he was in no position to slip away for a brief encounter with a senior mafioso in hiding while on a visit to Sicily, without the fact being noticed by his bodyguards or a dozen TV cameras following him around. Pino Arlacchi, who is now a member of the Italian parliament and perhaps Italy's most respected expert on Cosa Nostra, believes that the meeting was plausible. 'It illustrated the supreme arrogance of those in power at the time. They thought they were untouchable.'

If Giulio Andreotti maintained a sibylline silence over the Mafia, another Christian Democrat embodied the attitude that you can only exorcise the devil by pronouncing his name. The role of the Mafia's chief exorcist fell to Leoluca Orlando, former mayor of Palermo, who defected from the Christian Democratic party in 1987 because of its links to the Mafia. He set up his own political movement called La Rete, the Network. Perhaps the choice of name was unfortunate for a party that was devoted to fighting organised crime, but La Rete became the political voice against the Mafia. It articulated in middle-class Sicily a sense of civic responsibility and civil courage that many thought had been lost for ever. During the election campaign for mayor of Palermo, which Orlando won with an astounding seventy-five per cent of the vote, his supporters described him as 'Orlando Furioso', comparing him to the swashbuckling hero from classical mythology. Leoluca Orlando may not be the most subtle, articulate or cunning politician, but his uninhibited anger at the state of politics in Sicily was a welcome contrast to the previous rulers, who masked their hypocrisy and lies with verbal garlands. Orlando was refreshingly blunt. He hammered home his message with dogged determination, in Italian as well as in English, for the benefit of foreign news organisations like the BBC. Every month Orlando would discover a new sound bite with which to feed the rapacious animal of Western television. 'We are a *normal* people. We want to live in a *normal* city,' he would repeat mantra-like. Or: 'The Mafia has entered the Italian state like a Trojan horse.' Dismissed by his opponents as hot-headed and rhetorical, Orlando understood two important things: firstly ordinary Sicilians were sick and tired of living under the shadow of organised crime; secondly the Mafia was merely the most malignant manifestation of a problem that existed all over Italy.

In its mildest form this was called the *cultura dell'appartenenza*, the culture or mentality in which individuals seek security and protection from a hostile world and an indifferent state by belonging to a group that protects their interests. This mentality evolves into the *cultura della raccomandazione*, where nothing is achieved without the recommendation or patronage of a powerful person. The logical next step, according to Orlando, is the Mafia, a mutual aid society based on blood vendettas, violence and illicit earnings. Leoluca Orlando is not universally admired. His small party almost splintered over accusations that he behaved in an autocratic manner. Orlando has never really managed to give a convincing answer to the questions of how he, as a former Christian Democrat and mayor of the capital of Sicily, was able to avoid dealing with the Mafia. Hard-bitten cynics wonder how anyone in Palermo can receive seventy-five per cent of the vote without being backed by the mob, but Orlando has always said that his support results from his anti-Mafia stance.

Cosa Nostra has experienced its own revolution. For a brief period Rome was dominated by parties that apparently did not rely on votes bought by the Mafia. This freed government to introduce a number of stringent anti-Mafia measures, allowing them to confiscate trillions of lire in Mafia property and to conduct a witness protection programme that encouraged almost one thousand mafiosi to 'repent'. Ordinary Sicilians gained the courage to vote according to their conscience and not according to someone else's interests. The most important ingredient of this 'revolution', which paralleled that of *tangentopoli,* was the one that had always been missing in the past: the battle against *mafiosita*. *Mafiosita*, literally 'mafiosity', is a quintessentially Sicilian term, invented by the writer Leonardo Sciascia who died in 1989, perhaps the most perceptive observer of the Sicilian psyche. He distinguished between 'Mafia', the criminal organisation, and *mafiosita*, the mentality that allowed the organisation to thrive. This mentality was founded on the culture of suspicion, produced by generations of invaders and the worship of patronage, that was a hangover from feudal society. The battle against *mafiosita* was a fight for modernity and it could, according to Sciascia, only take place in the mind of every individual Sicilian.

I discovered my own definition of *mafiosita* in the most unlikely place: Palermo's General Hospital. This sprawling establishment is a surreal shrine to the corruption, superstition, inventiveness, neglect, generosity and violence . . . in other words to the warped humanity that is Sicily. Enter the large central gate and walk past a statue decked in flowers of Padre Pio, the friar turned miracle healer. Turn left and you'll be on the lawn next to the casualty unit. A flock of ten sheep are grazing nonchalantly on tufty weeds. A street urchin selling fortune tickets for good luck and carrying a yellow canary in a box waits patiently by the helicopter pad, where patients are flown in from Sicily's outlying mountain villages. He's in luck. A helicopter lands. The sheep disperse. As the stretcher is lowered from the helicopter and disappears into an ambulance, the urchin makes for the patient's relatives. An old woman buys a ticket displaying the face of a saint. She knows that her ailing husband will need all the luck money can buy to survive in Palermo's General Hospital.

Dr Marco Colimberti, one of the hospital's leading heart surgeons, who is leading a campaign to uncover corruption and professional malpractice, put on his white coat and took me on a tour in December 1993. We stopped at a building site surrounded by barbed wire. 'This is the new emergency ward, or rather this *should* be the new emergency ward.' A concrete monstrosity in the Mafia's favourite style (square and ugly), construction on the building began ten years before. The hospital's new wing still hadn't been completed when I visited it. Not because the money had run out. Tens of billions of lire had already been spent on it. Billions more would be. As the doctor explained, the faulty design ensured an almost endless string of repairs and fresh starts and thus a lavish flow of lire. This is common practice in Sicily – a standard way for the politicians to rake in bribes and for the construction business to secure lucrative contracts. At the time of my visit almost half the deputies in Sicily's regional parliament were being investigated for similar crimes.

The emergency ward may have been incomplete but it was being used. At night prostitutes plied a thriving trade on the mezzanine, where the rough cement floor glistened with used condoms. The first and second floors were littered with spent syringes. Dr Colimberti hated night shifts. 'It's too dangerous to walk from one pavilion to another,' he said. Fabrizio Chiodo, another heart surgeon in his early forties, was also afraid. He on the other hand had two bodyguards and sometimes, when talking, nervously fingered a Beretta pistol under his white coat. 'Just to check it's still there,' he would say.

The General Hospital is a dual homage to Fellini and Mad Max. The carabinieri gave Dr Chiodo his pistol and his armed escort after he received death threats in January 1993. The judiciary believes the threats came from the Mafia. Dr Chiodo had been indiscreet enough to tell Palermo's magistrates about one of the most lucrative scams in the hospital's famous cardiac surgery unit. Although the unit had three operating theatres and twenty-five surgeons, in the early 1990s it performed only 150 operations a year. This was very few compared, for instance, to a hospital in the northern city of Brescia where eight surgeons were performing 800 operations per annum.

The shortfall is due to the fact that the great majority of operations take place in private clinics staffed by surgeons from Palermo General Hospital. Investigators found that the waiting lists contained at least forty people who had already died and scores who had never lived. The purpose was to tell desperate patients that they would have to wait for years before they could receive the necessary operation, by which stage they would already have died. But if they or their social security were willing to pay an extra eight million lire (£4000) there was a way out.

Once they had agreed, a transfer was arranged quickly in the hospital's ambulances to one of a chain of private clinics. The operation was performed under immaculate conditions by surgeons from the hospital. The average salary of a Sicilian surgeon is seven million lire a month. For each private operation he receives another four million. At the time, the judiciary believed some of the clinics were owned by the Mafia and were used to launder drugs money. So far twelve surgeons, one owner of a private clinic and several government health officers have gone to jail for their involvement in the scheme.

Dr Chiodo's bodyguards followed him everywhere. When he was operating they hovered outside the theatre. In a hospital that employs over a thousand doctors and two thousand five hundred nurses Dr Chiodo had very few friends. He had broken the *omertà*, the vow of silence, brought the hospital into ill repute and spoilt the extracurricular activities. The doctor had some powerful enemies on the hospital's ruling administrative committee. All of its twelve members belonged to Palermo's premier Masonic lodge. In fact more doctors belong to the lodge than to the medical branch of the CGIL, Italy's main trade union federation.

On the final stage of our tour Dr Colimberti took me to a special parking lot for ambulances. A group of drivers were standing around smoking cigarettes. 'They are waiting for the dead,' the doctor explained. The vehicles are in fact hearses masquerading as ambulances – waiting to pick up the deceased to take them back to their homes 'where they can then die in peace'. For many poor Sicilian families a faked death at home is still preferable to a real death in hospital. And in Sicily death encourages potential beneficiaries to flout the law in the most imaginative and ingenious way. Because a corpse already issued with a death certificate cannot be taken back home, the doctors are bribed by the undertakers not to certify someone as dead. Each doctor works with a group of nurses and hospital porters who are retained by one of the rival funeral companies. They are paid a monthly fee or retainer as well as a percentage on each living corpse. When someone is about to die, the porter alerts the undertaker, who then gets in touch with the family. Sometimes the patients are picked up from hospital when they are still alive. In most cases they are already dead.

In order to pass through the police checkpoint at the hospital gate, the dead body in the fake ambulance is even fitted with an IV drip. The police don't seem to mind the fact that the fake ambulances are travelling in the wrong direction, away from the hospital. 'The system works relatively smoothly,' Dr Colimberti explained. 'Different undertakers service different wards.' In the interests of social peace and harmony they have even worked out a timetable. But sometimes the system breaks down. Last February two 'ambulances' from rival companies arrived to pick up the same body. There was a shoot-out. Dr Colimberti called the police, who finally arrived after twenty minutes and told him not to worry. No arrests were made.

Some of the doctors, surgeons and administrators running the hospital's various scams have been less lucky. In 1994 twenty suspects were arrested and charged with fraud, bribery and corruption. The changes at the hospital, the arrests, the inquiries and the new, more honest management cannot be seen in isolation. They are like so much else in Italy today: the consequence of political upheaval.

At times the battle against the Mafia and *mafiosita* even took on the forms of a popular rebellion. Francesco Rovelli, a professor of sociology with a round face and a gentle smile, is one of Orlando's fervent supporters. He sat in the flouncy lobby of Palermo's Excelsior Hotel, sipped a sweet coffee and ate one of the cool and sticky Sicilian cakes that testify to the mixture of cultures on this much-invaded island. The Cassata Siciliana, peppered with glazed fruit, laced with liqueur and covered with a fluorescent green icing, bears the signature of Arab, Bourbon, French and Austrian patissiers who accompanied one invading army or another. Sicilian desserts are the after-taste of invasions. But their sticky sweetness also serves as a reminder that all invasions in Sicily have failed and that logic, enterprise and initiative have eventually succumbed to the seductive powers of this sensual island. 'Until we start demanding our rights as citizens and stop looking for privileges or patronage, we will not have rid ourselves of our innate *mafiosita*.' The professor's face assumed the pained expression of a self-flagellating monk. 'What's needed,' he continued, 'are not just arrests, jail sentences and secure cells for the mafiosi but a popular revolution.' As we spoke an extraordinary din began to invade the velvet cosiness of the hotel lobby: drums, trumpets, whistles, helicopters, screeching voices on distorted loudspeakers and the verbal avalanche of half a million people, walking past our hotel. 'The racket of a witch-doctor driving out *mafiosita*, said the professor. It was 25 June 1992, the day of the biggest anti-Mafia demonstration in Sicily's history. The demonstration had been organised by the Italian Trades Union Federation. Thousands of people had been bussed in from all over Italy. But most of the demonstrators were ordinary Palermitani who had come to participate in this act of collective therapy. Tens of thousands of people who ten years ago would only have whispered the 'M' word in private were allowed to scream 'Mafia!' and listen to it echo through the narrow streets of the city. In many ways the rally had the same sensation of mental liberation that electrified the demonstrations which swept through Leipzig in October 1989 and helped to bring down the East German regime of Erich Honecker.

In Palermo people were not just demonstrating against a crime syndicate, but against a whole regime of connivance in which politics had become the shield for the Mafia. This regime had not only killed, stolen, smuggled or extorted, but had gagged ordinary Sicilians, had ruined their landscape with ugly construction, had polluted their sea, frightened off investors and had stifled their economy. A popular revolution seemed to be unfolding in Sicily at the same time as voters were turning their back on the Socialists and Christian Democrats in northern Italy, where the judicial stampede against corruption had already begun. The Piazza Politeama, where the four columns of demonstrators converged, was a sea of flags and banners, many of which thanked Antonio Di Pietro and the Milan 'Clean Hands' magistrates.

The demonstration had been inspired by the murder a month before of the country's leading anti-Mafia judge, Giovanni Falcone, his wife and three of their bodyguards. They were killed on 25 May 1992 by a huge bomb planted in the shallow draining duct under a stretch of the motorway near the village of Capaci between Palermo airport and the city. The explosion, which was set off by remote control from an olive grove above the motorway, tore a crater five metres wide and two metres deep into the tarmac. The first car, containing the bodyguards, was flung over one hundred yards to the other side of the motorway and landed in a vegetable garden. A group of Austrian tourists travelling in the opposite direction in their rental car were seriously injured. Falcone's car, driving at 145 kilometres an hour, crashed headlong into the asphalt that had buckled under the explosion like a crumpled carpet. The judge had insisted on driving the armoured car himself. His driver, who was sitting in the back, survived.

Falcone and his wife could have survived as well, had they worn seat-belts.

These technicalities became irrelevant as popular anger mounted. In brazenly eliminating their most formidable opponents, the bombers also created a martyr whose death galvanised the protest. During the funeral, in which thousands crammed into Palermo's cathedral, mourning turned to rage. The young widow of one of the five bodyguards launched a tearful attack against the political establishment in Rome and accused it of negligence in the fight against the Mafia. When they left the service the cabinet ministers were heckled by angry crowds. As the Mafia remained invisible the anger was directed against those who were widely despised as the mob's political patrons.

The murder of Falcone was intended as a specular display of the Mafia's power and its ability to eliminate its enemies. But it turned out to be a grave miscalculation. The bomb had shown that Cosa Nostra was on the defensive, forced to resort to dramatic displays of violence which were completely out of character. In 1991 Falcone himself had written: 'Newspapers, books and films all concentrate on the cruelty of the Mafia. Certainly it exists but not as an end in itself. Men who commit gratuitous atrocities provoke disgust within the organisation. Participation in an act of violence is usually rigorously logical, and it is this logic that makes Cosa Nostra the feared organisation it is.' By the Mafia's own standards the bomb at Capaci was a display of unnecessary violence. Moreover, police search teams discovered cigarette butts around a small cluster of olive trees on a hill overlooking the motorway. It emerged that the men who had set off the bomb by remote control had waited several days for Falcone's motorcade. Traces of saliva on discarded cigarette butts enabled the police to acquire a DNA print of the smokers. A year later eighteen people were arrested in connection with the killing of Falcone. The murder had been sloppy work by the mob's standards.

Two months later the Mafia compounded its problems by killing another leading anti-Mafia judge. On Sunday 19 July Paolo Borsellino, who had been one of Falcone's closest colleagues and had inherited his mantle, went to visit his mother in the centre of Palermo for afternoon coffee and cakes. When he left her flat a car bomb exploded on the street outside. It killed Borsellino and four of his bodyguards. Instead of intimidating the public, the second killing brought even more people out on the streets. The popular revolt gathered momentum. As the Mafia's mystique began to crumble, the *omertà*, the notorious code of silence which had protected the organisation since its inception and had undermined the search for witnesses, began to be breached not just in Palermo, but in more remote areas too. In the town of Capo D'Orlando on the northern coast of Sicily local businessmen formed a commercial association, a kind of anti-Mafia Rotary Club. Its purpose was to resist the *pizzo*, the extortion money which the Mafia demanded in return for protection. The only thing the money offered protection from was of course the Mafia itself. The association included businessmen, grocers, jewellers, bookshop owners and estate agents, each of whom was represented by a light-bulb that was hung from a kind of Christmas tree of defiance on the hill above Capo D'Orlando. The Mafia had tried to stamp out the roots of this revolt by burning down one or two shops.

But the intimidation didn't work. The silent protest continued. I asked the head of the association, the avuncular owner of a toy shop in the central square why he had taken this courageous step. 'The recession,' he replied. 'I can't afford to pay the *pizzo* of 800,000 lire (about £350) a month any more. And the Mafia doesn't take market forces or a decline in sales figures into account.' Capo D'Orlando bristled with carabinieri. We were staying in the Turtle Hotel, a kitsch palace on the waterfront where the windows had been fitted with security bars in the shape of wrought-iron turtles. Five carabinieri officers were permanently on guard, because the hotel owner was preparing to go to court and give evidence against the local Mafia family. Capo D'Orlando soon started a trend of defiance. Business associations were founded in Santa Agata, Enna, Nicosia and Gela.

Two and a half thousand years ago Gela was a thriving colony of Graeco-Roman culture on the southern coast of the island where the bougainvillaea grows in bushes as tall as trees, where the air is scented with jasmine and orange blossom and where a stiflingly hot wind called the Afa blows up from the Libyan Sahara and creates the leaden mood of an eternal siesta. Gela is about ten kilometres further south than Tunis but such geographical references are irrelevant in a place that hails from Dante's *Inferno*. Nowhere is the contrast between the stunning beauty of the Sicilian landscape and the jaw-dropping ugliness of its towns greater than here. Set along a spectacular coastline that sweeps up the hills behind it, Gela once boasted a seafront lined with palm trees and one of Europe's broadest, cleanest and whitest beaches. Now the city plays host to a disused oil refinery and some of Sicily's most vicious crime families, whose local version of the Mafia is called the *Stiddha*.

Today Gela is under military occupation. It hasn't had a mayor in years. The only public service there is the army. The customary carabinieri are outnumbered by soldiers from the Alpine regiment who patrol the city in armoured vehicles and trucks fitted with machine-guns on bipods. Army helicopters hover above like menacing insects. Judging from the expression of fear on the faces of the soldiers I saw, the Italian army had not won the campaign for the hearts and minds of Gela. The Alpine uniform of a peaked Tyrolean hat with a long drooping feather simply confirmed the soldiers' status as unwanted aliens. I had been taken to Gela by Carlo Averna, the owner of a factory at nearby Caltanisetta that produced Sicily's most famous Amaro, a bitter-sweet digestive drink made from a secret recipe of herbs. I met Signor Averna while he was taking part in a special course sponsored by the Italian government teaching Sicilian businessmen how to resist *mafiosita*. In a pink castle built at the end of the last century on the Monte San Pellegrino in Palermo, businessmen like Averna were brought together with officials from Sicily's public administration, and taught the rules of the free market and private enterprise. The object of the classes, which were held once a month, was to combat the climate of distrust which had helped to create the Mafia in the first place and which the Men of Honour knew how to exploit to their advantage. Averna gave me a simple but telling example. 'It is almost impossible,' he said, 'to get the fax number of another company in Sicily over the phone, without personally knowing the person you are talking to. We are a very enclosed society. Our instinct tells us to trust only those who belong to our family, our clan, our company.'

Averna was in his forties and had inherited the company from his father. Sixty per cent of his sales were on the domestic market, the rest mainly in Germany where the brown digestive treacle had become very popular. Although Averna was run like any other modern European business, its owner felt completely isolated in Caltanisetta. Since the sulphur mines had been closed his was the only factory in a town with over thirty per cent unemployment. Signor Averna told me he had been approached by the local Mafia but refused to pay the protection fee of five million lire a month. Now he was waiting for the next visit.

He was one of the founders of the Gela business association. On the day I visited Gela the association was burying one of its members. Gaetano Giordano owned a small chain of perfumery shops. One day he was driving his son to school, when his car was sprayed with bullets. Giordano had known he was in danger. In January he had opened another perfumery on Gela's high street. Two weeks later he received a visit from a stranger who demanded four million lire 'as a contribution to the neighbourhood watch scheme'. In March Giordano still hadn't contributed and the tyres of his car were shot up. In April they tried to burn down his house. In May the Mafia killed him.

The funeral procession of over 3000 people, headed by the son who survived the attack, wound its way solemnly through the cement maze of Gela. Many of the streets had not been asphalted. Piles of rubbish blossomed in the overflowing gullies, scrutinised by dogs and cats. The mourners included most of the 800 members of the local business association carrying the club's coat of arms. But they were outnumbered by those who stood on the pavement or sat on their balconies and just watched in silence. There was none of the jubilant defiance that had marked the funeral rallies of the judges in Palermo. Gela was the Mafia's natural habitat. The only employer with a future here is the Mafia. For a town with thirty per cent overall unemployment and fifty per cent of young people out of work, Gela had a disproportionate number of young men driving around in BMWs or open-top sports cars.

As I stood in front of the perfumery watching Gaetano Giordano's son lay a wreath, I heard a thick Brooklyn accent. 'This town is apocalyptic.' I turned round to see a teenager with a baseball cap, an alien apparition. Greg Bertini was eighteen years old and was just finishing high school in Gela. His father had moved back to his birthplace after his business collapsed in New York.

'What kind of business?' I asked.

'Import, export,' Greg replied.

'What's it like living here?'

'There is no future for any of us. Most of my class-mates already work for "them".'

I wasn't sure whether Greg was sending me up, or whether he had a well-developed sense of drama. He clearly looked uneasy. I asked him a little more about his family until he finally made his excuses and disappeared into the crowd. Since my visit in 1993 the carabinieri have arrested more than 400 people in Gela alone. Most of the male members of the town's four top Mafia families are in jail. Gela is the twilight zone of Italy. I had to pinch myself to remember that it was part of the European Union. Since the murder of Gaetano Giordano no member of the business association has been killed or threatened. But how long was it going to last?

'We *were* witnessing a Sicilian spring! Now the spring is in danger of being snuffed out!' Leoluca Orlando, the mayor of Palermo, was sitting in a cool room of the Villa Niscemi, a seventeenth-century summer palace on the outskirts of Palermo. Orlando uses the villa, which was sold to the city of Palermo in 1987, as a temporary daytime office. He arrives in his screeching motorcade of armoured cars, jumps out, pursued by his eight permanent bodyguards, and disappears into the marbled entrance hall of the villa. The mayor of Palermo is forever running away from an enemy he cannot see, whose movements he cannot predict, but whose intentions towards him are by now clear. The opulent rooms of the Villa Niscemi had tiled floors. The walls were decorated with exquisite frescoes in bright pastel colours. Sugary Venetian glass chandeliers hung low from the ceiling, adding an air of faded grandeur. Most of the rooms were abandoned and the magnificent furniture in others covered in a thick layer of dust. In one of the bedrooms towels were still draped over a rack. It looked as if the villa had suddenly been deserted, its inhabitants forced out by some plague. In another room the mayor's body-guards were lounging on the chaises longues, pistols stuck in their belts, like the bored retainers of a warlord.

Orlando uses the Villa Niscemi as his political 'surgery'. The waiting room was full of people, looking for help, advice and probably also personal favours. Outside the heat was intense. Inside the stuffy air was aflutter with women fanning themselves. Orlando, who was always known for his bounding energy and enthusiasm, looked drawn and tired. His usually swarthy face was pale. His eyes were red with lack of sleep, the bags under them the size of walnuts. He was sweating profusely in the midday heat. *La vita blindata*, the 'armoured life' of bodyguards and armoured cars, was clearly beginning to take its toll.

Orlando's brief honeymoon with politics was over. For example, he had just been accused by a *pentiti* of conniving with the Mafia when he held the office of mayor in the 1980s. His party, La Rete, had been crushed at the polls by Silvio Berlusconi's brand-new Forza Italia Party. The voters of Sicily had shown an extraordinary degree of fickleness. Five months after the left-wing parties like La Rete and the Democratic Party of the Left had triumphed in scores of Sicilian cities during municipal elections, they were already being abandoned by the voters. Some accused the Mafia of infiltrating Berlusconi's Forza Italia and buying votes by the bucketful for the tycoon. Others blamed the demise of the left on the fact that after four months in office they hadn't achieved much. Another explanation was that the bourgeois revolution against the Mafia, the battle against *mafiosita*, had simply run out of steam. Orlando believed that his revolution had been hijacked by Silvio Berlusconi and the right with its 'empty promises of instant prosperity'. Perhaps it was a combination of all these factors. The fact is, though, that in the middle of 1994 the tide seemed to be turning back in the Mafia's favour.

The victory of the right coincided with a consistent campaign of intimidation against a number of left wing-mayors in Sicily who had been elected vowing to fight the Mafia. In Piana di Albanesi the office of the PDS, the former Communist Party, was burnt down; in San Giuseppe Iato the PDS mayor, a woman, woke up one night to find her car in flames. Altogether there were over a dozen incidents of intimidation. Paolo Cippriano, the mayor of Corleone, was the first holder of that office not to belong to either the Christian Democrats or Socialists. Born in Corleone, he had worked for a student's cooperative doing community work before going into politics. He walked out of his house one morning in February to find a severed calf's head on the doorstep, a very traditional Mafia warning, usually followed up by another warning and then death. 'One shouldn't exaggerate these antics,' said the thirty-two-year-old mayor. Wearing jeans and a check shirt without a tie he looked like the foreman of a radical workers' committee that has billeted the town hall after the revolution. 'What *is* worrying to me and my colleagues is that we can feel the ground disappear from under our feet. We feel increasingly isolated here, and we don't think that we are getting the right moral support from the new government in Rome.'

In 1994 this became a common complaint, especially amongst mayors and municipal councillors all over Sicily who had been elected during the heyday of the anti-Mafia parties. Although Prime Minister Berlusconi said he was intent on fighting the Mafia, coming from him the message didn't carry the same conviction as it did from his immediate predecessors. The main reason for this is that a large number of former politicians who had been in parliament for the now-discredited Socialists or Christian Democrats had found a new and easy home in Forza Italia, Berlusconi's party. Hundreds of Forza Italia clubs which had been hastily set up to orchestrate the media tycoon's lightning election campaign were also suspected of having been infiltrated by people associated with the Mafia culture. When Forza Italia swept the board at the national elections in 1994, something which coincided with a wave of attacks against left-wing parties, it was not surprising that mayors like Cippriano felt intimidated and isolated. No one suggested that the bomb and arson attacks were organised by Forza Italia, only that the Mafia saw its opportunity to scare those who had openly campaigned against it.

What impressed me most about the mayor of Corleone was his accessibility. He occupied a vast office in the town's gloomy *municipio*, which had clearly been designed to keep people out not invite them in. But the door was open and every two minutes someone else came in for a quick chat. The room was filled with the trophies of power collected by his predecessors: a large moth-eaten banner made of red velvet displaying the city emblem, a lion clutching a bloody heart in its left paw. One wall was decorated with the portraits of previous mayors. One stood out. The caption read 'Bernardino Verro 1866–1915'. A dedication had been added: 'The farmers of Corleone remember that from him they received the first light of thinking about the dignity of the world. He was killed for his beliefs on November 3 1915.' One couldn't help but wonder whether a similar dedication would one day be written under the portrait of the present mayor.

'The reason why we haven't been able to follow up last year's successes, why the so-called "revolution" has suddenly fizzled out, is the economy,' Cippriano continued. 'Unless we can get the economy sorted out the Mafia will always find fertile ground for recruitment.' In many ways Sicily faces the same catch-22 situation as a former Communist country like Russia. The aim of social reform is to make individuals responsible for their own prosperity within the boundaries of the law, to break the long tradition of relying on someone else to deliver prosperity, protection and patronage. This involves starving Sicily of the subsidies which have fed straight into the Mafia economy. But a climate of increasing unemployment and hopelessness is tailor-made for the Mafia. Subsidies have already been cut in Rome and there are signs that the vicious cycle is continuing. Again there are no statistics to underpin this theory, just individual examples. Perhaps the most striking occurred in February in the eastern Sicilian city of Messina. Police arrested Janos Ferrara, one of the local Mafia bosses. The news spread rapidly through the neighbourhood that he controlled. When the boss emerged from the local courthouse, where he had been questioned by magistrates, to be transferred to jail, he was greeted by an angry crowd of two hundred people. Young men, old men, women, children, entire families were shouting from behind a metal barrier that had been set up to separate them from the entrance to the courthouse. The crowd was demanding the release of their local mafioso. 'Ferrara gives us jobs and food', read one banner. In this case at least, *Mafiosita* seemed to have triumphed.

There were other indications that the spirit of defiance was evaporating. In November 1994, a week before the Pope came on his visit to Sicily, a priest was addressing a congregation in his church in Palermo. When he told his worshippers, as he had done on many previous occasions that they had to stand up against the Mafia the reaction left him dumbfounded. The entire congregation of about a hundred people got up and left the church.

'Cosa Nostra,' wrote Falcone, 'has the strength of a religion and its actions are the products of an ideology of power and a subculture.' The Mafia has become an alternative state. Ironically it has had the same time to mature as the Italian state. Both were created in the 1860s. But the Mafia has turned out to be a much more flexible, adaptable creature. Its rules, customs and organisation are more durable than any individual mafioso. Many Mafia experts are convinced that the organisation continues to thrive despite the thousands of arrests that have been made in recent years. As one of them put it, comparing the Mafia to a famous international company: 'Just because you arrest the board of British Telecom, that doesn't mean that you finish off BT.' Cosa Nostra has also shown that it still has the power to intimidate with a few well-placed messages. A threatening phone call to a journalist, a severed calf's head nailed to the door of a priest, or an anti-Mafia memorial defiled. In November 1994 the memorial plaque to Giovanni Falcone and Paolo Borsellino, which had been put up in the square that now bears their name in Corleone, home of the Riina family, was stolen. 'Another attack against the opponents of darkness!' thundered the *Repubblica*. Public opinion was once again mortified. Later it turned out that the plaque had been stolen by Toto Riina's pudgy eighteen-year-old son. Anywhere else in the world the theft would have been a brazen schoolboy prank. In Sicily it was an attack against humanity, because it conjured up a whole string of associations, messages and implied threats. The Mafia exists no doubt, but after a century of intimidation it has also ensured that much of its menace is in the eye of the beholder.

9

The Conspiracy of Truth

Leonardo Da Vinci gazed gloomily on the scene of destruction around him. Michelangelo had been hit by some shrapnel in the foot. The blast of the explosion had chipped Vasari's left ear. Botticelli was lucky to be unscathed. The statues of Italy's Renaissance artists stood in the courtyard of the Uffizi Gallery in Florence like stunned spectators after the outrage. The ground was covered in a crunchy carpet of broken glass and fragments of masonry. The air was thick with hot dust. Rescue workers wearing face masks were carrying some of the damaged pictures to safety. Bewildered tourists who had stayed in hotels nearby were moving out and wheeling their suitcases through the mayhem. On 27 May 1993 someone had parked a large car bomb in a small Fiat 500 outside the Academy of Giorgiophiles, the oldest agricultural institute in the world, which forms part of the Uffizi complex. The blast, which ripped through the historic centre of Florence in the early hours of the morning, could be heard in nearby Fiesole, about five miles from the centre of the city. It caused one part of the five-storey sixteenth-century building to collapse like a house of cards. Fabrizio Nencioni, the caretaker, his wife and their two daughters lived on the top floor. It took all night to dig their bodies out of the rubble.

Part of the devastation looked like the work of an earthquake. The rest like Bosnia. Shrapnel had lacerated the façades of the honeycombed houses in the narrow Via dei Pulci, the Road of Fleas. Red roof tiles had been blown off, leaving the bare wooden staves looking like fishbones. Three satellite dishes put up by the Italian network RAI were towering above the rescue operation.

The blast had been turned into a media event as only the Italians know how to stage. Every few minutes another minister arrived in a convoy of sirens and flashing blue lights to pay his respects. The Prime Minister's helicopter landed between the statues of David and Neptune in the Piazza della Signoria. On one of the television monitors that had been set up near the site of the blast, one could see a game-show host introducing his programme with a one-minute silence in respect for the dead. Three Playboy bunny girls stood with their heads bowed and tails drooping.

The Florence bomb wasn't the only one to shake Italy that summer. A car bomb in Rome's elegant Parioli suburb almost killed Maurizio Costanza, the host of a popular television talk show. Another bomb in Rome tore off the façade of one of the city's most beautiful churches, San Giorgio in Velabro, a twelfth-century Romanesque church in the shadow of the Palatine, which was very popular amongst Romans for weddings. The third bomb, which exploded almost at the same time, damaged the façade of the Basilica of St John Lateran, the seat of the Pope in his capacity as Bishop of Rome. On the same night a booby-trap car bomb in Milan killed four people, including two traffic wardens and a North African immigrant. The car, stuffed with explosives, had been planted near one of the city's most famous galleries.

Although some of the bombs claimed casualties, the police thought that these were accidental. All the devices exploded in the middle of the night in areas which were normally deserted. Their targets were primarily cultural. Italy's post-war history is pockmarked with terrorist attacks against trains, banks, military installations, government offices, ministers and ordinary citizens. But never before had anyone bombed the 'untouchable': the country's cultural soul. Perhaps the bombs were a devious attempt to destabilise society by striking the one institution that had not yet been compromised. One of the terrifying and terrorising aspects of these attacks was that no one knew exactly why they had occurred and who was behind them. Once again the mist of conspiracy settled on the country. The bombings of summer 1993 became the latest in a long line of unsolved *strage*, literally 'assaults', which run through post-war Italy like a dark subplot.

A group calling itself the 'Armed Phalange' claimed responsibility for the 1993 bombings. The government dismissed the claim as bogus. Instead the Interior Minister Nicola Mancino blamed the Mafia. But the Mafia doesn't go in for terrorism based on fuzzy notions of destabilisation. It tends to liquidate its enemies with precision. The minister's theory wasn't taken seriously by the public and many of the newspapers. Demonstrators in Florence filled the Piazza della Signoria near the Uffizi with banners declaring *Stato Assassino*. They were accusing the state of having bombed itself. Theories proliferated and ripened into conspiracy theories. The most common one was that the bombings in Florence, Milan and Rome signalled a return to the 'strategy of tension' of the 1960s and 1970s. The aim of this strategy was to destabilise democracy by creating panic and then to set up in its place an authoritarian military regime or a Fascist state, in other words, to create order through disorder. This recipe for social change has by and large been the speciality of right-wing terrorism.

To foreigners, Italy's left-wing terrorism is well known, particularly its most famous incarnation, the Red Brigades, who kidnapped and executed the former Prime Minister Aldo Moro. But right-wing terrorism matched the scope of the left. In the 1960s more than 100 right-wing organisations sprang up. Many of them were just gangs of Fascist thugs, espousing the cult of violence and picking fights with their opposite numbers on the left. But a dozen or so were hard-core terrorist groups that bombed buildings and people. They shared the Fascist faith in the purifying and liberating effects of violence and they were responsible for some of the worst terrorist outrages in modern Italian and European history. In December 1969 terrorists blew up a bank in Milan's Piazza Fontana, killing sixteen people. A year later a train was derailed in Calabria, killing six people. In 1974 an anti-Fascist demonstration in the northern city of Brescia was bombed, resulting in eight deaths. Later the same year the express train Italicus was attacked, killing twelve. In August 1980 a bomb exploded in the waiting room of the railway station at Bologna. Eighty-five died and 200 were injured – one of the bloodiest act of terrorism in Europe in the post-war period. The explosion occurred one day after four suspects from an extreme right-wing terrorist group had been indicted for the bombing of the Italicus train. The finger in all these bombings was pointed at right-wing terrorists. But after years of trials, retrials and acquittals only a handful of people have been convicted and sent to jail.

While left-wing terrorists held people's trials, issued manifestos and felt the need to justify their violence intellectually, right wing terrorism has always been shrouded in mystery. The suspicion arose in the 1960s that right-wing terrorists were acting with the connivance of the Italian Intelligence Services and deviant elements within the Interior Ministry. A number of intelligence agents were linked to the Piazza Fontana bombing, for instance. They were tried, convicted and then acquitted on appeal. In many cases the authorities had acted with much greater ferocity against left-wing terrorists than against their colleagues on the extreme right. This impression was reinforced by other conspiracies and plots. The notorious P2 Masonic lodge of Licio Gelli, which was uncovered in 1980, aimed to set up an alternative power structure in Italy. It counted amongst its members the heads of the Intelligence Services as well as senior figures from the army and the carabinieri. The impression emerged that the state was plotting to overthrow itself, in order to dispense with the tedium of democracy. This was also part of the 'strategy of tension'. Having been buried and almost forgotten for a decade the theory resurfaced last year after the bombings in Florence and Rome. The theory was plausible. After all, Italy had experienced the bloodless decapitation of almost an entire political and business élite. After decades at the helm the old guard weren't just going to relinquish power without a fight. But in the absence of suspects and firm clear motives the counter-revolution remained veiled in the opaque haze of mystery. The effect was as unsettling as the sudden and inexplicable appearance of an epidemic in the Middle Ages. It found easy prey in the country's fertile imagination.

The suspicion blossomed that some members of the government were trying to put a halt to Italy's 'silent revolution'. No suspects were ever named. No one was arrested. No evidence was found. But a few days after the Rome bombing Prime Minister Carlo Azeglio Ciampi sacked the chiefs of SISME and SISDE, the two Intelligence Services, and put the organisations directly under his command. Slowly the plausible but unproven web of conspiracy began to be woven in the public mind. Perceptions were, as ever, more important than facts. The conspiracy weavers were out in force.

In October 1993 an extraordinary woman called Donatella de Rosa burst onto the national stage with allegations that a coup was being plotted in the upper echelons of the military. Diminutive, elegant and in her mid-thirties, Miss de Rosa appeared every night on television chat shows and thundered against the plotters. She claimed that five senior generals were plotting to overthrow the government and establish a military junta. The five included the Army's Chief of Staff, General Gofreddo Canino; the military commander of the Tuscany and Emilia Romagna regions, General Biaggio Rizzo; and General Franco Monticone, the commander of Italy's rapid reaction force, who also happened to have been Miss de Rosa's lover. There were only two things to underpin these allegations. One was that Miss de Rosa had allegedly been given a bribe of 450,000 dollars by General Monticone, to ensure that she wouldn't reveal the incriminating contents of her pillow talk with the commander of the rapid reaction force. The second, still more flimsy, was that Miss de Rosa, who is endowed with large blue eyes, said she had spotted a well-known right-wing terrorist called Gianni Nardi in her hometown of Udine. Nardi was thought to be responsible for the Brescia bombing of 1974 and had fled to Spain in the late 1970s. He was supposedly killed in a car crash in 1980, but Donatella de Rosa now claimed that he was alive and that according to her military sources he had carried out the bombing of the Academy of Giorgiophiles.

Miss de Rosa's allegations were outlandish, bordering on the nutty. But the police took them seriously. Nardi's body was exhumed in Spain. They discovered that the dead terrorist had not wandered from his grave since he had been put there in 1980. Yet the allegations had more serious repercussions. One of the generals implicated by Miss de Rosa was dismissed by the then Defence Minister, Fabio Fabbri. General Monticone, Miss de Rosa's former lover, was investigated by magistrates for plotting against the state; and General Canino, the Chief of Staff, resigned over the way his friends and colleagues had been treated by the government. In the absence of a single scrap of evidence or a single charge, such actions were dramatic to say the least. In Britain or the United States, accusations of coup plotting by the country's senior generals would have either been dismissed out of hand or taken so seriously that they would have led to a massive outcry from the public, a large-scale criminal and governmental inquiry. Hours of news and talk-show footage would have been devoted to the subject. The credibility of the democracy and its institutions would have depended on it. In Italy the episode produced little more than a collective shrug of the nation's shoulders. Donatella de Rosa mesmerised Italy for about two weeks. Then one day she suddenly disappeared from view, her performance having come to an end. She was briefly arrested for misleading the magistrates. Now she is no doubt waiting in the wings to be asked back onto the stage of conspiracies. She has become part of that neo-reality of attempted coups, Masonic lodges, secret societies and 'illustrious' corpses that envelops Italy like an ether, often too fantastic to be proven, always too plausible to be dismissed. The thought that the worst terrorist outrages ever committed have remained unpunished and that the secret services, the Interior Ministry and the army were all plotting to overthrow the democracy which they had been paid to defend, would put an unbearable strain on many other societies. Not so in Italy. The rumours of a military coup were not taken seriously enough to bring people out on the streets, but they did lead to the dismissal of a number of senior generals. Instead of demanding an explanation the allegations and their consequences were merely absorbed into the mysterious atmosphere of conspiracies and counter-conspiracies that intoxicates Italian society. The Italians take coups in their stride. In a society where everything is plausible, the citizens eventually lose their sense of outrage.

Karl Marx said the Russians were unable to stage a revolution because they were illiterate. Stalin said that Communism would fit the Germans like a saddle fits a cow. The biggest obstacle to collective social change in Italy is not the features normally attributed to the Italians. Italian society is less chaotic than outsiders would like to think, less individualistic and much more conservative. The real problem is that dogma will always be undermined by the need to complicate matters. Dialectic will be diluted by mystery. The Italians have an instinctive aversion for the obvious. To take events at face value is an admission of stupidity. Everything has a hidden reason, which only the most intelligent people will be aware of. There is even a word for it: *dietrologia*, literally 'behindology'.

Dietrologia is not just an intellectual sport, it is also a political staple. The seven-time former Prime Minister Giulio Andreotti has been accused of collaborating with the Mafia. The magistrates investigating him say the only way he could ensure perpetual re-election for his Christian Democratic Party in Sicily was to buy votes with the help of Cosa Nostra. Mr Andreotti's lawyers have a different theory. The Cold War is over. Communism has collapsed in the Soviet Union and the Italian Communist Party, once the biggest in the West, no longer poses a threat to Nato and the stability of Europe. The Clinton administration, more puritanical and thrifty than its predecessors, is loath to support the political system masterminded by Giulio Andreotti and friends now that the justification for it has ceased to exist. The United States wants to get rid of Andreotti. It plants a Mafia turncoat on the Italian judiciary to discredit the statesman. The proof for 'this destabilising conspiracy hatched in foreign circles', as one of the former Prime Minister's associates called it, was obvious: the day Andreotti was forced to defend his reputation before his peers in the Senate, the head of the CIA James Woolsey flew to Rome to meet with his Italian counterparts. It was widely assumed that he had come to plot the downfall of Don Giulio. In fact this theory was so plausible that even Andreotti's detractors started to believe the conspiracy. As conspiracy theories go, this one contained all the right ingredients for a great vintage: the Mafia, a statesman who prays every day, a foreign power, the CIA. The frenzy was deflated when the Information Service of the United States embassy told reporters that Mr Woolsey's trip had been planned well in advance and that, 'in any case, with all due respect' the CIA had more pressing problems to consider, such as the instability of the Soviet Union, the clandestine traffic of nuclear materials to the Middle East and the war in Bosnia.

The less important a country is, the greater seems to be its propensity for conspiracy theories which cast it as the protagonist.

To give an example: a right-wing landowner from Puglia in southern Italy, whom I met at a dinner party in Rome, patiently explained to me the real reason why the former Communist Party had adopted the policy of privatisation. 'Achille Occheto – the former head of the party who never stopped being a Communist apparatchik, despite the end of the Cold War – was blackmailed into accepting the principal of privatisation for Italy's slumbering state industries by a Jewish lawyer in New York. This lawyer,' the acquaintance continued, 'was acting on behalf of President Boris Yeltsin of Russia. Yeltsin used him to get some of the money back which the old Soviet Union had lent to its Communist satellites around the world. The Kremlin gave billions to the Italian Communist Party. Its successor, the PDS, was of course in no position to pay back the money, let alone to admit publicly that it had ever received it. A compromise was brokered by the lawyer. Mr Yeltsin would get some of the money back. It would be supplied by big Italian business. Why? Because in 1993 the Italian business community was desperately casting around for a new political ally. The Christian Democrats, Socialists and Republicans had all disappeared or become unelectable thanks to the corruption scandal. Silvio Berlusconi had not yet appeared on the political stage. Converting the former Communists to capitalism was the only option.' According to my acquaintance, several large companies paid off some of the Communists' debt in return for a commitment to continue the privatisation programme. This would allow them to purchase shares and buy up the family silver sold off by the Italian state. My head was spinning.

Dietrologia, which stems from a mystical aversion to the obvious, is not confined to the political arena. I may be accused of peddling a worn-out cliché but no day goes by without some reminder of Italy's enchantment with the Mysterious. The novelty is not that the Italians believe in hocus-pocus, witchcraft or black magic, it is that they treat them in such a matter-of-fact way. An example: after returning from a holiday last year my friend Tamara was watering her plants outside her flat in Rome's Trastevere quarter. It was summer and many of the plants had withered. Suddenly her next-door neighbour appeared at the window and shouted: 'Your plants are dry because your period is too strong!' Tamara was my contact to the nether world of healing, yoga, pranotherapy (laying on hands) and general quackery. First she joined a Siddha yoga class in Rome and then a healing course. Her school used to organise national healing congresses in Milan, which were attended by hundreds of Italians from every region, social background and age group. On her return journey from one of these weekend 'heal-ins', she was sitting on a train to Rome. Suddenly the woman sitting opposite her said she had a sharp pain in her arm. My friend Tamara set about healing her, which involved 'purifying her aura' with gentle strokes. Instead of moving to the next railway carriage or hiding in acute embarrassment behind their newspapers – as they would have done in the United Kingdom – her fellow passengers formed a queue. They also wanted to be healed.

Italy's faith-healers appeal to the supernatural and superstitious while using the tools of modern technology or the electronic medium. There are scores of tiny commercial television channels offering phone-in exorcisms, death curses or just run-of-the-mill recipes to ward off the evil eye. Agony aunts have been replaced by television sorcerers and soothsayers. For emotional problems try Signora Francesca on Palermo's tarot card and horoscope channel. From the comfort of your own living room you can watch Signora Francesca deal out and read your tarot cards. Her gaze into the future will cost you 2540 lire per minute, plus VAT. For those who are too embarrassed to purchase crystal balls, black hoods, chains or the tools necessary for a home exorcism like squirting plastic Madonnas that can be filled with holy water like toy pistols, there is always the CEAMS, the European Centre for Superior Experimental Magic, a mail-order company. It is impossible to put a precise figure on the total number of self-professed wizards, clairvoyants and fortune-tellers. There are hundreds of small regional black magic circles. ARPE, the Association for Parapsychological and Esoteric Research, has about 120 members. It operates in the Adriatic holiday resort of Riccione. According to the ANDDI, the Italian National Institute for

Magicians, there are 6000 registered magicians or wise men working in Italy. The country alone boasts 20,000 registered pranotherapists – people who lay on hands. They produce an annual turnover of 250 billion lire worth of business. Devil worship has become one of Italy's most vibrant growth industries. There are more registered magicians per capita in Italy than in Haiti, the home of voodoo.

The occult has increasingly become an urban phenomenon. Turin, the city of Fiat, 'northern' productivity and Germanic efficiency, is reputed to be the black magic capital of Italy, encapsulating the apparent contradiction between a modern society and occult practices that are more at home in the Dark Ages. Perhaps the climate of almost perpetual mist and the city's mysterious covered arcades have helped the occult to prosper here. Perhaps the Turinese just need a reprieve from the never-ending quest for profit. Perhaps they are just rich enough to afford a weekly dose of black magic. But Turin is not alone. The Yellow Pages of Rome, Milan and Bologna are stuffed with the telephone and fax numbers of wizards and witches. Example:

TIZIANA – Specialist in Curses
Defeat your rivals in business
and love for ever. Ring 06 653 5060
or (for emergencies)
cellphone 0336 74 40 82.

Much of this activity is, however, clandestine and advertised by word of mouth. Therefore it has been impossible to determine the exact growth of the occult industry. A report entitled *The Devil's Cash*, published by the Italian research institute Eurispes, states that 'Magic is today a business with a vertiginous turnover.' It estimates the number of 'magi' between 12,000 and 20,000, most of them men. Meanwhile 12 million Italians, most of them women, are estimated to seek their services every year. The report concludes: 'In Italy vast and ongoing modernisation has not swept away the age-old superstitions and eccentric beliefs which have their root in ancient history.' Professor Luigi Satriani, an anthropologist from Rome University, believes that the occult has filled the vacuum left by the Catholic Church. The writer Umberto

Eco believes the obsession with the occult, the supernatural and certain forms of designer Buddhism expresses the yearnings of an urban society that has rejected one creed after another. In his novel *Foucault's Pendulum* the writer describes a generation that had left their Catholic faith in the 1950s, their political idealism in the 1970s and the pure consumer culture of the 1980s. The 1990s seem to be open season for any mystic, soothsayer or quack who can supply the meaning of life for a price.

This manifestation of decadence isn't of course confined to frustrated city dwellers. It also feeds off a rich rural tradition in the south, where religion, the worship of saints and faith-healing have always gone hand in hand. In the Calabrian village of Guarda Sanframondi, for instance, young men parade through the town at Easter wearing crowns of thorn. They run along a path of the imaginary twelve stations of the cross. At every station these post-pubescent self-flagellants stop and beat themselves with stones until they are covered in blood, delirious with pain and half dead. This ritual has survived since the Middle Ages, although the Vatican frowns on such exaltation through self-inflicted pain. Near the town of Nola, a sprawling industrial satellite city creeping up the slopes of Vesuvius – against the flow of lava – there is a small forest of oak trees. Here within the roar of the autostrada the forester and his wife heal hernias and enhance fertility once a year. They take their 'patients', mostly adolescent boys, to the forest and choose one of the young oak trees. The forester slits open the trunk, prises it apart and inserts two wooden staves about forty centimetres long, thus creating the shape of a vagina. When the patient has got undressed the forester and his wife pass him to one another through the tree trunk like a sack of potatoes. They do this six times. Every time a pass has been completed the forester mutters a quick prayer and crosses himself three times. When the ceremony is complete the staves are taken out of the trunk and a picture of the Madonna is inserted in their place. The trunk is then closed and tied together with wax string. If the tree continues to grow the patient's hernia will be cured and he or she will become more fertile. If the tree dies the cure will die with it.

The supernatural feels most natural in Naples. Life in Italy's southern metropolis, which is located in the shadow of a live volcano and perched uneasily on a geological fault-line, prone to earthquakes, has always been a bit of a lottery. The city has been prey to natural disasters, the last one being the earthquake at Pozzuoli in 1980, as well as to centuries of poverty, disease and crime. In the dank urban maze of Naples the piles of uncollected rubbish blossom like some luxuriant fungus, the traffic lights work rarely, the city has one of the highest population densities in the world and the city council has even seen fit to appoint an 'Assessor for Normality'. His job is to oversee that the lifelines of the city, from transport to rubbish collection, work to give a semblance of normality. It is not clear whether this is normality by the standards of Cologne or Calcutta. Nevertheless he seems to have had some success. At least Naples no longer suffers the once regular alarms about the poisoning of milk and water supplies that had been tampered with by the Camorra.

Naples has, not surprisingly, always been at the crossroads between devout Catholicism and superstition. Thousands of Neapolitan house façades are decorated with luminous shrines to the Madonna flashing in garish pinks and fluorescent greens. The Church of Gesù Nuovo, one of the most beautiful in the city, contains a shrine to Giuseppe Moscati, the 'holy doctor'. Beatified by Pope John Paul II in 1987 Professor Moscati achieved sainthood thanks to his healing methods and his humility. Death has not halted his good works. One room near the church's apse contains a replica of the professor's surgery and study, with all the original furniture. In another the walls are covered with hundreds of small frames. Each one contains a body part in thin moulded silver, a photo of the donor and a dedication. 'Dear Professor Moscati, my right leg has been giving me too much pain now for three years. Please help me!' The dedication in an almost illegible scrawl is written underneath a four-inch silver relief of a leg, wearing stockings and what looks like an old-fashioned shoe. Judging from the silver body parts that adorn the wall, the saintly doctor has been asked to heal arms, ears, hearts, fingers, toes, stomachs, noses, eyes, foreheads, buttocks, lungs, chests and in many cases a composite of several. One 'patient' had almost his entire body in silver parts displayed in a large frame. 'That would have cost him about 450,000 lire,' the lady behind the counter explained helpfully. The dispenser of body parts was a small Neapolitan housewife wearing a kitchen pinny. She produced a box full of silver lungs, chests, ears, arms . . . the only organs she didn't have were sexual ones. 'That wasn't really St Moscati's department,' she pointed out.

Neapolitans are much happier to entrust their lives and their health to the supernatural health service than to the one subsidised by the state. This is not altogether surprising. The Carderelli Hospital in the centre of Naples has more in common with Bedlam than with modern health care. And some of the city's most lurid corruption scandals were nurtured in the health service: the Neapolitans have learnt to rely on miracles. Nothing else really works for them. The most obvious example is the biannual liquefaction of the blood of San Gennaro, the martyr, in Naples cathedral. In 305 San Gennaro, the patron saint of Naples, was thrown to the lions in the Pozzuoli amphitheatre after which, being rejected by them, he was beheaded by Roman soldiers. A solid trickle of his blood is preserved in a phial, kept in a reliquary behind the altar. Twice a year the phial is taken out of its casing. On those days the crystals of blood should have turned into a dark brown liquid. Sceptics believe that the liquefaction occurs when the weather is hot enough for the crystals to turn into liquid in the hands of the bishop clutching the phial. But no one is asking for a scientific explanation. The secret is to believe, putting scepticism to one side. Thousands of Neapolitans still do. If the liquefaction doesn't occur at all, disaster is bound to strike as it did in 1944 when San Gennaro's crystallised blood refused to liquefy and Vesuvius erupted. In 1993 the liquefaction was two weeks late. There were scenes of mass hysteria around the cathedral as a crowd of four thousand men and women sobbed and screamed. *Tangentopoli* had intervened, it was widely believed.

With such important miracle shrines it is not surprising that the occult profession has flocked to Naples in abnormally large numbers. Above the central bus station in Naples there is a large luminous billboard. It advertises the services of Professional Magician Gardelio: 'Expert in communication with the dead, hypnotist, exorcist, pranotherapist and legal adviser'. His 'surgery' was located behind the central bus station on the second floor of a seedy block of flats. An assistant in her twenties opened the door. I should have made an appointment. The waiting room was packed with visitors, mostly women, many of them with children. Two policemen were sitting in the corner, nervously playing with their caps. Some clients leafed lazily through magazines, which had been laid out in a neat fan shape on the coffee table. One of them was a mail-order catalogue for the black magic trade. On the open page there was an advertisement for the plastic 'squirting Madonnas' – 'An Essential Accessory for a successful Exorcism'. The stifling heat was redistributed by a swivelling fan. I thought for a moment I had entered a dentist's practice. But the walls were decorated with the *mago*'s trophies. A newspaper article explained how he had liberated a thirty-year-old carabiniere officer from the Devil. The picture showed the officer dressed in a T-shirt and looking exhausted, his father, mother and the magician. They were shaking hands and smiling, as if they had just won the lottery. Next to the framed newspaper clipping was an elegant certificate, according to which Mr Gardelio had taken part in a European Community Workshop for small-scale entrepreneurs.

'Signor Frei, you will be seen now,' the secretary called into the room. I felt faintly embarrassed. Gardelio's surgery was bathed in red light thanks to a red lampshade and red plastic sheeting taped over the window. I was led inside, with a mixture of bemusement and awe. The eclectic magician who could drive out demons, cast evil spells and give legal advice stood behind his desk. A small portly man with long black hair tied in a pony-tail, he wore a yellow silk blouse and black trousers with razor-sharp pleats. A large glistening medallion nestled on his hairy chest. Miniature skulls and items of clothing were assembled on one table. The other displayed a collection of half-molten candles in human shapes. Behind a glass vitrine on the shelves I could see a twisted silver foil that looked disturbingly like a human shape. 'What is that for?' I asked. There was a slight pause. The *mago* looked irritated. 'That,' he said in a quiet, almost inaudible voice, 'was the wrapper of my lunch sandwich.' For a moment the spell was broken and the *mago* resumed the session. I had after all paid my 100,000 lire an hour for basic consultation.

I asked about the price list. The fees ranged from 800,000 lire (£320) to ward off the evil eye, to two million lire (£900) for an exorcism and 20 million lire (£9000) for casting a deadly curse. I asked him what proof he could give me of his magical abilities. He showed me the stigmata on his right hand, a thumb-sized scab which he said had started bleeding when he was ten. Magic mixed with Catholicism: the classic Neapolitan recipe. His healing power, he told me, emanated from his hands. By way of a demonstration he stood up, threw back his head, spread out his arms, clenched his fists, closed his eyes and, breathing heavily, crunched his knuckles. They made a terrifying sound. More bruiser than healer, I thought. Ten years ago most of the magician's clients came to him because of 'matters of passion' – warding off rival suitors, preparing love potions, a little spiritual detective work for suspicious spouses or simple crystal ball matchmaking. 'But,' said the magician, 'the recession and the political crisis ended all that. I get lots of people worried about money, about losing their jobs. I have even had a politician who was afraid of losing his seat in parliament.' 'Did the spell work?' I asked. 'Not in his case,' the magician admitted. Italian politicians are not embarrassed to admit that they go to faith-healers. Bettino Craxi used to pay regular visits to a society sorcerer. His brother went one step further and joined an ashram in India.

Some of the self-appointed healers and exorcists are absurd, others are dangerous. Several tragic incidents have focused the critical attention of Italians on their obsession with the evil spirits and the paranormal. In August 1994 a Sicilian fisherman was tortured by his brother and father, who had suspected him of being possessed by the Devil. Another Sicilian fisherman died after drinking a potion prescribed by a sorcerer that was supposed to bring good luck to his boats. In 1988 two young men killed themselves in an occult ceremony that was interrupted by a police raid. The authorities fear that scores of incidents are unreported. Of those that are known, the case of the two-month-old Maria Ilenia in September 1994 was without doubt the most tragic.

Maria Ilenia was the only daughter of Michele Politano and

Laura Lumicisi. The couple were both farmers in their early twenties. They lived on the outskirts of Polistena, a dusty and desolate town in the southern province of Calabria. The family occupied a half-built four-storey house, one of the typical dwellings of raw cement and steel girders. On every floor a small effigy of St Francis twinkled under a neon light in a glass box. The Politanos were devout Catholics. In fact, when the police came to search their house they discovered numerous articles of their devotion. On the blood-splattered table in Maria Ilenia's bedroom there was a picture of Christ on the cross, a map with charts and demonic emblems and a bucket filled with five litres of holy water from Lourdes. There was a small wooden crucifix and a transparent plastic Madonna filled with holy water. The police also found two photocopied pages of a manual on exorcism; they were there to remind Maria Ilenia's great-uncle Vincenzo Fortini, who was leading the ceremony, of his mantras: 'Oh Jesus, free her from the torment and corruption of this evil spirit, illuminate her with your grace and goodness.'

Two years before, the Politanos had become convinced that their house had been possessed by the Devil. They told neighbours that they were being tormented by shadows and strange noises. They said that the temperature in the house frequently dropped to freezing, even in the sweltering summer. Laura attributed the death of her father to the Devil, rather than to the lung cancer diagnosed by the doctors. The couple had already spent hundreds of thousands of lire on attempts to cleanse the house of evil spirits. Uncle Vincenzo, who was in his forties and lived near Rome, had already been summoned several times to help. Mr Fortini had taken courses in spiritual healing and considered himself to be an expert on the Devil and a qualified exorcist. But even he couldn't stop the noises and the fluctuations in temperature. Then, in 1993, the Politanos decided to have a baby. Laura had been told that the presence of an innocent child in the house might ward off the evil spirits. But as soon as Maria Ilenia was born she started screaming. What other parents would regard as natural was seen by the young couple as proof that the Devil had now also possessed their daughter. They despaired and in August they asked a local exorcist to help. They found the number in the Reggio di Calabria Yellow Pages. Francesca Gian-anti spent two weeks in the house burning incense and praying. She was paid one million lire. Nothing changed. In fact the more incense filled the baby's room, the more she screamed. Finally on 14 September the Politanos decided to call their uncle in Rome. On Sunday night eight members of the Politano family, including the uncle and the girl's parents, began the ceremony to exorcise the child. It lasted until seven in the morning. At one stage, Maria Ilenia's twenty-three-year-old father, moved by the sight of his screaming daughter, tried to stop the torture. He was stopped by his wife and brother-in-law. In the early hours of the morning the uncle became ever more desperate as the child refused to stop crying. He told the police that he tried – literally – to kick the Devil out of Maria Ilenia. Shortly after dawn the two-month-old infant was dead. On Monday morning the family was arrested. Neighbours had alerted the police. The Politanos were devastated, consumed by remorse for the death of their daughter. But they were still convinced that the child had been possessed by the Devil. Asked what proof they had, the uncle told investigators that Maria Ilenia was crying when she was doused in holy water. The doctor at the local hospital who had performed the autopsy said that Maria Ilenia's face was badly scratched. She was bleeding from the mouth and from the anus. Apart from that, her tiny body looked unbruised. But when the doctor opened her up, he discovered that her internal organs had been mashed 'as if someone had thrashed a wall with her body'.

The death of Maria Ilenia was particularly gruesome. She was killed by her own family, the victim of her parents' ignorance and obsession. How was such a thing possible? A survey conducted by the *Repubblica* newspaper at the time showed that one in three Italians feared the Devil. This appeared to be a substantial increase compared to 1991, the previous time that such a survey had been conducted. Furthermore a growing number of people believed that the Devil was not just an abstract evil, but the incarnation of *Male*, the Bad. Professor Luigi Satriani, a well-known anthropologist at Rome University, blames the Catholic Church. Under Pope John Paul II, he says, the Catholic hierarchy has underlined the presence of Evil as a physical being. The

Pope speaks frequently about *Il Maligno*, the Evil One. This, the professor believes, has led some people to think of Evil in the form of a person. The word *Maligno* is frequently used during the exorcism ceremony itself.

The Church is naturally shocked by accusations that it has anything to do with the rise in black magic. Don Gabriele Amorth, one of the scores of official exorcists appointed by the Vatican, said if the Calabrian family had suspected the presence of *Maligno*, they should have gone to the Church and not sought what he called 'an instant solution through an unqualified exorcist'. The Catholic Church does not regard exorcisms as a weird aberration but as a spiritual service to the community. It is an integral part of the ministry. Father Amorth receives on average one hundred requests for exorcisms a week. He said he can't cope with the workload, which has doubled in the last three years. The Father refers most of the requests to a medical doctor or a psychiatrist. But if the symptoms persist – symptoms like inexplicable headaches, stomach cramps and cold sweats – he will deal with the case. The Father's main grievance with the exorcism of the two-month-old Maria Ilenia was not that it took place, but that it was done without the guidance of the Church. It was left to amateurs.

In times of difficulty and crisis people have always resorted to the occult. The traditional soothsayers have been replaced by prantotherapists, or hand-healers. Sheep entrails have been replaced by the telephone and the fax. Apparently Prime Minister Silvio Berlusconi has been one of the few Italian heads of government and party not to live by the horoscope or to consult a medium. But the new bimonthly magazine *Magicamente* gave him the benefit of their science anyway. In their first edition (August 1994) they predicted that the tycoon – born 29/9/1936, a Libran – would weather the long-standing crisis in the coalition thanks to Jupiter imposing his *epidekatea* on the waxing moon. The article went on to predict a healthy balance of trade surplus and, more alarmingly, an increase in interest rates. But taking the long-term view the magazine predicted that Italy's economic recovery would peak in 1999, the year in which a total eclipse of the sun could be expected in the sign of Leo. By that time Mr Berlusconi may of course have long abandoned politics and returned to business. Indeed the tycoon Prime Minister, who likes to think of himself as a man of great logic and clarity of thought, would probably dismiss any horoscope, however glowing, as claptrap. But although the Prime Minister may not consult the stars he is in fact a closet consultant of entrails and displays all the basic requirements. Silvio Berlusconi sees conspiracy theories where others see simple mistakes. He detects plots against him and his government where others suspect incompetence or just the vagaries of the market. For instance, an increase in American interest rates by the Federal Reserve in the summer of 1994 which unleashed a wave of speculation on Wall Street, driving down the value of the lira, was portrayed as an international conspiracy to knock Italy. According to some members of the government the conspiracy had been hatched by the 'vitriolic international press', Communism and the Jewish lobby, three not necessarily obvious co-conspirators. This betrayed not only an alarming degree of paranoia, it revealed an inability to accept the consequence of one's own actions.

'To you we are all a bunch of superstitious eccentrics, in the grip of some quack or faith-healer,' my friend Anna Bruna, a petite Neapolitan with fiery red hair, told me, angry with my theories about Italians and their predilection for conspiracy theories, plots and the supernatural. 'If you want a true view of our supposed culture of superstition you should ring up my former teacher Professor Dilario. He has just completed an important work on the use of sodomy in fertility festivals in the Campania.' She paused. 'But don't call him today. He's a Capricorn. I think he may be going through a rough patch.' The longer I live in Italy, the more I feel that this is a country of unselfconscious paradoxes: the cult of the family in a society where a negative birth rate is threatening the family with extinction. The family as a source both of strength and of weakness. A country which has more laws than almost any other in the world but where the law is constantly being flouted. A society of seemingly anarchic individualists – if you look at their driving – and sticklers for etiquette and petty rules – if you consider their coffee-drinking habits and obsession with titles. Italy: on the one hand a highly active democracy, judging from its voter participation and lively political debate, on the other a quasi-feudal society, judging from the stranglehold once exercised by political parties; a successful economy, thriving in a sea of systematic corruption; a country where the omnipresent patrols of carabinieri with machine-guns, or – in the case of Sicily and Calabria – soldiers with armoured vehicles, remind you of a police state, but where one-fourth of the territory is effectively under the control of organised crime. And finally a highly sophisticated, technologically minded society with more cellphones per capita than Germany or the United States, where Devil worship, the occult and belief in the supernatural are on the increase. Italy is both highly pragmatic and alarmingly illogical. Some of these paradoxes are of course not confined to the Italian peninsula, but here they seem to manifest themselves in a more dramatic way. Perhaps this stems from the fact that Italy is both a very old culture and a very new country.

10

Forward to the Past

The city of Pontida flickered in the midday heat. The surroundings were veiled in thick smoke that rose from the bonfire in front of the fortress. The methodical and menacing beating of drums grew louder and louder. Suddenly the knight on horseback, his sword aloft, burst into the courtyard. He was followed by what could only be described as a crude makeshift tank, pulled by two bullocks. This machine was called the *carroccio* and it was decked in the Lombard flag. The line of foot-soldiers in armour broke up immediately. Some ran for cover, others, more courageous, took a stand. One of the soldiers screamed as he discarded his heavy helmet and vizor, revealing an ugly grimace. The drumbeat became faster. The dust thicker. The red and golden banner of the Holy German Emperor Frederick I Barbarossa was trampled into the dried mud. Cries of *Libertà, Libertà* (Freedom, Freedom) rose above the din of metal. Young men, draped in white flags, stormed into the courtyard behind the horse. Their faces were painted white with a red cross in the middle and their grimaces of rage must have looked terrifying to the foot-soldiers, who, although better armed, seemed only half as determined. The sun was relentless. The dusty air was pungent with sweat and horse shit. The Emperor's troops flagged. They were fighting someone else's war, far from home. Suddenly everything seemed to end without a single clash of arms or blow. Amidst groans of pain and murmurs of surrender the soldiers in armour collapsed like marionettes whose strings had been severed. Two men dressed in strange square garments that made them look like floppy model towers toppled to the ground. Someone laughed. Then someone else shouted: 'Fuck you! That's my foot!' The bullocks which had been pulling the *carroccio* now took off their heads to reveal two sweaty human faces. It was a Sunday morning in June 1992 and the battle of Legnano, 1176, had been won, yet again, by the Knights of the Lombard League, founded originally in 1167, and then again in 1982.

Today Pontida is a dreary town south of Milan. In 1167 representatives from the cities of Venice, Padua, Brescia, Mantua and Milan met there to take the oath that formed the Lombard League. Nine years later they defeated the Imperial troops of Frederick Barbarossa at Legnano. The battle is still celebrated by the zealots of the Lombard League every year. The historical pageant has become a party-political rally. The habit of dressing up in crusader uniforms to wield axes and cudgels is like the annual re-enactment of the battle of Hastings by the British Battle of Hastings Society. The difference is that the defeat of King Harold has not inspired a political party which has swept the Conservatives from power and dwarfed the Labour Party. The King Harold Party does not control the industrial heartland of England, and it does not threaten to turn Britain into a loose federation, creating fears that the country is in danger of becoming another Yugoslavia. In Italy, the Northern League does. It is one of Western Europe's more remarkable political movements, feeding on widespread anger with corruption and on a peculiarly Italian obsession with history as a living inspiration. Dentists dressed in codpieces and reciting Lombard poetry are also one of Italy's many answers to the end of the old world order.

The leagues began springing up all over northern Italy in the 1980s. They remained on the outer fringe of Italian politics until 1992, when the Northern League entered parliament with dozens of deputies. The Northern League is an umbrella organisation for a number of regional leagues, principally from Lombardy, the Veneto and Piedmont, who joined forces in 1990. Because the umbrella movement is heavily based on the regional identity of its component leagues, it is by nature schismatic. Originally the leagues articulated a search for a new ethnically pure identity, a disillusionment with consumer society and a return to a patchwork of independent states in pre-Risorgimento Italy. Some leagues, especially the Lega Veneto of the rumbustious Franco Rocchetta, developed strong ethnic overtones, or what one commentator called 'a sense of ethnic ecology'. Mr Rocchetta once told me that he thought the Venetians should spearhead the League movement because they had the purest ethnic pedigree. 'The Lombards' (the dominant group in the Northern League), he said, 'were upstarts and newcomers. They descended from the Celts and they only arrived on the Italian peninsula in the ninth century.' As the Northern League gained more and more power and eventually became a party of government in April 1994, it ditched some of its zanier ethnic ideas and their exponents, including the ethnically pure Signor Rocchetta.

The fact that a party as important as the Northern League is inspired by events that took place almost 800 years ago, uses the language and emblems of the twelfth century and manages to become the most popular party in the richest, most advanced part of Italy, is not just eccentric, it is an indictment of Italian unity. The rise of the Northern League raises some serious questions about the health of a nation that was born just over one hundred years ago, and that never felt completely comfortable being one nation-state. But then who does these days? The collapse of the old world order, the end the Cold War and its division of the international community into two principal blocks, the global village of high technology, optic-fibre communication, high speed travel, mass migration – there are so many forces and 'events' that have put a large question mark over the nation-state, the most basic political unit of the post-Enlightenment world. Recent conflicts, from the war in the former Yugoslavia to Rwanda and the pathetic attempts of Chechnya to gain independence from Russia, have all thrown up questions that had remained dormant for much of the Cold War. When is a state a nation? Does a state have the automatic right to become a nation? Have migration, satellite communication and economic interdependence rendered the nation an irrelevant, old-fashioned concept? If tribe is more important than nation, then why do so many national borders cross tribal divisions? If all borders are absurd, why do they exist at all or why do we not acknowledge and respect their inherent absurdity and stop trying to move them? These questions are linked to an identity crisis that seems to have afflicted much of the planet after the end of the Cold War as it grapples for a new and not yet defined 'world order'.

This identity crisis doesn't always have to lead to violence. Sometimes consternation will do. The North American Free Trade Area, NAFTA, seems like a logical extension of the American market so some, like a threat to national identity, North American jobs and the economy to others. The European Union is tortured by the gulf between its ambitions and its limitations. The German government wants to create a Federal Europe but can't even create a genuinely united Germany. It says it wants to adopt a single European currency, but the one national symbol its people hold dear and can display with unabashed pride is the Deutschmark. The British government is afraid that monetary union will mean a loss of national sovereignty, but the country's economy is already slavishly tied to the Bundesbank. Does the increasing integration of Europe mean that Britain has become a British nation within a European state? And whose sovereignty is it anyway? British sovereignty? Scottish sovereignty? English sovereignty? Welsh sovereignty? Westminster's sovereignty?

Italy has been afflicted by the identity crisis in a peaceful yet more existential way than most other Western nations. The fault-line of the Cold War ran through Italy, the country with the largest Communist Party in the West. Internally this fact created a rigid balance between right and left. Italian unity was not questioned as long as the country was firmly embedded in the Western Alliance on the front line against Communism. The questions 'what is Italy?' and 'who are the Italians?' were put on ice. But these are questions which have troubled Italy ever since people first started talking about it as one country. Metternich, the Habsburg foreign minister at the time of the Congress of Vienna in 1815, famously dismissed Italy as 'a geographic expression'. Count Cavour, the Piedmontese Prime Minister whose machinations allowed Italy to be born, spoke better French than Italian. He never dared travel further south than Florence. Massimo D'Azeglio, the author, painter and philosopher of the Risorgimento, said gloomily in 1861: 'We have made Italy. Now we have to make Italians.' Today one can say the opposite. Italians have been made, but Italy seems to be unravelling. More than 130 years after unification the country has not been able to heal the genetic fault it inherited at birth: the north/south divide.

If anything the gulf between Milan and Naples, Turin and Reggio Calabria is getting wider. The statistics speak for themselves. Unemployment in Calabria, Campania and Sicily currently hovers between twenty and thirty per cent. In Lombardy, Veneto and Piedmont between five and ten per cent. Northern and central Italy have some of the highest productivity rates in the European Union. If the European average is 100 then Lombardy has a per capita GDP of 122. Germany has 113.8 by comparison; the United Kingdom 106.3. However, Sicily and Calabria fall below the seventy mark. They are almost half as productive as the industrial heartland of the north. Eighty per cent of Italy's direct taxation comes from the north, twenty per cent from the south. Eighty-four per cent of the national social security contributions come from the north, sixteen per cent from the south. The gulf is as dramatic as the difference between eastern and western Germany. But while the two halves of Germany are gradually beginning to merge, Italy's north and south are drifting further apart.

This is surprising when one considers the history of the last five decades. Since 1945 six million 'southerners' have migrated to the industrial heartland of the north. Without their labour the economic miracles of Lombardy and Piedmont would not have happened. The south provides the market for much of what is produced in the north. The division is further diluted by the 'centre', the regions of Tuscany, Emilia Romagna and Umbria. The first two are the traditional fiefdom of the Italian Communist Party – a tradition that has more to do with their anti-clericalism at the time of the Papal States than with the proletarian Utopia. And yet these regions have achieved a standard of living that in some cities like Siena and Bologna is higher than the average in the north. But the perceived gulf between north and south is growing wider.

This development has been accelerated by *tangentopoli*, which folded the national umbrella that the ruling parties had provided for five decades. Until 1992 Christian Democrats or Socialists from opposite ends of Italy and dramatically different income brackets could still find common cause in their party. The parties maintained high levels of subsidies in the poorer south not so much to ensure an equal distribution of wealth but to woo southern voters. For instance the agricultural sector in southern Puglia was one of the most heavily subsidised in Europe and the local agricultural associations and their supporters rewarded the party with votes. When the Christian Democrats became discredited and the subsidies started to dry up the agricultural community transferred its allegiance to the neo-Fascist MSI.

Now for the first time since the creation of the post-war republic the economic gulf between north and south is mirrored in the political landscape. Here lies the novelty. The Northern League of the rabble-rousing populist Umberto Bossi has become the voice of plebeian anger in the industrialised north. The neo-Fascists have thrived on southern fears about being left behind. The League is the party of discontent for the *ceti medi*, the professional middle and lower-middle classes who are fed up with Rome and its corruption and with paying their taxes into an inefficient state machine that squanders them on the south. The real issue is not whether the Northern League is separatist, regionalist, federalist or just pro-autonomy. When speaking to a hard-line audience in Bergamo, Signor Bossi is separatist. When speaking to the Venetian League he is a regionalist. When in Rome he is a federalist and when in Sicily he becomes pro-autonomy. Behind all these adjectives there lies one continuous theme: the end of national solidarity, the glue which has held Italy together as a nation state. Supporters of the League argue that an Italy divided so dramatically between a poor south and a rich north cannot be squeezed into the straitjacket of national unity. They argue that this is unfair to the northerners, who carry the financial burden, and to the southerners, who have come to rely on state subsidies like a crack addict relies on his drugs. The Italians call this addiction *assistenzialismo*, the culture of economic dependence. Maurizio Menegon, the treasurer of the Lega Veneto in Venice who owns a small glass factory on the island of Murano, summed up the League's grievance when he told me in November

1993: 'We catch more fish than they do. But instead of giving them our fish we should teach them how to cast their own rod.' This is the sort of advice that makes Sicilians or Calabrians boil with anger.

But the dwindling spirit of national solidarity caused by the collapse of the party system is not the only factor that has undermined Italian unity. The other is Europe. In the ever closer union of the European Union, national borders have become increasingly irrelevant. While the people of Bradford may worry about losing their national sovereignty, the people of Bergamo can't wait to lose theirs. For them there is only one thing worse than being raped by Eurocrats in Brussels and that is *not* being raped by Eurocrats in Brussels. The European Union offers liberation from the central government in Rome, as long as it intervenes less in people's lives than the Italian state. Marco Formentini, the Northern League mayor of Milan, worked for the European Commission before going into Italian politics. In March 1994 I interviewed him in the spacious mayor's office in Milan's gloomy city hall. Sitting on a huge swivel chair surrounded by overpowering old master paintings, Formentini put it like this: 'We believe in a united Europe of fifty regions like Lombardy, Bavaria or Wales. And not in the Europe of twelve nations.' This concept may still drift in the realm of wishful thinking but the possibility of European union exerts a magnetic pull on cities like Milan, a pull away from Rome. I have made a habit of asking supporters of the League where they belong. The most common answer is: 'First I'm Lombard – or for that matter Piedmontese, or Venetian – then I'm European, and then I'm Italian.'

I followed one group of League supporters who came up with this common refrain to a bar in a small village in Lombardy. Umberto Bossi, the party leader, had just addressed a public rally. He had condemned the south for its laziness, Mafia culture and corruption. To clamorous applause he had ranted that Italy had to become a loose federation. The scene was a frenzy of white and red Lombard flags. However, this was also the night Portugal played Italy in a qualifying game for the World Cup. The bar where we had gone for a drink after the rally was packed with League supporters. Everyone cheered the Italian team as if their life depended on it. During the World Cup similar scenes of national football hysteria and soccer patriotism took place in the most radical Lombard strongholds. The genius of Silvio Berlusconi and his team of advertising executives turned party managers was to realise that Italy's national identity is alive and kicking on the football pitch, and that 'Forza Lombardia' (Go for it, Lombardy!) doesn't have the same ring as 'Forza Italia'. Berlusconi tried to revive the concept of Italy by talking about Italy as the 'Italian family', by talking about his cabinet as the 'national team'. Millions of Italians are quite capable of cheering the national team during the World Cup while refusing to contribute their taxes to the nation's coffers or placing their trust in the central government in Rome. Their regionalism is one way of expressing their distrust or dislike of any central government that imposes itself upon them. For instance, I have come across a number of hard-line League supporters who will march across Italy to demonstrate against the corruption of the Italian government, call for a separate northern republic and tell Sicilians to go to hell. But when I, a foreigner, asked them why Italy was so corrupt, they rallied around the flag and became defensive about their nation. The key issue is not the outright rejection of Italy but how to accommodate the country's variety and regionalism in a looser-fitting national garment. Unfortunately, many southerners, especially those who support the hard-right wing National Alliance, are quick to interpret northern calls for an Italian federation as betrayal of the nation.

While the Northern League uses the prospect of a closer European Union to justify an Italian federation, the neo-Fascists in the south do precisely the opposite: they think only a strong and united Italy can survive in a more integrated Europe. The National Alliance – the successors to the neo-Fascist Italian Social Movement – has always had a substantial following in southern cities like Naples or Catania. But together with Berlusconi's Forza Italia movement it now rules most of the south, especially the regions of Puglia, Campania and Calabria. The rebirth of neo-Fascism is a complex and fascinating phenomenon which I will deal with in a later chapter, but one of the important reasons for its rebirth is southern fears about being abandoned by the north.

Every time Umberto Bossi lambasts the south for being lazy and corrupt, the neo-Fascists gain strength. At a neo-Fascist rally in Lecce, the baroque city on Italy's festering heel, a demonstrator wearing a black bomber jacket and dark shades – at night – explained: 'My father sacrificed his life for Italy during the war. Most of my family work in the car factories in Turin. My sister is married to a Milanese. And now they – the Northern League – want to separate. It's treachery.'

One of the bizarre aspects of the feverish debate about north and south is that no one can agree about the border. A Palermitano is adamant that Rome belongs to the cold-hearted north driven by efficiency and productivity. Many Milanese regard Rome as the deep south, the embodiment of all the 'southern' clichés from the impenetrable thickets of bureaucracy, the laziness, the oriental wiliness and the untrustworthiness to the Mafia. Even Umberto Bossi, whose political identity rests on it, doesn't know for certain. Although he proposed to split Italy up into three republics: Padana in the north, Etruria in the centre and the Republic of the south, he neglected to point out where the borders should be. Interpretations differ. The European Community's Development Aid programme believes the border runs along the dividing line between Lazio, the region around Rome, and the Campania to the south and the Abruzzi mountains to the east. David Willey of the BBC, who has lived in Italy since the early 1970s, insists that the border between north and south lies somewhere near his holiday home in Cortona in southern Tuscany. This was the old border between the Papal States and Tuscany, and the popes were responsible for some of the worst aspects of modern Italy, especially the reluctance of individuals to take responsibility for their actions. In other words the border between north and south exists mainly in people's minds. In one week alone in October 1993 I was given four different reasons for the divide. A baron in Naples blamed it on the Spanish Bourbons whose occupation of the Two Sicilies confined southern Italy to the dark ages and the Inquisition until the middle of the last century, by which time it was too late to catch up. A taxi-driver in Palermo blamed it on the Risorgimento, which he called a capitalist exploitation by the industrial north of the agricultural south. An anthropologist in Rome remarked cynically that Italy should never have been one country anyway since it was in fact home to three completely different peoples: Celts in the north, Etruscans in the centre and Greeks in the south. An emaciated waiter in a fish restaurant in Bari thought it was a question of diet. 'The northerners are too aggressive,' he said, 'they eat too much red meat.'

Some would even argue that the division between north and south has nothing to do with geography. Italy is in fact a mish-mash of Northern European and Southern or Mediterranean values, which have produced a schizophrenia at the heart of the Italian character. Since the unification of Italy in the 1860s, the Italians have been trying to diagnose and cure the north-south divide like some genetic defect. It's as if the elegant Italian boot concealed a club-foot. The American social historian Robert Putnam has tried to explain today's differences between the north and the south by looking at yesterday's civic traditions. In essence he believes that the causes can be found in the eleventh century when northern Italy broke up into self-governing 'communes' and city-states, and the south came under the control of the Holy Roman Empire. There the rule of Frederick II the *stupor mundi,* was the most enlightened in Europe at the time. Norman Sicily already had a highly developed bureaucracy. Frederick founded Europe's first state university in Palermo. The Emperor himself was a Renaissance man – three centuries before the beginning of the Renaissance. He was an accomplished poet, an amateur civil engineer who took a great interest in everything from fortress designs to irrigation systems. Under him Sicily also enjoyed an unprecedented degree of religious tolerance and the strong Moor-ish influence in the architecture that dates back to Frederick and the rule of the Normans in Sicily is testimony to the fact. The Emperor's rule was indeed enlightened, but it was also highly autocratic, creating a feudal style of 'vertical dependence' between the subject and his ruler. The northern communes meanwhile developed 'horizontal ties between the citizens' and thus a civic responsibility. In effect what distinguished cities like Venice, Florence and Siena from Naples or Bari was the extent to which men were allowed to govern their own lives through laws and associations. Thirteenth-century Florence was not, of course, a democracy. It was ruled by an oligarchy of families. Half the Florentines lived like slum dwellers. The streets were bristling with violence and class warfare. But the principles of mutual aid and economic collaboration were established in that period. People felt increasingly that their well-being depended on the well-being of the community, rather than on the protection of a ruler. This nascent civic responsibility expressed itself in the formation of guilds, clubs, mutual aid societies, fraternities, cooperatives and in the rule of law. Fourteenth-century Bologna, the intellectual capital of communal Italy with one of the world's oldest universities, had 50,000 inhabitants. two thousand of them were lawyers. Wealth and power in the northern communes was based less on land and more on commerce and finance. This created a bond of economic interdependence, accompanied by a high degree of social mobility.

In 1303 Verona created Europe's oldest guild structure with its own charter. 'A violation of the statutes,' Putnam writes, 'was met by boycott and social ostracism.' At the same time Florence had ten guilds, seven of which dealt with export. A medieval version of the neighbourhood watch committee, called *vicinanze*, flourished in these cities, as did 'tower societies' that provided mutual security from invaders. Siena was a paradise for the committee man. There were 860 city posts for 5000 adult males in fourteenth-century Siena. They dealt with everything from refuse collection to banking. Banking in itself illustrated the importance of 'horizontal' ties since it was based on credit. And credit, which derives from the Latin word *credere* (meaning believe), relied on trust and stability. Siena became one of the banking capitals of late medieval Europe, with the result that in 1993 the city's bank, the Monte di Pieschi di Siena, celebrated its 500th anniversary as the oldest surviving bank in the world. The bank is partly administered by the city authorities, and the fact that Siena has had a Communist mayor since 1945 is not a weird contradiction but perfectly consistent with a tradition where the Communist Party and now its successors, the PDS, have always represented civic pride and the art of self-government. Siena's brand of Communism, which stems from anti-clericalism, is quintessentially bourgeois and would no doubt have made Marx spin in his grave. The famous Palio horse race which takes place in the shell-shaped Piazza del Campo every summer is much more than a spectacle for the tourist industry. The teams of horsemen are formed by the city's ancient guilds and the race is seen by the Sienese as a ritual celebration of their independence and civic pride, as well as a good romp in the heat and an excuse for a hearty meal. Such pageants are, of course, not confined to central and northern Italy. But in southern Italy, festivals like the famous Festa dei Jii in Nola or the omnipresent Easter parades are more mystical affairs celebrating patron saints or invoking good harvest weather and fertility.

The mystery of Putnam's theory is how the civic spirit born in the late Middle Ages was able to survive centuries of wars and pestilence. In the 1656 plague half the population of Venice, Florence and Bologna died. Tuscany and Umbria were for centuries ravaged by invasions and border disputes. The landscape, now dotted with medium-sized factories and coveted by German dentists rich enough to afford a small farmhouse, was scarred by centuries of poverty until the 1950s. A friend of mine who was born near Siena in 1947 has said that his village was so poor, his family couldn't even afford to eat pasta. They were fed by an uncle who worked as a waiter in a Rome hotel and stole food for his Tuscan family once every two weeks. Now the family has made a small fortune selling herbs, porcini mushrooms and extra-virgin olive oil for export. In the last century Florence and Verona were picturesque but crumbling cities, stuck firmly in the pre-industrial age. Naples meanwhile was a teeming metropolis. The city was four times the size of Florence and three times as big as Milan. It entered the industrial age full of promise. In 1818 Naples launched the first steamboat in the Mediterranean. In 1839 it opened the first railway on the Italian peninsula, a five-mile track from the city centre along the coast to Portici. In 1880 it had a funicular railway and a few years later a steel plant. However, none of this amounted to a genuine industrial revolution. The railways and steam engines were not launched to satisfy the needs of a rising entrepreneurial class but to flatter the egos of the

Bourbon rulers, desperate to show off their commitment to progress.

In 1984 a Neapolitan aristocrat and his wife set up an association called Napoli 99. The Baron and Baroness Barraco chose the number 99 because it refers to the year 1799. Inspired by the French Revolution and supported by French Revolutionary forces, the people of Naples ousted their Bourbon ruler King Ferdinand in that year and proclaimed the Parthenopean Republic. For a brief period the city became a chaotic island of democracy. But the Neapolitan Jacobins lacked the support of the peasantry outside the city and their revolution was essentially imported from France. It collapsed like the French Revolution when Napoleon came to power. By 1815 Ferdinand was back on his throne as the King of the Two Sicilies. For the Barracos, 1799 represents the great 'Missed Opportunity' of Italy's south. 'This was *our* chance to create a civic responsibility. And we flunked it.' Their mission today is a modest one: to reopen most of the cultural treasures in Naples which have been closed due to a lack of custodians to look after them, the threat of theft or sheer neglect. There are more than 200 boarded-up churches in Naples. The city has 2000 municipal gardeners. But the 100 hectares of park-land are in a pitiful state. Until recently the gardeners collected their salaries from the municipality but no one expected them to do any gardening for the city. They were too busy running their own private enterprises from garden centres to tree nurseries. What appalled Baron Barraco was that most Neapolitans didn't even seem to mind that their cultural heritage had become a No Access Area. Instead of clamouring for change they accepted the woeful status quo. 'We suffer from a severe lack of civic pride and responsibility,' the Baron told me. 'We have been trapped in a vicious circle. Because the Neapolitans haven't cared enough, it has been easy for politicians to rape the city in search of political patronage. No one stopped the unfettered construction of bridges, motorways or ugly high-rise blocks, which were essential for providing jobs and buying votes.' Corruption was fuelled above all by the billions of lire in emergency aid that flooded the Naples area after the 1980 earthquake. Unfortunately only a small proportion of the money made its way to the thousands of people left homeless by the earthquake. Most of them were still living in portacabins in 1990.

Thanks to Napoli 99 scores of churches and parks have been reopened to the public and Naples invited the rest of Italy to witness its artistic treasures in an 'open weekend' in May 1993. The city's new mayor, Antonio Bassolino, a member of the Democratic Party of the Left who narrowly defeated Alessandra Mussolini, the Duce's granddaughter, seems to be fulfilling some of his election promises. His administration discovered that one of the reasons for the city's moronic traffic chaos is that most of the 1400 traffic wardens, who are paid by the Neapolitan authorities, rarely venture out onto the streets. As one of them put it: 'There was no point. The traffic was too bad. Better to leave it alone.' The traffic wardens were free to pursue another job, while already receiving a salary from the state, as well as enjoying all the privileges and clout bestowed upon them by their jobs as uniformed civil servants. It is against such self-interest disguised as resignation that the Baron and his wife, not to mention untold others across the country, are battling. Italy lacks an event like the French Revolution or a document like the American Constitution or an institution like the House of Commons that enshrines the pride and the values of the entire nation. The Risorgimento is regarded as a great feat of self-determination by some and a calamity by others. Italy's post-war Constitution is a beautiful but much-flouted document. Unlike the Deutschmark, which has become a symbol of national unity in a country where many are still reluctant to wave a German flag, the lira has too many noughts to be taken seriously.

More than 130 years after the foundation of modern Italy and Italians are raiding their history in search of a national identity. Those looking for a sense of civic responsibility have scoured the more obscure corners of their past for a model. The Barracos have chosen the year 1799, relevant for Naples. Siena looks back to the fifteenth century, when the Monte di Pieschi bank was founded at the height of the city's power. Not surprisingly outbursts of civic pride are accompanied by historical pageants. Central and northern Italy are a paradise for accountants, dentists or plumbers who like dressing in codpieces once a year to carry lances or torches through the main square, to joust or shoot crossbows in honour of their ancestors. These festivals have naturally become tourist attractions, but they are above all a historical ritual for the local population. The choice is mind-numbing, especially in the month of May. In Umbria alone there are thirty-five different festivals in cities and hundreds more in villages. You can go to Assisi to see troubadours serenading in the streets in memory of St Francis, the city's most famous saint who was a playboy before he abandoned family wealth for monastic poverty. In Narni citizens don medieval garb to commemorate their patron saint, Juvenal. Young men representing the city's three ancient guilds compete in a game that involves lancing a ring which is suspended from a rope in the Piazza Maggiore. Your next stop on the pageant trail could be Gubbio with its Festival of the Giant Candles, then on to Cascia to light your own candle for the Holy Rita. After that to Orvieto for the Festival of the Doves and if you have any energy left you could flit back to Gubbio for round two: the cross-bow Palio. The Northern League, which looks back to twelfth-century Milan and Mantua for inspiration, must be the first example of a historical pageant turned political party.

Italians love political trinkets and Lombard history has provided the League with a booming kitsch industry. Every League rally is accompanied by a curious array of vendors who do a roaring trade in the movement's paraphernalia: Lombard League badges, displaying the party's mascot, the mercenary general Alberto Da Giussano. With his legs akimbo and his sword held high, the figure graces boxer shorts, handkerchiefs, watch-faces and even lingerie. There are toy models of the *carroccio*, the ox-drawn medieval version of a tank with which the League warriors defeated the armies of Frederick Barbarossa. *Il Carroccio* has also become a nickname for the Northern League in Italian news-papers. For the wishful thinkers there are blue hardback passports for the imaginary Republic of the North, as well as fake postage stamps in denominations of a currency that doesn't exist – the lece – but that can be bought at an exchange rate of one-to-one with the Deutschmark, Europe's hardest currency. The passport vendor, who clearly hopes to be a border guard one day between Lombardy and Tuscany, was attached to the party's bellicose symbol. He rolled up his sleeve to reveal a string of tattoos of Lombard knights fighting their way up to his hairy armpit. But despite its barbarian growl the League is also very petit bourgeois. Other items on sale included a video of the wedding of Mr Bossi, a full set of League crockery and League doilies. The League has built its own personality cult around the raucous Mr Bossi. At one party congress I saw someone selling cigarette ends, smoked and stubbed out by the party leader, a bargain at 1000 lire or approximately 45 pence apiece. This curious addition to the annals of political hero worship can only gain value, because Mr Bossi gave up smoking two years ago.

In 1993 the Northern League became the most popular party in Italy's rich industrial north. In Milan, the country's business capital and once the powerhouse of the Socialist Party and its leader Bettino Craxi, the League won forty-two per cent of the vote in the summer of that year. Not since Mussolini's Fascists has a party here been so popular. The League's genius was that it combined a political revolt against corruption with a much more ancient rebellion against the capital. The *leghisti* despise Rome both as the incubator of political corruption and as a central power that siphons off northern taxes and dilutes northern identity. In a country where history has always been recruited to legitimise a new political movement, the League's historical pageants are more than just fun and games. They are to Umberto Bossi what Rome's imperial past was to Benito Mussolini: an ideal from a distant era, as inspiring as it is inaccurate. An exhibition in Milan's town hall, timed uncannily to coincide with the election for a new mayor in 1993, hammered home the point. The period of the city's commune in the twelfth century was depicted as the flowering of Milan, when civic culture produced flourishing guilds, a sewage system and stunning Gothic churches. The spirit of the commune had been unleashed when the Lombard League produced a series of military victories, such as the one at Legnano, and forced the Holy Roman Emperor to make a number of important concessions. He guaranteed the city of Milan and its allies the right to govern their own affairs, to collect and spend their own taxes and to be subject to their own laws. Ironically the exhibition also proved how the same historical event can be manipulated by different people for precisely opposite ends. In 1849 Verdi wrote an opera entitled *The Battle of Legnano*. The music was piped through the exhibition rooms on crackly loud-speakers. But the opera had been composed at the height of the Risorgimento, when Italy was being unified by force. It was supposed to celebrate Italian unity in the face of outside aggression from the Austrians, and the ability of the fledgling nation to stand up to foreign invaders. Today the same music is used to symbolise the struggle of Milan, Brescia, Mantua and Venice to resist the compromises of nationality.

Much of the League's success as a protest movement is also due to its leader, Umberto Bossi. The fifty-one-year-old senator is a scruffy rake with unkempt hair and a crumpled suit who looks like a seedy encyclopaedia salesman and sounds like a cattle auctioneer. Bossi is a rabble-rouser and a street fighter who would be shunned in more polite times. During the upheaval of recent years he came into his own. On stage Bossi grabs the microphone as if he wanted to throttle it. His voice is gravelly, his chin brutal, his thick bulging lips look bruised and his speech meanders from insult to libellous injury. Bossi is proud to be gruff. It comes naturally, but it is also politically calculated. In a country where the ruling parties have masked their abuse of power with an abstract and abstruse vocabulary, Bossi's blunt indiscretions were refreshingly irreverent, if not always subtle or funny. He has called the former Prime Minister Ciriaco De Mita 'pig ugly', com-pared the moustachioed leader of the former Communist Party to a 'truffle pig' and described Silvio Berlusconi, his putative coalition partner, as 'Berluskaiser', the self-appointed emperor, who didn't know the meaning of democracy. Bossi slammed the neo-Fascists as 'unreconstructed blackshirts and liars'. His style of rhetoric is perhaps best encapsulated by the Northern League's rallying cry: *C'è l'ho duro!* 'I've got a hard-on.' A slogan embla-zoned on the front of one of the League's more popular souvenirs, pairs of jockey shorts, it is presumably meant to instil a sense of euphoria into the wearer. Some have pointed out the connection between the League's imaginary erection and the unsheathed sword of its mascot, Alberto Da Giussano. 'The intention,' one of the party's supporters once told me, 'is to create the impression of a party thrusting ahead.'

Rage is the lifeblood of Bossi's politics. Born in 1941 in a village near Varese, he was brought up in a family that struggled to stay above the poverty line. His father was a textile worker and sold the milk produced by two cows that he owned. His mother, who came from a poor peasant family, found a job as a concierge when the family moved to Milan. Umberto was one of the first of his generation to go to university on a state grant. 'I had a difficult, tedious childhood,' he told the journalist Giorgio Bocca. 'I saw the cosy world of my parents collapse around me. And I couldn't digest the new things around me.' In a country that was transformed in a few decades from a predominantly agricultural society to an industrial one, this admission of culture shock could have come from millions of Italians, many of whom now support the leagues.

In his teens Bossi drifted from one casual job to the next, trying his hand at everything from teaching to playing the electric guitar in a rock band. Bossi read medicine at Padua University but dropped out before completing the degree. However, he kept the fact from his first wife, Gigliola, whom he had married while at university. After giving up medical school he still used to leave the dinner table and follow up emergency calls that had never been made and rush off to treat fictitious patients in clinics that didn't exist. While many of Bossi's contemporaries were turning either to the extreme left or to the extreme right, he became a born-again Lombard. At the instigation of a friend who ran the student's league for Valdotaine, the largely French-speaking region around Val D'Aosta, Bossi rediscovered his Lombard roots. He took up night classes in the Lombard dialect, which must be one of Italy's ugliest, and wrote Lombard poetry, turgid ballads extolling the virtues of the hardy Lombard spirit. In the late 1970s he founded a journal called *Lombard Autonomy*, which folded soon afterwards, saddling Bossi with debts. Then, in 1981, Bossi met the man who would become the League's ideologue and with whom he would form one of the more unlikely couples in modern Italian politics. A law professor in his late seventies, Gianfranco Miglio was one of the first to desert the Christian

Democrats for the League. His imposingly bald head is covered by a Bavarian-style feathered hat. He carries a cane and wears thick tweeds, giving the impression of a Habsburg landowner, preserved in aspic.

Professor Miglio belongs to that rarest of modern breeds: the Teutonophile. He adores Germans and is a great believer in German myths from punctuality to efficiency. He also thinks that the German Federation should be the role model for a future Italy. In fact, according to Miglio, Italy in its present state defies nature. Sicily and the south should, in the professor's own words, 'be abandoned to their destiny'. Italian unification was a historical error. The argument is as follows: the Risorgimento was imposed on the people of the Italian peninsula from above by what Miglio and Bossi call 'a war of conquest'. Unlike German unification, which started with the *Zollverein*, the customs union between Germany's many principalities and kingdoms, and was driven from below by an increasingly assertive bourgeoisie, Italy had unification thrust upon it by Piedmont. Garibaldi and his Red Shirts were cheered in Sicily not because the peasants wanted unification but because of promises of bread and land. In 1861 most Italians were farm labourers who lived on pittance wages and a staple diet of bread, water and vegetables. They had little idea of what was meant by Italy. Some Sicilians thought that 'L'Italia' was in fact La Talia, the wife of King Victor Emmanuel. Massimo D'Azeglio, the elder statesman of Italy at the time of unification, thought that the annexation of Naples amounted to sharing a bed with someone who had smallpox. In 1861 he wrote: 'In Naples we drove out a king in order to establish a government based on universal consent. But we need sixty battalions to hold southern Italy down and even they seem inadequate. What with brigands and non-brigands it is notorious that nobody wants us there.' The Risorgimento had little to do with the romantic nationalism and spirit of liberation cherished by the philosopher Giuseppe Mazzini. One hundred and thirty-three years after unification these issues have returned to haunt Italy.

The League's supporters are a mixture of zealots, protest voters left homeless by the collapse of the Christian Democrats or Socialists and opportunists. It's a fluid following and many people who voted for the League in 1993 probably defected to Berlusconi's Forza Italia Party in 1994. But a large number of voters are fiercely loyal to Umberto Bossi. I met some of them in the foothills of the Alps. Gardone Val Trompia, about an hour's drive north-east of Milan, is the home of Beretta, Europe's oldest arms factory. Beretta is still the biggest local employer. Thousands of League supporters had packed into the small square festooned with geraniums and the League's red and white colours. Bossi was two hours late as usual, but his bedrock supporters were not going to desert him even at eleven o'clock on a cold March night. Those who didn't crowd into the main piazza watched from their balconies and windows, wrapped in blankets. The people of Gardone cared about two issues above all. They wanted separation from the south and to prevent a ban on hunting in Italy, because this would curtail their favourite hobby and endanger the demand for hunting rifles and thus their jobs. Who better to address these fears than their local candidate, Vito Gnutti?

Gnutti, who was appointed Minister of Industry in 1994, comes from an old family of arms manufacturers and today owns one of Italy's biggest trigger factories. I asked one of the supporters, a teenager, why she had come to the rally, and what she felt about separation from the south. 'We want a separate republic,' she said. 'In the schools here we want northern teachers, not southern teachers. There are too many southern teachers now. This is not right.' I asked what was wrong with southerners. 'I don't hate them,' she replied, 'but they are lazy. They are corrupt. They bring Mafia here.' Her sentiments were echoed by the graffiti all over Lombardy. 'Southerners out.' 'Calabrians, Sicilians go home.' These sentiments represent the lunatic fringe of the Northern League. They are Umberto Bossi's most loyal supporters but also the ones who will marginalise him in national politics if he fails to distance himself from them. What distinguishes the Northern League from Le Pen's National Front or Franz Schoenhuber's extreme right-wing Republikaner in Germany is that they are as concerned about internal migration from the poorer areas as immigration from the Third World. 'They treat us like the Moroccans,' Gianni Carelli, a Milanese taxi-driver told me. 'Bossi is a racist. That's why I voted for Berlusconi.' The driver was a second-generation immigrant from Puglia in the south. He spoke with a Milanese accent. He had never lived in southern Italy. But the rhetoric of the League had brought out the southerner in him. It had also cost Bossi another vote. The localism of the Northern League, with its racist, anti-'southern' overtones, is both a strength and a weakness. It has given the movement a well-defined regional identity that goes hand in hand with a 'northern' reluctance to pay taxes to the central government in Rome. However, it has also limited the League's appeal. In 1992 Umberto Bossi stood for election in Sicily and Rome as well as in Lombardy. His percentage of the vote outside his turf was tiny. Bossi and the League are loathed south of Rome, where they have rekindled traditional southern fears about being neglected, disdained and browbeaten by the north.

Nevertheless Umberto Bossi's revolution has been hijacked by Silvio Berlusconi. As a Milanese tycoon he has all the credentials of a rich northerner necessary to impress right-wing voters in Turin or Venice, but his appeal stretches far south well beyond the reach of Lombard regionalism. The greatest danger for Bossi is that as the local hero of Lombardy, he will be celebrated by zealots in crusader uniforms but abandoned by the 'Gucci revolutionaries' that have given his movement economic clout. I went to see some of the League's fur-clad 'sansculottes' in the sedate and beautiful city of Mantova. Famous for being Virgil's birthplace as well as for producing Italy's best butter, Mantova was a member of the Lombard League in 1167 and was the first city to be ruled by a League mayor in 1992. Signora Poggialli was one of the original Jacobins. The owner of the Café Centrale, this middle-aged matron was weighed down by chunky gold jewellery and burdened by a beehive hair-do. Over a cup of Earl Grey with a twist of lemon, she explained how she was at the forefront of Italy's new revolution, how the League's victory in Mantova will be remembered like the storming of the Bastille and how those corrupt politicians in Rome should 'all rot in jail or worse. I will *not* waste my taxes on that bunch of thieves,' she hissed. 'I didn't have the heart to ask the terrifying Robespierre of Mantova what her contributions to the national coffers were. As a self-employed café owner, she belonged to one of the most notorious tax-dodging brackets in Italy. Despite her bloodcurdling support of the League in 1993, when I met her, a year later, Signora Poggialli was voting for Silvio Berlusconi's Forza Italia Party. She, like thousands of other voters in the north, had been scared off by the League's rabble-rousing rhetoric and found refuge in the more clubbable ranks of Forza Italia, where codpieces and lances have been replaced by blue blazers and cellphones.

There was something endearing about the League's unorthodox array of politicians: Umberto Bossi, the street fighter; Roberto Maroni, the Interior Minister with designer stubble and dark Trotsky spectacles who used to relax by playing the piano in a Milan jazz club; Irene Pivetti, the powerful and devoutly Catholic speaker of the chamber of deputies who was appointed to that illustrious position at the tender age of thirty-one, and had all the old master paintings of nudes removed from her office; Francesco Speroni, the former Alitalia flight engineer who became Minister of Institutional Reform, responsible for drawing up legislation that would transform Italy into a loose federation of states. When I went to interview Minister Speroni in the summer of 1994 he was sitting at his vast desk flanked by Italian flags, trying to land at Chicago's O'Hare airport. The minister was playing on his flight simulator, he was wearing a Harley Davison biker's tie, cowboy boots and a huge silver belt buckle, embossed with the sword-wielding emblem of his party.

The heart of the Northern League may reside in Lombardy, but its political ambitions have migrated to Rome. Bossi's dilemma was that until an Italian federation has been created with substantial powers devolved to regions like Lombardy, he had no interest in confining his political power to the north. He did not want to become the Italian equivalent of the late Franz Josef Strauss, the Bavarian Premier who spent the last twenty years of his life trying to persuade Germans that he was a national leader while wearing a feathered Bavarian hat and lederhosen. The Northern League was caught uneasily between its regional allegiances and voters and its national political ambitions. This balancing act ended with the appearance of Bossi's fellow Lombard, Silvio Berlusconi, who was a much more credible national leader and whose party Forza Italia stole millions of votes from the Northern League in 1994. This rivalry between Bossi and Berlusconi, two unlikely allies who had decided to join forces in government, was the factor that more than any undermined Italy's ruling coalition in 1994.

By attacking his allies, Umberto Bossi was also trying to redefine the political character of his movement. But the more he ranted the more he frightened the mainstream voters of his movement, who have come out of the protest phase and are now looking for stability and ways of benefiting from the end of the recession. Nothing could be more damaging in this climate than the threat of tax revolt which Bossi has launched periodically in recent years. The closest anyone has come in recent years to bankrupting the Italian state was when Bossi called on his followers to boycott BOTS, the high-yield treasury bonds with which the Italian government finances its vast budget deficit. The Italian state borrows from its own people, which is like a pilot borrowing money from the passengers for the fuel. This also explains why Bossi's call to boycott BOTS could never have worked. The passengers had a vested interest in keeping the plane flying. If Bossi is feared by the Italian mainstream voter, he is also distrusted increasingly by the Lombard puritans. One of them is his own sister Angela. Angela Bossi and her husband were founding members of the Lombard League but became disenchanted as the movement grew more and more powerful and began to exchange the threat of separatism and secession with the gentle notion of federalism. Angela Bossi has none of the political spark of her younger brother. The picture of bucolic round-face simplicity, she relies heavily on her husband for even the most basic political questions. He tends to whisper the right answer into her good ear. Another problem is that their movement is threatened by physical extinction. Mrs Bossi has founded the Alpine Pensioners' League. Their emblem shows an old man with a feathered hat and a stick walking up a very steep mountain. Mrs Bossi may not pose a grave political threat to her brother but she is a reminder of the inherently schismatic nature of regionalist movements. By the end of 1994 the Northern League was in danger of splintering into a myriad of movements, ironically recreating the fragmented map of regionalism which originally inspired its narrow horizons.

The Lega Veneto had split off from the parliamentary group of the Northern League, and even the stalwart Lombard deputies created a schism over the question of when and how to topple Prime Minister Berlusconi. The grand project of Italian federalism had been almost wholly forgotten in the daily political battles for survival. With the country and the economy teetering on the abyss, the murky machinations of the Northern League, who threatened almost every day to topple the government, looked like the guerrilla tactics of a splinter faction in the Lombard Rotary Club. Umberto Bossi proved himself to be a masterful and ruthless political tactician but the more he schemed the more he was seen, to quote one newspaper, as 'a political terrorist who threatens to blow up the whole country, just to save his own party'.

The Italians have a wonderful word for the high-pitched form of local patriotism that the leagues came to embody. They call it *campanilismo*, which translates literally as 'churchbellism'. It means that your loyalties and interests extend no further than the echo of your local church bells, which is not very far at all. The word is a polite way of calling someone a parochial bigot, blinkered from the outside world. As the Italians are reassessing the value of their nation-state, this breed of 'Little Lombards' or 'Little Venetians' has multiplied. 'Small is beautiful' is their philosophy. They tend to dislike outsiders of all kind, be they North African immigrants, tourists or Italians who don't hear the chime of the same bells. Venice has become their spiritual capital. Last year the Venetians held a referendum on whether to separate from the mainland city of Mestre, thus ending a municipal marriage engineered by Mussolini in 1926. The Venetian league which is behind the referendum, believes that the requirements of Venice and Mestre would be much better served if the two cities were separate. They are indeed an odd couple. Mestre is an industrial nightmare. Instead of canals there are slag-heaps; instead of gondolas or vaporetti, buses and cargo trains. The palazzi of Mestre are high-rise blocks, fuel tanks and refinery funnels billowing black smoke into the murky sky.

Meanwhile La Serenissima has become like an elegant but shrivelled dowager duchess, inching towards the great lagoon in the sky. Mass tourism and exorbitant house prices have driven the majority of Venetians over the water to Mestre. Many still work in Venice during the day. At rush-hour you can see them trudging along the canals like forced labourers or crowding onto the water buses heading for Piazzale Roma, the large landing station from the mainland, easily recognisable by its huge multi-storey car park. From here it is a mere hop to the urban hell of Mestre. Venice seems to have given itself a licence to rip off everyone, even Venetians. Everything is expensive in Venice. The consequences for the city's population have been more devastating than the Black Death of 1665. The population has dropped from 200,000 in 1961 to just over 60,000 in 1993. At night Venice is as deserted as a ghost town. The city that hosts one of Europe's most important film festivals has only four cinemas. Davide and Christina, a couple who own a bookshop near the centre, and who were lucky enough to have inherited a house, complained that all their friends had moved away. They had no social life, because it was too complicated to leave the lagoon city at night. They had become prisoners in the most beautiful city on earth. Venice, they said, wasn't dying, she was already dead. By separating her from Mestre all hopes of bringing down house prices and luring back some of the Venetians are likely to fade away. Venice will become a theme park for tourists. 'Everyone will become a tourist,' said Christina, 'even the people of Mestre. And those of us who are left will probably be made to wear traditional Venetian costumes. For us life will become one long historical pageant.'

Fascist Hang-ups

My girlfriend and I live in the old Jewish 'ghetto' of Rome, an area between the Tiber Island and the Capitol. The ghetto was created here in 1515 and 'opened' in 1870, when Rome ceased to be under the control of the Popes and became the capital of a united Italy. The narrow dank streets are patrolled by mangy cats and scented by sweet smells wafting from the local bakeries clustered behind the city's synagogue. The synagogue is a large square-domed building, completed at the beginning of the century when Rome had a Jewish mayor. It is surrounded by heavily-armed policemen, a security measure introduced in 1985 after a car bomb exploded in the street behind the synagogue, killing five people. The ancestors of the families who moved here over four centuries ago still live and work in the ghetto. The area still specialises in the traditional Roman Jewish trades such as laundries, textiles, mattress stuffing, household goods and some of the city's best restaurants. The sense of continuity is underlined by the ancient Roman columns that stick out of the pavement in the Via di Portico D'Ottavia and by the frieze fragments from the temple complex that the Emperor Augustus dedicated to his sister Octavia. They now grace the entrance to Bar Toto, my local; they were built into the wall in the fifteenth century when most of this quarter was a heaving vegetable market. The famous Medici Venus, a beautiful Roman sculpture depicting the goddess, was found underneath a pile of rubbish and vegetable compost that had accumulated over the centuries. The quarter is a testament to the fact that no aspect of the past is ever completely eradicated in Rome. Near the ancient Theatre of Marcellus, an amphitheatre that was turned into a block of flats in the fifteenth century, there is a memorial slab. It commemorates the victims of Fascism, the hundreds of Jewish Romans who were shot or sent to concentration camps by the Nazis who occupied Rome with the support of Benito Mussolini in 1943. The backdrop of continuity in the ghetto is appropriate because in the last three years it has looked as if, for the neo-Fascists, history was repeating itself, as a farce.

In October 1992 there was a commotion in the ghetto. A group of skinheads had come to the area in the middle of the night and daubed the walls with swastikas and invitations for the 'Jews to get out'. The following day two hundred or so young Jewish men decided to retaliate by paying the skinheads a visit. They got on their mopeds, many of them wearing their skullcaps, drove to the Via Domodossola in a notoriously right-wing quarter of the city and raided the offices of a small group of neo-Nazis. A few people were beaten up, some furniture was destroyed and there was a threatening response from the skinheads, who vowed to avenge what one of them called 'this violation of our political rights'. Jewish community leaders denounced the Jewish raid as a dangerous provocation. The number of policemen around the synagogue was increased. For several days the atmosphere was tense, as the inhabitants of the ghetto braced themselves for retaliation. But the response never came. The skinheads seem to have been stunned by the unusually robust response of their victims. A few months later, however, graffiti started to appear again on some walls in the ghetto. This time it read: *ANTI-Fascismo Mai Più!*, 'ANTI-Fascism Never Again!' The victimisers had become the victims. Violent thugs became consumed with self-pity. The jackboot had been replaced by the open-toed Birkenstock sandal. Meanwhile neo-Fascist members of parliament were pleading for understanding. Mussolini, they complained, had been misunderstood. The Duce had really been a frustrated democrat. Politicians and supporters of a movement that once worshipped the purifying effects of violence now complained that they were being persecuted. History seemed to be taking an absurd twist.

The bruised sensibilities of Italy's neo-Fascists have coincided with their sudden return to power after fifty years in the wilderness. The neo-Fascist MSI – Italian Social Movement – has formed part of the ruling right-wing coalition under the new name of Alleanza Nazionale, or National Alliance. The architect of this conversion is Gianfranco Fini, the young and immensely popular leader of the party, who has left the margins of Italian politics to soar in the opinion polls, even eclipsing Silvio Berlusconi in popularity. In 1994 Fini went on a goodwill tour to the United States to reassure the Jewish Community and American legislators that they had nothing to fear from his movement. Back in Italy he laid wreaths in memory of the victims of Fascism, sounded as reasonable and mild-mannered as a Swedish social democrat. His declared policies of peace and harmony would have sat comfortably with any Rainbow Alliance. But in 1992 the same Fini was singing the old Fascist songs surrounded by thugs in black shirts giving him the old Roman salute.

The neo-Fascists were marginalised as long as the *partitocrazia* was in power. The consensus between centre left and centre right, the solidity of the ruling coalition and the cooperation of the Communist opposition meant that the neo-Fascist MSI could be ignored. Apart from a few half-hearted attempts at *rapprochement* the neo-Fascists were always excluded from power by the arithmetic of coalition government. Once the coalition evaporated and the *partitocrazia* caved in under the weight of corruption and misrule, the MSI was poised to pick up the pieces. Thanks to its marginal role the party had never had the opportunity to be tempted by bribery. A bribe to the neo-Fascists was, on the whole, a bribe wasted. After all, the party had no power on the national level. Furthermore, the neo-Fascists managed to absorb millions of voters left homeless by the discredited Christian Democrats, especially in southern Italy. The party had trebled its electoral base. In cities like Rome, Naples and Bari, where it had a traditionally strong showing – around eight to ten per cent – in depressed working-class areas it has become the biggest or second biggest party. Rome narrowly avoided electing Gianfranco Fini as its mayor in the municipal elections of November 1993. But in the first round of the elections the party emerged as the most popular in the Italian capital with over thirty per cent of the vote. The pollsters had miscalculated the final result by around ten per cent. The reason was that many of the voters who were questioned when they left the polling both were too embarrassed to admit that they had voted neo-Fascist. It didn't take long for the old taboos to be swept away, however. The neo-Fascists had come out of the closet. The square-jawed face and dark glare of the 'Redeemer of the Heavens', as the Duce used to be known, began to appear on magazine covers all over the country. A rash of Mussolini publications, from 1000-lira summaries of his life to cartoons, video biographies and cassettes of his speeches, started to appear in news-stands. The book retailers Feltrinelli noted that the number of publications dealing with Fascism and Mussolini had trebled in one year to 2300. The Duce was back in fashion. So, too, was his voluptuous thirty-year-old granddaughter, Alessandra.

In 1994 she was elected to parliament for her second mandate. Her surname was no longer an embarrassment, but her main political asset. The neo-Fascists have become clubbable, not to say fashionable. After the municipal elections in Rome in November 1993 in which the National Alliance emerged as the biggest party in the Italian capital, posters started to appear on the city's walls and billboards. They were advertising a Mediterranean cruise in the company of the neo-Fascist leader Gianfranco Fini. The cruise ship was the *Achille Lauro*, the same one that was hijacked by Palestinian terrorists in 1984 and which was to sink in December 1994 off the coast of Somalia. The ship was named after a former mayor of Naples, an extreme right-wing populist who was also one of Italy's wealthiest shipowners. The berths were sold out as early as February. The neo-Fascist travel bureau, next to the party's modest headquarters, was doing a roaring trade in tie-pins with the party emblem, a small, almost self-effacing flame in the Italian colours – red, white and green – that flickers eternally for Il Duce. There were similarly emblazoned lighters, handkerchiefs and watches. And for those who couldn't get on the cruise there was always the neo-Fascist ski weekend in the Abruzzi mountains or the rambling weekend with lectures on the fauna and flora of the mountains east of Rome. The neo-Fascists know how to enjoy themselves and they no longer have to do it in private. They have come out of the closet. In Germany the extreme right-wing Republikaner are making gains at the polls, especially in the depressed inner-city areas; in France Jean-Marie Le Pen of the National Front has managed to dictate the national agenda on immigration policy. Once a fringe politician, he became a serious candidate for the French presidency. All over Europe issues such as immigration, long-term unemployment and economic insecurity have helped the right and in some places the extreme right. But Italy is unique as a country that defeated Fascism five decades ago only to find its spiritual heirs re-elected democratically to power.

The presence of a Mussolini in parliament and the neo-Fascists in government have forced Italians to re-examine their past of five decades ago. The Fascist era had been covered under the blanket of post-war political consensus. Whereas the Germans at least made some attempt to ask how the rape of democracy, human rights and civilisation had been possible under Hitler, the Italians opted for a collective amnesia. One could justifiably argue that Nazi Germany had more reason to atone for its sins than Mussolini's Italy. Nevertheless the Italians spent little time after 1945 asking why their fledgling democracy had collapsed so swiftly in the early 1920s. One indication of this wilful amnesia is the fact that the history taught in Italian schools barely touches on the subject of Mussolini and Fascism. While textbooks devote entire chapters to the Italian Risorgimento, the period between 1922 and 1945 gets an almost perfunctory mention.

Initially this attitude had less to do with self-censorship or the whitewashing of history than with a desire to heal the country's internal rift. Between 1943 and 1945 Italy was torn apart by what amounted to a vicious civil war between Communist partisans and the remnants of Fascism. The situation was further aggravated by the fact that the Nazis who occupied northern and central Italy after the fall of Mussolini punished Fascist Italy for deserting Germany just as the fortunes of war were turning against it. Field Marshal Kesselring, the Nazi commander of occupied Italy, not only sent 18,000 Italian Jews to their death in German extermination camps, he also deported almost one million Italians to Germany for forced labour in the Reich's factories. 'The German generals sought revenge for Italy's betrayal,' the historian Richard Lamb has written in his book on the subject, 'they wanted to treat her like Poland and the occupied countries.' The Nazis' humiliation of their former Fascist allies gave all sides after the war a common enemy. It may even have helped to heal some of the rifts. In any case a pragmatic decision was made in 1946 by Italy's allies, the Catholic Church, the Christian Democrats and even the Communists to reconcile former enemies. Palmiro Togliatti, the leader of the Italian Communist Party who lived in exile in Moscow during the Mussolini years, became Minister of Justice in 1946 for a year. It was the first and the last time that the Communists were to hold a ministerial post. Togliatti, who sought a *modus operandi* with the Christian Democrats, signed a decree abolishing the policy of *epurazione*, or purification, which had been introduced only a year earlier and with which fascist elements were supposed to be weeded out of the bureaucracy and brought to trial.

The decision may not have been entirely the result of considered political judgement. *Epurazione* turned out to be a resounding failure. It purged low-ranking members of the Fascist rank and file while those responsible for some of the worst abuses of Fascism were left untouched. A grotesque distinction was made between 'ordinary tortures' and 'those that were particularly atrocious'. Thanks to this distinction many appalling crimes went unpunished. One, involving the electric torture of a partisan's genitals applied through a field telephone, was pardoned by Italy's highest court because 'it only took place for intimidatory purposes and not through bestial insensibility'. While Togliatti's general amnesty ended a policy that had become distorted and unfair, the fact that the decree to ditch it had been signed by the head of the Communist Party who was forced into exile by Mussolini was a remarkably nimble act of reconciliation. Many former partisans never forgave the leader of their party, especially since many more efforts were made by the Allies and the Christian Democrats to exclude Communists from power than former Fascists. Officials of the former Fascist administration of the Republic of Salo benefited widely from the republic's recruitment policy. Some never even left their jobs. In 1960, sixty-two out of the sixty-four prefects, the principal representatives of the central government in the provinces, had been senior officials in the Fascist regime. All the 135 police chiefs and their 139 deputies had been functionaries under Fascism. Despite the continuity of Fascist officialdom the Fascist Party was outlawed. Its successor party, Italian Social Movement, which took its name from the 'Italian Social Republic' – the official title of Mussolini's Nazi puppet state – was tolerated but marginalised. One of its defects was that it was founded in 1946 after the Italian Constitution had been written. The MSI was the only mainstream party in parliament which had thus not participated in the drafting of Italy's liberal Constitution. It compounded the situation by maintaining an ambiguous stance towards democracy. Until the late 1980s the MSI advocated an alternative to the 'system'. Nevertheless because the right and the left had both decided to bury the country's Fascist past the MSI was able to linger inoffensively on the margins of Italian politics, as a kind of mutual aid society for survivors from the Fascist regime.

This cosy *modus vivendi* disappeared with the *partitocrazia* and the return of the neo-Fascists to power after five decades in the wilderness. The anaesthetic of amnesia had worn off. History was whitewashed or blackened according to which side you belonged to. Essentially the left tried to show that Gianfranco Fini's party, now called the National Alliance to attract more moderate elements of the right from the former Christian Democratic Party, was the direct heir to Mussolini's blackshirts. Meanwhile Silvio Berlusconi and the neo-Fascists themselves wanted to prove that they were no longer Fascists. At the same time Fini insisted that Mussolini should not be demonised. The simultaneous rejection of Fascism and the continued worship of Mussolini amounted to a puzzling trapeze act for the leader of the National Alliance. It was necessary because Fini had to satisfy both the hard-liners who represented the bedrock of his party and the general public nurtured for decades on the taboo against neo-Fascists. The other reason was that Fini had to cling to the memory of Mussolini as the main feature that distinguished him from the right-wing movement behind Silvio Berlusconi. The media tycoon with his slick campaign and television power threatened to gobble up the parties on the right, who were now thrown into an identity crisis.

As Fini became more and more adept at his ideological trapeze act, the past was being haggled over. The Mussolini years, which had been so studiously ignored for decades, were now being dissected and debated on television, in the newspapers, in the piazzas. One historical document in particular re-awakened ghosts from the past that many thought had been buried for ever. In April 1994, shortly after the victory of the right in the national elections, Italian state television showed the so-called 'combat film'. This black and white film shot by an American soldier who had entered Milan in April 1945 with the Allied forces had been unearthed at the Library of Congress in Washington, DC. It showed some of the most painful and gruesome moments of Italian wartime history. One was the lynching of Mussolini. The Duce, his mistress Claretta Petracci and a dozen or so Fascists still loyal to him had been caught by Communist partisans trying to escape across partisan lines into Austria, disguised as retreating German soldiers. Mussolini was wearing a German Wehrmacht coat and an ill-fitting helmet, which failed to hide his distinctive features and jutting chin. It is not certain where or under what circumstances Mussolini and his entourage were executed but the 'combat film' shows clearly what happened next. The bodies were taken to the Piazzale Loretto in the centre of Milan. A huge seething crowd had gathered. The bodies were kicked and spat at. A collection was organised to pay for the funeral. Then a group of partisans hung Mussolini and the others by the feet from the metal awning of a petrol station in the square. As she dangled head down, Claretta Petracci's skirt had fallen over her bruised and bloodstained face to reveal her underwear. A priest pinned the skirt back up. The names of the executed were scrawled on the awning with an arrow pointing to the corresponding pair of feet. Mussolini's name was in large capital letters. Later the cameraman found the bodies abandoned on a platform at the nearby train station. This time there were no crowds. The cameraman propped Mussolini, whose face was squashed, up against a wall and put his dead girlfriend next to him, with her head resting on his shoulder. The two looked like ghoulish lovers relaxing after a picnic. A name-tag with the name Mussolini and the number 168 written on it dangled by the side.

The mutilation of the bodies of Mussolini and his entourage had been described many times in graphic detail, but its depiction on film, first shown in 1994, made a powerful impact. To many neo-Fascists it illustrated how one of the greatest Italian statesmen had been betrayed and defiled by his own people. The violent death of Mussolini became a symbol for what the neo-Fascists regard as the hypocritical 'anti-Fascism' of the great majority of Italians who had worshipped the Duce until 1943. Intoxicated by nostalgia, they failed to see that the Italians were also punishing the Duce for his gross incompetence, for the fact that he led Italy into a disastrous war for which it was ill prepared, allied to a country that ended up humiliating it. As if to mirror the debate that had been fuelled across the country, RAI invited a panel of former partisans and Fascist sympathisers to see the film with a studio audience. The debate became more and more heated, the participants squirmed as the gruesome past was dredged up once again before their eyes. Hatred between left and right that had been dormant for decades suddenly flared up again.

Any attempts by neo-Fascists to revise history with the 'combat film' were soon undermined by the second instalment. This showed the aftermath of the massacre of 335 civilians, Communists, partisans and Jews by the Gestapo and the SS in Rome in March 1944. The massacre in the Ardeatine caves outside Rome was organised to avenge the killing of thirty-two SS soldiers in the centre of Rome, when on 23 March Italian partisans had detonated a bomb in the Via Rasella while a company of SS soldiers marched past. Hitler was so angered by the attack that he originally wanted fifty Italians killed for every dead SS soldier. Field Marshal Kesselring, the commander of German forces in occupied Italy, persuaded Hitler that the ratio of revenge had to be brought down to ten Italians for every dead German. The head of the Gestapo in Rome, Herbert Kappler, had told Kesselring that he could find 320 Italian prisoners who had already been condemned to death. When he examined his records he found that there were only three. Working all night on the list, Kappler could only find 270 Italians in German custody in Rome. He asked the Italian Fascist Police Chief in the capital, Pietro Caruso, to make up the shortfall of fifty. Caruso, with the permission of Buffarini Guidi, Mussolini's Interior Minister, obliged the Gestapo. A raid was organised on the Jewish ghetto, where fifty innocent civilians and another twenty-five 'for good measure' were rounded up and taken with the other prisoners to the Ardeatine caves. There they were led into the caves in groups of five, listening to the screams of the group in front of them, and shot in the back of the head by SS officers. The Wehrmacht had refused to take part in the operation.

The shooting lasted six hours. In an affidavit to Field Marshal Kesselring's trial at Nuremberg, Major Kappler, who was in charge of the operation, described how he ordered his men to get drunk on brandy after the massacre. In a matter-of-fact way he recalled how he led one reluctant German private into the cave 'in a companionable way' and how together they shot a group of prisoners in the head. Six hours later, when the shooting had ended, German army engineers blew up the caves in an attempt to bury the evidence. When the Allies liberated Rome later that year the caves were opened and the decomposed bodies were retrieved. This is the scene shown in the documentary film: hundreds of wives, girlfriends and mothers being led to the Ardeatine caves to identify corpses. Mass was celebrated outside the caves and then the women were led into the caves one by one. Ten minutes later they emerged into daylight crying, screaming, devastated by the sight of their relatives reduced to bones. Despite the resentment felt by the Italian Fascists for their German occupiers, the film was a reminder that Nazi atrocities in Italy were committed with the connivance or cooperation of the Fascist authorities. Before the Germans marched into Rome, Mussolini himself had urged Hitler not to spare the city's palaces and Roman ruins, if their destruction was the price of occupation.

The film elicited a powerful response on both sides of the old ideological divide. Newspaper headlines warned about a creeping revisionism. Thin-skinned neo-Fascists pleaded: *Anti-Fascismo Mai Più*. 'Anti-Fascism Never Again.' History had become politicised, the past had once again merged with the present. A country that had pretended Fascism never existed five minutes after the fall of Mussolini now found itself divided by history. On 25 April 1994 – Liberation Day – the Democratic Party of the Left, who had just lost the elections, were determined to win the moral high ground by organising a massive demonstration in Milan, ostensibly 'for national reconciliation and against Fascism'. The real target of the rally was of course the right-wing government that had just been elected. Never before had such a large rally been organised on Liberation Day. Over 200,000 people streamed into the streets in torrential rain. The Italians are masters at organising rallies and they weren't going to be daunted by the wet weather. A colourful carnival of union banners, brass bands, party leaders, party hacks with red flags, hooded anarchists, reformed Communists, unreconstructed Marxists and tens of thousands of ordinary umbrella carriers made their way to the Piazza del Duomo in front of the cathedral. It was an extraordinary turn-out. One housewife told me she had been driven into the streets by the neo-Fascists: 'We must not let them forget the past.' A taxi-driver said he was 'marching for democracy', another man said that he was frightened by 'the return of ghosts from the past'. The only right-wing leader to take part in the procession was Umberto Bossi and the Northern League's mayor of Milan, Marco Formentini. Both were heckled as they arrived. Some demonstrators shouted 'Racists, traitors and Fascists'. Meanwhile in Rome the leader of the neo-Fascist party, Gianfranco Fini, went to a Remembrance Mass and later preached reconciliation to the press. A spokesman for Silvio Berlusconi announced that the tycoon was staying at home with his family in their villa at Arcore outside Milan. Berlusconi followed the events of the day on television and later went to his private chapel to pray for social harmony in the company of his family and a few close friends. Two weeks later he finally announced the line-up of his cabinet which included five ministers from the National Alliance. None of them were hard-liners from the former MSI. But nevertheless they belonged to the neo-Fascist camp. The left-wing *Manifesto* newspaper greeted the announcement with a solid black front page. This depicted the neo-Fascists' victory as a kind of coup staged by ghosts from the past. The fact was that five million Italians had voted for the National Alliance. Under the agreement reached with Berlusconi's Forza Italia Party and the Northern League, they fielded no candidates in the north of Italy, but they became the dominant party in the south. Moreover Gianfranco Fini, who knew how to look on in dignified silence while his coalition partners squabbled in public, rose steadily in the opinion polls. By the summer of 1994 he had become the country's most popular politician.

With him a new breed of very old politicians burst from the closet. Fini was born seven years after the death of Mussolini. Some of his associates were not only alive when the Duce was in power, they ruled with him. Ajmeno Finestra was one of them. Diminutive and feisty, the seventy-three-year-old neo-Fascist mayor of Latina was elected in December 1994 with a resounding majority. His party had received fifty-seven per cent of the votes, an unprecedented amount for any list in Latina. The voters had rallied to the neo-Fascists' call for order and clean government, as they had done in scores of other cities. Finestra had invited me to lunch at the local tennis club to celebrate his victory. The freckled terracotta walls were decorated with art deco lights and stylish photographs of Mussolini and of Latina's Fascist architecture, which the mayor had commissioned. Twirls of *nouvelle cuisine* pasta – black spaghetti with pink salmon sauce – were served on large plates, accompanied by white wine or the 'lightly fizzy' mineral water that has become fashionable in Italy. The murmur of *sotto voce* small-talk was drowned out now and again when Finestra raised his voice to hammer home a point to the city's new cultural officer, a frail-looking woman seated on his left. Slimline cellphones rang with great regularity. Latina's neo-Fascist élite was sitting down for a high-fibre, calorie-controlled lunch.

The mayor is a former sports teacher and local businessman. Despite his age he still does fifty press-ups a day and has a horse called Charlie. He owns the local fitness club and opened the first physiotherapy centre in the region, which he believes may account for the fact that so many handicapped people voted for him. Finestra seems like a thoroughly good chap. Why, I asked the mayor, had he won? He put his hand on my shoulder, and said: 'A winning smile? People think I'm a nice guy.' The mayor smiled winningly, displaying two rows of small but perfect teeth. His gold-rimmed, half-moon spectacles gave him the air of an eminent dental surgeon. 'And,' he continued, 'people respect me as an honest man.' Thanks to the corruption scandal and decades of festering lies, half-truths and empty promises the Italian voters rate honestly very highly. And Ajmeno Finestra is disarmingly honest, even about his past. He was proud to have been a Fascist, he told me. But he abhors the term 'neo-Fascist'. 'This sounds like neo-Nazi. We are not Nazis. Mussolini was never a Nazi.' The voice crescendoed. The rest of the table fell silent. 'Not *neo*-Fascist', the mayor corrected me, '*post*-Fascist.' OK, I thought, post-Fascist. Neo, post, crypto, quasi . . . the fact is that the party that was founded in 1948 to carry the torch of Fascism into the future still clings to the man who inspired it.

In 1946 the mayor with the winning smile was tried for ordering the execution of a dozen Communist partisans. Finestra had served as a lieutenant in Mussolini's army and as a government official in the notorious Republic of Salo, the Duce's puppet state set up by the Nazis behind German lines in 1944. He was found guilty and received a sixteen-year prison sentence. Shortly afterwards he and 36,000 other Fascists were released from jail under the general amnesty signed by the then Justice Minister Palmiro Togliatti, the head of the Communist Party. In the climate of forgiveness Ajmeno Finestra went on to prosper first as a businessman and then as a politician. Before becoming mayor he was also a parliamentary deputy for the MSI.

Latina provided the perfect setting for Finestra's comeback. The city of 120,000 people is Fascism preserved in cement. Originally called Littoria, it was founded by Mussolini in 1932 as a Fascist model city and as part of the Duce's settlement programme for the Pontine Marshes, a vast flat expanse south of Rome. The marshes had been drained by Mussolini in the late 1920s and were one of the dictator's few successful economic projects, revered by neo-Fascists as much as those famously punctual trains. Littoria was populated with destitute families from all over Italy, poor peasants from the Veneto and Calabria, unemployed blue-collar workers from Lombardy, dispossessed Italians from Istria on the Dalmatian coast. Like elsewhere in Italy most of

Latina's former Fascists switched their allegiance to the Christian Democrats. Nevertheless the city always harboured a quiet adoration for the Duce, whose monumental architecture still serves as a powerful reminder of the city's founder. In fact Latina must be one of the few Italian cities where Fascist architecture is conspicuous by its beauty. The square-jawed Palace of Justice or the jackbooted cathedral, straddling the square between the skull-like dome of the House of Youth – the inscription is as legible as it was fifty years ago – and the box-like Veterans' Home are Latina's architectural highlights.

The rest is a monument to post-war *abusivismo* and the excesses of the *partitocrazia*. Latina has been scarred by a particularly virulent bout of unfettered construction. The brutalist church spire competes for ugliness with a vast water-tower that rises out of the urban sprawl like a cement mushroom. The maze of red-brick and grey cement tower blocks, worthy of any Eastern European satellite town, are the fruits of four decades of political corruption, based on the unholy alliance of a Christian Democrat city government and a pack of unprincipled building magnates. After the war most of the city's former Fascist supporters switched to the Christian Democratic Party, which managed to maintain an absolute majority for almost five decades. Clientelism further strengthened the party's hold over the city and its electorate. Votes were shamelessly bought and sold for political favours and, according to the editor of the local newspaper *Latina Oggi*, more than thirty per cent of all jobs in Latina's medium-sized industries depended on the Christian Democratic Party. This accounts for the fact that some thirty-four per cent of the electorate still voted for Christian Democrats in the municipal elections of 1993, despite the corruption probes. It takes more than a trial and public disgrace to break the old bonds between client and protector.

Inevitably Latina too became engulfed in the corruption scandal. Twenty-one out of the city's forty town councillors were arrested for bribery. The mayor was put under investigation. The city government was dissolved and the affairs of Latina were run by a state prefect, a Pisan despatched from Rome. The Christian Democrats had not only left a cement nightmare. They had also bankrupted the city, by pouring billions into a fleet of buses that never ran and a refuse collection network that remained mostly idle. The exact size of the city's debt is still a mystery. The outgoing Christian Democrats had been careful to shred some of the more incriminating files. As in so many other cities Ajmeno Finestra, the neo-Fascist candidate, emerged as the only 'Mr Clean' by dint of never having been in power. Honesty and a clean record may not be the only requirements for running a city with a huge deficit and social problems, but for now it's a pre-requisite for getting elected. What the mayor's programme lacks in detail it makes up in presentation. Addressing an audience of citizens and journalists, he began his acceptance speech in the marble chamber of Latina's town hall in a dulcet tenor only to be swept up by a dramatic crescendo in which the words *ordine, disciplina* and *honestà* fizzed and popped like flares in a firework. Much like the Fascist movement itself, its successor the MSI promised everything to everyone, often in total contradiction. It adopted the spirit of vagueness which Mussolini fostered for pragmatic reasons: 'Fascism,' he once said, 'is a synthesis of every negation and every affirmation. Ideologies are a luxury for intellectuals only.'

The National Alliance says it supports a free market but also has pledged to protect the jobs of government clerks in smoke-stack ministries or workers in some of the country's wasteful state enterprises like the much-hated SIP, the national telephone company. Italy's legions of clerks and state employees, now more beleaguered than ever, have always been the neo-Fascists' most fertile recruiting ground. The party appeals to rich and poor, to monarchists and republicans. It incorporated the old Italian Monarchist Party in 1960, even though it favours a strong presi-dential system along Gaullist lines. At an election rally in a vast circus tent on the outskirts of Rome, Gianfranco Fini, the party's youthful leader, was applauded by both skinheads in black shirts and ladies in fur. As thousands of young supporters jumped up and down like football hooligans, the ageing Prince Ruspoli, a well-known salon post-Fascist, sat serenely in his chair clutch-ing a wooden cane tipped with a golden helmet – a replica of Mussolini's helmet – and stared up at the podium with a tear rolling down his cheek. This motley alliance of followers doesn't always see eye to eye. At the church service commemorating the anniversary of Mussolini's March on Rome in Predappio, the Duce's birthplace in the hills of Emilia Romagna, I was standing between a skinhead with a mohican and an elderly woman in a green hat with feathers. As the fur-lined Fascist sang along to one of the old songs, the representative of the younger generation merely hummed. He obviously didn't know the words. The old woman was outraged, lent over to me and whispered: 'Is *he* one of us?' pointing to the young man, with a note of disgust in her voice. She was appalled to hear that he was.

The party's basic stance is that of right-wing movements everywhere: it is tough on law and order wants to restrict immigration; although a lay movement it has a high esteem for church and family abhors unconventionality in whatever form; is highly suspicious towards social and sexual minorities, divorce, abortion, every form of social permissiveness and – oddly enough – vivisection. It worships the Italian nation, believes in a strong centralised state and a presidential form of government, as in France or the United States. If it wasn't able to restore the vanished era of Fascism, it was at least able to keep its memory alive. Before taking its place in the ruling coalition one of the party's main functions was to organise Fascist festivities on important anniversaries like the March on Rome. These pageants tended to be colourful, harmless and often absurd events. The only neo-Fascist torchlight parade I have ever seen involved fruit salads. At a large dinner for over 1000 party faithful the chef revealed his political affiliations in the dessert. Out of each bowl of sliced kiwis, apples and oranges rose a clenched silver fist with a small gas flame. The lights were dimmed and the bowls were carried in by a procession of strutting waiters. Verdi's *Aida* blared out of the loudspeakers. The faithful stood up and saluted the fruit salads.

That's the innocent side of the party. The key question mark is its commitment to the Italian Constitution and democracy. In the past the party has been ambiguous on this sensitive subject. At its congress in 1973 it adopted 'an alternative to the system'. It condemned the use of force to change society, but never explicitly recognised the Italian Constitution. The party also has a more shadowy tradition to live down. Some of its deputies and high-ranking officials have been implicated in coup plots and other acts of subversion fostered by Italy's murky secret services. One MSI deputy with a shadowy past was Sandro Sanducci. A former official in the Republic of Salo – like Ajmeno Finestra – he took part in the farcical coup attempt led by Prince Valerio Borghese in 1970. During the Republic of Salo the Prince had headed one of the most ferocious armed groups, the Decima Mas, which was virtually independent from the Fascist government and worked closely with the Nazi occupation forces. At one time Borghese even threatened to imprison Mussolini who was increasingly concerned about the independence of these gangs of thugs. On 7 December 1970 the Prince assembled 200 of his armed followers from the National Forestry Service on the outskirts of Rome. The plan was to occupy the television station and the Interior Ministry. But the coup soon descended into black farce with key commanders disagreeing and fighting amongst themselves. Most of the forestry workers abandoned the coup and went home for dinner. But some, it was later admitted by Giulio Andreotti, who was Defence Minister at the time, did enter the Interior Ministry. The government also had information that a right-wing terrorist group possessed plans to poison water supplies with radioactive material, which was to be stolen from a nuclear reactor in northern Italy. Even more worrying was the fact that the investigations into the coup implicated the head of the intelligence services, General Vito Miceli. Miceli was arrested on suspicion of subversion, accused of knowing about the plot and charged with conspiracy. In 1974 he was acquitted for lack of evidence. In 1976 he was elected to parliament as a deputy for the MSI. In 1980 his name was discovered on the membership list of the legendary Propaganda 2 Masonic Lodge of Licio Gelli. The lodge was described as a 'creeping coup' because it tried to set up an alternative power structure, and a parliamentary investigation discovered that it was also familiar with the Borghese plot. Another man who casts a black shadow on the National Alliance is Pino Rauti. This former hothead was elected as the party's secretary in 1990. Three decades earlier he had founded the extreme right-wing organisation Ordine Nuovo (New Order). As the defence pondent of the right-wing newspaper *Il Tempo* he had often lectured on military affairs in the United States, including one paper on 'Techniques and possibilities of a *coup d'état* in Europe' given to the US Naval Academy at Annapolis in 1961.

The list of unsavoury relics was long. Guido Leto, head of Mussolini's secret service in the Republic of Salo, was cleared of all war crimes and then promoted in 1946 to director of Italy's police schools. Giuseppe Pieche was a general in the Fascist carabinieri, who had helped coordinate Italian military assistance to Spain's General Franco and to Croatia's Ustashe dictator Ante Pavelić. Freed by the amnesty, he was later put in charge of the Interior Ministry's fire department, a front for his real job in police intelligence. General Pieche's main task was to oversee the retirement policy of the police force, under which former members of the pro-Communist resistance were 'retired' at the tender age of forty and former Fascist policemen at sixty. With such a cast of characters it's not surprising that the MSI's loyalty to the Italian Constitution has been called into question again and again. The party is only now trying to emerge from the twilight of illegality. Its former leader Giorgio Almirante fostered a dual tactic of overt democratic respectability and covert encouragement of the 'strategy of tension'. Under its new leader Gianfranco Fini the NA has ditched its rejection of the 'system' and has bent over backwards to be accepted by the political mainstream.

Gianfranco Fini is without doubt the biggest attraction of the party, especially for those supporters who are not motivated by nostalgia for the pre-war brand of Fascism. Fini has an unlikely background for a neo-Fascist. He was born, seven years after Mussolini's death, in Bologna, the capital of Italian Communism. His family were wealthy, professional, middle class and – typically for this city – voted Communist. When I interviewed Fini he told me that he turned to the neo-Fascist MSI in 1968 because they were the only party that represented a real opposition to the Communists. 'Even then I was branded a Fascist for my anti-Communism.' With his good looks, his smooth tanned skin and his round professorial spectacles, Fini stands out amongst the pitted and cowed grimaces, more usual in the ranks of the MSI. The party which has been more the home of Italy's political and social outcasts had always borne the stamp of insecurity. Its members have usually radiated resentment against just about everything: the rich, the poor, foreigners, northern Italians. In such company the tall, handsome and supremely confident Fini is an implausible figure.

Today Fini plays down his admiration for Mussolini. Shortly after the 1994 elections he told a reporter from the weekly magazine *Panorama* that in his opinion 'Mussolini had been the greatest statesman in Europe'. While the rest of Europe was commemorating D-Day Fini told another magazine that 'the liberation of Europe by the Americans had meant the loss of Europe's identity'. What, one wondered, was Fini thinking of? Was he shedding a tear for the identity represented by Hitler and Mussolini? The fact that Fini, who is an extremely shrewd politician, was able to make one public relations gaffe after another raised the suspicion that he still worshipped at the Duce's shrine, even though, when pressed, he plays down his allegiance to Mussolini. 'So what *do* you stand for?' I asked the leader of the National Alliance. He sat back, smiled and said, listing the points on his fingers: 'Democracy, the only system for governing a people, social solidarity, the environment and of course peace.' Fini grinned as he finished the list. The pattern on his tie, I noticed, was of dolphins frolicking in gushing water. Mussolini is surely turning in his grave.

Highly intelligent and able, Fini has attracted many centre right-wing voters who would never have touched the MSI with a barge-pole, but were driven right by the collapse of the centre. Gianfranco Fini has become clubbable. He is at pains to describe his party as right wing, conservative, nationalist, anything but neo-Fascist. In December 1993 he launched the campaign to change the party's name to Alleanza Nazionale – National Alliance – with a visit to the Ardeatine caves. Fini has clearly distanced himself from the worst outrages of Fascism. Although he may have replaced black shirts with grey suits (dark grey) and the Fascist Roman salute with handshakes (firm ones) he has not been able to eradicate the thug element from his party or his election rallies. The party's young guard – short haircuts, bomber jackets, sunglasses and angry miens – still strut and shout in attendance. The figure of Mussolini still has a magnetic attraction for the party's members and for Fini himself. There initially was a pragmatic reason for the Mussolini cult. The National Alliance clung to the Duce in the same way that the Northern League adopted its mascot, the twelfth-century Lombard general. These are the figures and the traditions that distinguish their parties from Prime Minister Berlusconi and his right-wing constituency. But as Fini's star rose higher, and Forza Italia began to be absorbed by the National Alliance, Fini inherited a broader base of support.

But the National Alliance also occupies another important role. Its support is concentrated in regions stretching from Rome and Lazio south to the tip of Puglia, where it has become the voice of discontent. The NA is the southern answer to the Northern League. Its nationalism and its worship of a strong, united Italy are a cry for help from millions of Italians who fear that a Federation of Italy will force Campania, Calabria, Puglia and Sicily to drift towards Tunisia and away from the European Community. The fears of the traditional supporters of the former MSI, the white-collar workers and clerks of the heaving southern bureaucracy as well as the blue-collar workers in large cities like Bari and Naples, have now become the fears of a much wider part of the population. Their feistiest champion is the Honourable Alessandra Mussolini, the Duce's Neapolitan granddaughter, who has become a neo-Fascist Joan of Arc for the Mezzogiorno.

The rise of Alessandra is a Neapolitan family affair. When she entered politics in February 1992 she was 'presented' to the press by her father, Romero Mussolini, a well-known jazz pianist and the Duce's youngest son. Mussolini stood up and in a moving introduction he praised his daughter's intelligence and beauty and described her as 'my little songbird'. At this stage a phalanx of octogenarian Fascists seated in the back row clearly got carried away and stood up shouting 'Duce, Duce, Duce', with their fists in the air. Nowadays such public eruptions of nostalgic fervour wouldn't be allowed by the party leadership. Alessandra Mussolini was wearing a pink sweater and the diffident expression of a débutante at a coming-out ball. Had Alessandra not been a Mussolini she may never have entered politics. The MSI discovered her in the same way that someone comes across a precious family heirloom while rummaging through the attic. Ageing party hacks

with grey tired faces feed off her young blood like political vam-
pires. She embodies the MSI's spirit of rejuvenation, as if the
party's prayers had been answered. As one old Neapolitan woman
put it to me: 'The Duce has sent us a granddaughter!' La Mussolini is unashamedly proud of her grandfather and calls herself a
'Mussolinista', which is just about as silly as John Major calling
himself a 'Majorite'. As she weaves her way through the dank
urban maze of old Naples, she is hugged, squeezed and kissed by
fat mammas and gawped at by men. She is not embarrassed. 'Go
on, look! Have a good long look!' she seems to be saying.

In the picturesque squalor of Naples La Mussolini offers a
vague hope of improvement for people who have lost all faith in
government. In the dark teeming maze of old Naples some buildings are still propped by scaffolding after the 1980 earthquake.
Nothing has been done to repair them, despite millions of dollars
in relief aid from Rome and the EC. Most of the money has been
squandered by the city's politicians shopping for votes. I went
into one shop where an old man and his surly daughter were
making Christmas cribs. 'I am a Fascist,' said the man. 'I have
always been a Fascist and I am proud to be able to vote for the
Duce's granddaughter.' What will she do to improve your life? I
asked. The man paused, thought for a moment and then said:
'What can she do that's worse?' His daughter nodded in agreement. Everyone in Naples is hoping for a miracle. In the mayoral
elections of 1993 just under half the city voters thought it might
come from the neo-Fascists and Miss Mussolini, just over half
believed the Democratic Party of the Left and their current mayor
Antonio Bassolino. He was elected mayor but Alessandra Mussolini received more than fifty per cent of the vote in parliamentary
elections, a huge proportion by Italian standards. The other
family connection, equally important in Naples, is Miss Mussolini's aunt, the Hollywood star Sophia Loren, who was born in
Pozzuoli on the outskirts of the city. This counts for a lot here,
and the fact that Sophia Loren has publically criticised her niece's
politics has caused some bitterness in the Mussolini camp.

The granddaughter of the Duce abandoned a flagging career
as a part-time actress for politics. In a country more puritanical
than Italy Miss Mussolini's past would have created a public

relations nightmare and probably doomed her to political failure. In 1983 she posed for *Playboy*. In 1986 she undressed – completely, no panties, no gauze – for the German soft-porn weekly *Quick*. All of this is potentially embarrassing. Oddly enough it was never used by the opposition – perhaps because the pictures would have boosted her support. Miss Mussolini may be new to politics but she is not a wallflower. 'The Mouth from the South' cajoles, caresses and prods her audience like a Neapolitan housewife. The Black Madonna, as her foes call her, wags her finger at voters and rolls her big eyeballs like an actress in a cheap Chinese opera. She clearly feels the family's rhetorical calling. Being shouted at by La Mussolini is a terrifying experience. When I asked her on one occasion whether she would still describe herself as a Fascist, she screeched: 'You foreign journalists are all stupid! Stupid!' She almost spat the word. But for many there is something deeply embarrassing about this fiery, pouting matron. The anxieties, fears, hang-ups and inferiority complexes of men and women seem to melt away in her presence.

The future of the National Alliance and its attempts to become a moderate party of the right depend largely on the economic plight of the Mezzogiorno and big cities like Naples, Bari and Rome, where the party is now the most popular political force. Rising unemployment, mass lay-offs, problems over immigration are all likely to fuel the extremist elements which try to find a home in the National Alliance. Although deputies like Alessandra Mussolini and Pino Rauti are currently being marginalised, their hour of glory may still lie ahead. Like so much else in Italian politics at the moment, the National Alliance is in the middle of a delicate conversion process, whose path has not been fixed. The National Alliance does not represent a rebirth of old-style Fascism or totalitarianism. Democracy is firmly rooted in Italy. It will not be sacrificed as it was in 1922. Like Fascism, neo-Fascism is too woolly, contradictory and incoherent to provide the magnetic attraction of a genuine ideology. To be magnetic it needs a charismatic leader and, though intelligent, telegenic and articulate, Fini is no political messiah. First and foremost he is a man seeking recognition rather than upheaval. Decades in the wilderness have made his once ostracised party yearn for acceptance, a share of power and clubbability. Furthermore the party is only one of three coalition partners, who will probably invest most of their energies fighting each other rather than moulding society.

But doubts remain. If the neo-Fascists can be so blinkered about the past and overlook Mussolini's worst outrages and blunders, can one trust their judgement? Can one trust them to run anything more serious than a march to commemorate the Duce's birthday? So far Gianfranco Fini has thrived in the opinion polls, largely because he has maintained a serene silence while his partners have been throwing mud at each other. His grasp of many practical issues from the economy to foreign policy is distinctly weak. But the most worrying aspect of the National Alliance is not the dewy-eyed nostalgia of some of its members for Mussolini, it is the fact that the party's appeal is based on grudges, resentments and inferiority complexes. The self-confident and suave Fini gives a misleading impression. Visiting any constituency organisations of the National Alliance in Rome, Bari or Naples one is struck by an atmosphere of restrained menace. In the NA constituency support office in Rome's San Lorenzo district young men lounge around in smoke-filled rooms declaring their love for democracy and tolerance to the cameras. Meanwhile the busts of Mussolini are stacked high in one corner of the office; the walls outside are daubed with Fascist graffiti and slogans like 'Italy for the Italians', 'White order will prevail', 'Fuck off Darkies', to name but a few. An alarming increase in racist attacks in a country which has always been kinder towards its immigrants than France or Germany also indicates that Italian tolerance has its limits, especially as the number of illegal immigrants to the country continues to rise. Italy has over three thousand kilometres of open coastline, providing a relatively easy port of call for any Albanian or North African immigrant in search of a job picking olives or grapes.

The National Alliance has been trying to introduce tougher legislation on illegal immigrants, which are currently thought to number about 450,000 in Italy. A draft law, tabled in October 1994, proposed that all illegal immigrants who were under investigation for any crime, however petty, should immediately be expelled from Italy. Since their very status as illegal immigrants is a crime, this would theoretically mean mass expulsions. The reality is, however, more complex. Unless the Italian government is prepared to charter a fleet of planes or ships, the illegal immigrants are here to stay. Unless they can be better integrated into Italian society the tensions as well as racist attacks are bound to increase. The grass roots of the National Alliance are more extremist than Fini and his colleagues would care to admit. The question is whether the thugs now think they have a licence to flex their muscles against anyone who arouses their resentment? Many Italians have similar reservations about the Northern League and its petty localism and macho-morality. Both parties represent a culture of intolerance and what a well-known Sicilian sociologist has called a rejection of social solidarity. While graffiti in Milan tells the Calabrian factory worker to 'go home', graffiti in Calabria tells the Moroccan immigrant to get out of the country. Everywhere the quest for the underdog is on. The National Alliance is unique because it represents the direct heirs of a totalitarian regime that was ousted five decades ago, but its worship of law and order, its nationalism, its immigration policy also have their place in a European and North American context. They represent a growing disenchantment with post-war democracies in general, unable to ensure continuing levels of employment and well-being, but equally unfit to fill the gaping spiritual void left by a rampant consumer culture. For Italy the biggest danger lies in the combination of social resentment, represented by the National Alliance, with the television politics of the media tycoon Silvio Berlusconi.

12

Silvio Berlusconi, or The Triumph of Television and Soccer in Politics

Imagine a man who owns three television channels attracting almost half the nation's viewers, around 25 million people. The same man also controls sixty per cent of all television advertising. The advertisements made by his company Publitalia sell the products of the country's biggest supermarket and retail chains, Standa and Euromercato, of which he is also the owner. The food is eaten in tens of thousands of homes, in holiday villages and suburban satellite towns built by one of the country's biggest real estate empires, Edilnord, which is run by the man's brother. On the coffee table in front of the television are three magazines, including *TV Sorrisi e Canzoni (TV Smiles and Songs)*, the country's best-selling listings weekly. They're all published by Mondadori, a company, needless to say, owned by the man. His publishing house also owns twenty-five per cent of all copyrights on Italian authors. You have just finished watching one of the videos from the biggest film library outside Hollywood – courtesy of the man, of course – and now you're settling down to the final of the national soccer championships. But before you resume your television viewing, you may just want to read a pamphlet that has landed on your doorstep and tells you about life insurance. The company is called Mediolanum and a billboard displaying its name can be seen on the side of the stadium where AC Milan is about to be crowned as the country's undisputed soccer champion. You are watching Rete 4, one of the man's three national channels – and who is being carried on the shoulders of the star players after the triumphant match, cheered by tens of thousands of fans in the stadium and admired by millions in their homes? It's the owner of the team. It is the man. And in May 1994 the man also became the country's Prime Minister. The rise of Silvio Berlusconi from cruise ship crooner to tycoon, to prime minister of the world's fifth richest nation is a fairy-tale of power. It could only have happened in a country where the collapse of the previous 'regime' had left a vacuum, and where the concept of professional politics had become discredited by mammoth corruption. In an age when the traditional labels of Christian Democrat, Socialist or Liberal and the ideologies they represent have become meaningless or redundant, Berlusconi invented a new crass style of politics, inspired by football, patriotism and television.

The Milanese tycoon is not the first media mogul or tycoon to go into politics. He was preceded by the former Brazilian President Collor de Mello or the Americans William Randolph Hearst and Ross Perot. But Berlusconi has stylised the phenomenon more than any of his predecessors, creating a crass political language that reflects the death of orthodox post-war politics. His party was named after a soccer slogan, 'Forza Italia', or 'Go for it Italy!' His cabinet was called the 'Azurri', the Blues, a term nominally reserved for Italy's national football team. Far from being ridiculed, these new labels appealed to a large portion of Italy's sophisticated electorate. Demoralised by the bankrupt politics of the past the voters behaved like adventurous consumers happy to try a new glossy product. Berlusconi used advertising and marketing skills for political purposes, blissfully unburdened by any sense of political correctness. Secondly he turned Forza Italia into the world's first genuine *partito azienda* or company party. Its campaign was funded by the company and many of its parliamentary candidates were seconded from the board of management. The party pyramid resembles that of a corporation. In March 1994 the Italians didn't elect a Prime Minister but a chief executive of the Italy corporation.

When Roman generals returned to the capital from a successful battle and rode through the city in triumph, decorated by the Senate and hailed by the people, a servant known as the *lictore* used to stand behind them on the chariot and whisper into their ear, 'Remember you are not a god.' The first time I saw Silvio

Berlusconi it struck me that he too should employ a *lictore*. I had gone to Turin in December 1993, three months before the elections that brought Berlusconi to power and one month before he had even decided to go into politics. The occasion was the opening of Italy's biggest hypermarket, a cathedral to consumer culture in a country where most of the shopping is still done in small corner shops. The shopping mall was marooned in the middle of a never-ending building site. The streets had been cordoned off by policemen. Blue lights flashed eerily through the thick freezing fog. And Mr Berlusconi wasn't even coming by road. He prefers helicopters.

When he finally landed, an entourage of over a dozen body-guards with earpieces stepped with him out of the fog, as well as a retinue of bag carriers, advisers and beautiful secretaries with clipboards. It was hard to believe that Mr Berlusconi was merely opening a supermarket, albeit a very big one. The tycoon, one of the wealthiest men in Europe, is no taller than five foot eight and a half inches and yet compelling to look at. He expects you to gawp at him. He has one of the most perfect sets of teeth in modern politics. His skin is permanently tanned and has an almost orange tint that looks extraterrestrial, especially in winter. His face is round and pointed, strangely reminiscent of an exceptionally groomed, quick-witted mouse that never stops smiling. Berlusconi is unabashedly pleased with himself and has good reason to be.

Before he became a construction magnate, a media mogul and a football tycoon, Berlusconi worked part-time as a nightclub crooner on Italian cruise ships. A black and white photograph from the late 1950s shows a young and handsome Berlusconi wearing a white tuxedo and a white trilby holding a microphone stand at an angle and singing to an audience of seaborne pensioners. Today when he gives a public address he still holds the cordless microphone like Frank Sinatra. He sways gently on stage, as if steadying himself deftly on a slippery platform during high seas. Berlusconi puts even the most skilful baby-kisser and flesh-presser to shame with his startling ability to woo the voters, in the most absurd setting. In the hypermarket near Turin the old entertainer inspected a formation of giggling cashier girls in pink uniforms, standing next to a giant mortadella from the sausage stand. I thought for a moment he might even break into a song. Under the watchful eye of his entourage the Great Seducer hugged, kissed, patted and flattered his way from frozen foods to fresh fish and ended up in confectioneries, standing underneath a ceiling dripping with red, heart-shaped balloons. The ghost of Federico Fellini was with us.

Berlusconi had made a simple calculation. The Italians, he told himself, eat my food, they watch my television channels with their low-fibre diet of game shows, B-movies and very soft porn. Tens of thousands of them live in houses and flats that I have built, they go on holiday to the seaside resorts that I have constructed, they love my football team, surely they will also worship *me* if I go into politics. He was right. According to one opinion poll, Berlusconi was more popular than Jesus Christ among nine-to-thirteen-year-olds at the time when he decided to go into politics. His ratings amongst Italians of voting age wasn't bad either. Forza Italia, the party which he launched at a glossy ceremony in Rome at the beginning of February 1994, improved its approval rating in the opinion polls from six to thirty per cent in the space of two weeks. Forza Italia even beat the former Communist Party, the PDS, which had triumphed at local elections the year before and was confident that after five decades in opposition its hour of power had come. In short, Forza Italia became Italy's most popular party only one month after its creation. The elections brought it to power at the head of a right-wing majority of 366 deputies in the lower house and a slim working majority in the upper house. It was an extraordinary achievement, which said as much about the volatile state of the Italian electorate as about the marketing skills of the tycoon's party managers.

Silvio Berlusconi is a product of what's become known as *economia spettacolo*, business as showbiz and spectacle. This has created the hero worship of a small group of captains of industry, whose business exploits are celebrated like triumphs of human achievement and whose lifestyles are the subject of intense and jealous scrutiny. Demonised in the seventies as capitalist exploiters of the masses, men like Gianni Agnelli, the head of Fiat, and Carlo De Benedetti, the chairman of the computer giant

Olivetti, suddenly found themselves being idolised like football pin-ups in the eighties. This change in attitude probably stemmed from the declining fortunes of left-wing ideology and the corresponding rise in enthusiasm for life's achievers. As the veteran newspaper editor Indro Montanelli put it: 'The literature and iconography of business and financial success have now overtaken in popularity that once dedicated to women's breasts.'

While the 'yuppie' cult has faded away in other countries, in Italy it seems to have persisted. In fact it can be said to have experienced a rebirth with the rise of Silvio Berlusconi. The club of the *condottieri*, or soldiers of fortune, the term often used to describe the princes of Italian industry, is highly exclusive. The real stars are given nicknames. Agnelli, the grandest *condottiere* of them all, is the *Avvocato*, or the Lawyer, for the rather banal reason that he has a doctorate in law. De Benedetti is known as the *Ingeniere*, or the Engineer, for similar reasons. Raul Gardini, who committed suicide last year hours before the police were going to arrest him in connection with the Enimont corruption scandal, was known as the *Contadino*, the Peasant. The Ferruzzi empire which he headed was mainly involved in agricultural products like cereals and sugar. Berlusconi has two nicknames, *Sua Emittenza* and the *Cavaliere*. The first is a pun on the title of a cardinal and the Italian word for broadcasting. The nickname translates literally as 'His Broadcastingship'. The second nickname refers to *Cavaliere del Lavoro*, Knight of Labour, an honorary title bestowed upon successful businessmen in Italy. All the *condottiere* were indirectly involved in politics. Through the newspapers they owned and the parties they had adopted they tried to manipulate behind the scenes. Agnelli, De Benedetti and Luciano Benetton were members of the small but influential Republican Party. The *Avvocato* was one of the party's life senators and Luciano Benetton had a seat for the party in the upper chamber. Berlusconi's conversion to full-time politics came later in life at the age of fifty-four. In the words of Luigi Spaventa, the former Budget Minister who ran against him in the central Rome constituency last year: 'Berlusconi used to be involved in business and politics. Now he's involved in politics and business.'

The *Cavaliere* embodied upward mobility. But compared to the other *condottieri* Berlusconi had a humble background and an upbringing that was both austere and very ordinary. In the intensely snobbish world of Italian high business, which is based on family firms and dynasties, Berlusconi was always seen as an upstart. During the election campaign he received very little public support from his fellow captains of industry. Agnelli let it be known that he would prefer a victory of the left, which would continue the economic policy of the government of Carlo Azeglio Ciampi, a central banker with no political affiliations. Carlo De Benedetti went even further. He published an article in the *Financial Times* in which he warned about a victory of the right in apocalyptic terms. The *Ingeniere* loathed the *Cavaliere*. This was animosity fired by jealousy. De Benedetti had suffered in the corruption scandal. He had spent a brief spell in jail on charges of corruption and is still appealing against a six-year prison sentence for fraudulent bankruptcy in the notorious case of the Banco Ambrosiano, the Vatican's bank which collapsed in 1982 and which led to the death of Roberto Calvi, the banker who was found hanging underneath Blackfriars Bridge in London. De Benedetti could not understand how the media tycoon had avoided an *avviso di garanzia* and arrest. Their dislike towards each other came to a head when the Italian government awarded a lucrative contract for establishing a new cellphone net to a consortium led by Olivetti, the *Ingeniere*'s company. Berlusconi was leading the rival consortium. The award of the contract was made hours before the polls of the 1994 election closed. Fininvest claimed it was rushed through before the tycoon's victory. But the fact is that the government was probably doing Berlusconi a favour. He hardly needed another conflict of interest as he was about to become prime minister.

Despite his power, influence and money Berlusconi always saw himself as an outsider in the exclusive *salotti*, or salons, and banking circles of Milan. He had shunned the Confindustria, the Italian Employers' Federation, which he regarded as the arrogant fiefdom of rivals like Agnelli and De Benedetti, and in the spring of 1994 he even attacked the federation's ruling council as élitist and damaging to the interests of the small businessman, the much-heralded backbone of Italy's export economy. During the election campaign Berlusconi styled himself as the champion of small enterprises, despite the fact that his own empire represents Italian business at its most monopolistic. The tycoon liked to think of himself as an outsider, an attitude which may also have inspired his political affiliations before the collapse of the old parties. While Agnelli and other grandees became the patrons of the small but worthy and powerful – and corrupt – Republican Party, Berlusconi espoused the Socialist Party of his university friend Bettino Craxi. This had nothing to do with Socialist ideals. The decision owed more to the fact that the Socialist Party had become the political voice of the rich and powerful who, like Craxi and Berlusconi themselves, had not been born to greatness.

Berlusconi was born on 29 September 1936 and came from a typical Milanese petit bourgeois family. His mother Rosa was a housewife. His father Luigi worked as an official in a small Milan bank, the Banca Rasini. It was this bank that later launched Berlusconi in the construction business with his first loan. Berlusconi went to a monastic boarding school where he received a rigorous classic education. It was a spartan set-up, with fifty to one hundred boys sleeping in a dormitory. The emphasis was on good manners, discipline and a sense of duty. Schoolfriends remember Berlusconi as being hyperactive, fidgety, intelligent and cocky. The tycoon was very loyal to his school. He has kept in touch with some of his teachers and organised annual reunions in his sumptuous villa at Arcore near Milan. Above all he kept his friends, involving some of them very closely in his business empire. His schoolfriend Dr Adalberto Spinelli became the corporate psychiatrist of the Fininvest group. Berlusconi encouraged some of his closest employees and collaborators to subject themselves to the analytical scrutiny of the doctor at Sunday morning meetings in Arcore. Such corporate therapy sessions set the tone for his whole company and fostered an exceptional degree of loyalty, which proved immensely useful during the election campaign. For instance, the tycoon created awards for the best employees of the 130 companies that make up his empire. The winners received a sports car and were treated to the delights of the tycoon's villa at Arcore. They swam in the pool surrounded by an aviary of exotic birds, strolled through the parks and the private zoo of llamas and pet tigers. Berlusconi showed them his magnificent library and the permanent exhibition of Renaissance art. Together they watched films in the video room which has seven large screens. If the tycoon was particularly fond of his guests, he would entertain with old crooners from his cruise ship days in the underground theatre at the villa. More intimate gatherings might include a special tour of the family tomb. Modelled on an Etruscan necropolis the Berlusconi mausoleum is situated in a leafy corner of the tycoon's private park. One enters it by a narrow passage. Inside there are thirty-six burial niches for the male members of the tycoon's family, his closest friends and business associates. The women are buried elsewhere. Berlusconi wants to die like an emperor. He himself will rest in peace and splendour in the centre of the burial chamber under a huge granite slab, resembling a cheese-cake. The mausoleum is decorated, if that's the right word, with an abstract sculpture depicting what look like twisted torsos and heads.

This is the Never Never Land of Italian business and politics. The Berlusconi villa at Arcore is as mysterious as the secretive headquarters of an oriental sect. It is as gaudy as the palace of a Roman despot. Berlusconi has skilfully exploited the mystique of his palace for political ends. The public has only been allowed to see the villa's magnificent front façade, leaving the rest to the imagination. The villa has enhanced the tycoon's aura of power. Secondly Berlusconi has used it to make important appeals to the nation. The Prime Minister has turned one of his studies into a television studio. Interviews or announcements are filmed, lit and directed by his own technical staff. The camera lenses are all fitted with stockings to soften the focus – apparently this is quite normal in quality film-making – and the studio is suffused with a soft light that is kind to wrinkles. From here Berlusconi broadcasts directly to the nation, reassuring his voters or threatening his opponents. The use of direct television appeals as a means of communicating to the voters above the heads of parliament became increasingly frequent towards the end of 1994, when Berlusconi came under fire for his conflict of interest, and for the criminal inquiries into his companies, conducted by the Milan magistrates. These television addresses are carried simultaneously by all seven national networks, creating an eerie sense of uniformity. But by choosing his own villa as a venue for public addresses and recruiting his employees as party officials Berlusconi tried to remind the public that he is not part of the political apparatus but a self-made man. To his critics, however, it created the impression of a corporate dynasty, launching a hostile take-over bid on the whole country.

After leaving school the nineteen-year-old Silvio read law at Milan University where he met Bettino Craxi, a fellow law student who later became a close friend and godfather to his daughter Barbara. After graduating with a thesis on the legal aspects of advertising – a useful subject considering his later interests in the media – Berlusconi became a stand-up comedian and a night-club crooner. First he worked at the Tortuga, or Turtle, nightclub in the Adriatic resort of Rimini for 40,000 lire a night. Later he founded a group called the Four Musketeers and toured the Mediterranean on cruise ships. His best friend Fedele Confalonieri accompanied him on the piano. Another friend, Alberto Ciciatello, played the drums. Both have been working with Berlusconi ever since. When the media tycoon went into politics he put Confalonieri nominally in charge of the Fininvest empire. Ciciatello became the head of internal security in Fininvest. Both have a place reserved in Berlusconi's family mausoleum. Unlike the other grandees of Italian business Berlusconi didn't just have a family to run his empire, he also had a band.

Cruise ship entertainment has provided him with a deep well of inspiration. His 1994 political campaign looked as if it had been conceived on the dance floor of the *QE2*, and choreographed by George Orwell. When the veteran crooner launched his Forza Italia Party at a glossy ceremony in Rome – televised live on his own channels – he shmoozed with his audience of 2000 supporters as if they were a group of pensioners on a retirement cruise. As he paced up and down the stage, clutching his microphone with both hands, he looked up at the lights with a beatific smile. The same smile, extended to three feet wide, appeared on a giant video screen that dwarfed the entire auditorium. The video wall is to Silvio Berlusconi what the soap-box was to John Major. This was Big Brother meets Max Bygraves. The grand finale included a rendition of the Forza Italia anthem. For those who had forgotten the lyrics, the words flashed up on the big screen, karaoke style. 'It's time to grow, it's time to believe, it's time for Forza Italia.' Berlusconi used the same formula for every one of his election rallies. Another intriguing detail is that he always wore the same clothes: a dark grey double-breasted suit, a pale blue shirt and black and grey spotted tie. One day last summer, the Prime Minister changed his wardrobe to a blue suit, a white shirt and a red spotted tie. This was his summer uniform. An adviser of the Prime Minister told me once that this uniformity of wardrobe was meant to inspire confidence through continuity. The Berlusconi suit and spotted tie became the emblem of power and success. The more troubled the Prime Minister's government becomes, perhaps the more often he'll change his tie.

Berlusconi made his first trillion lire in construction, building blocks of flats and then entire suburbs on the ugly outskirts of Milan. His company Fininvest is still one of the largest private construction firms in Italy. Its speciality is futuristic satellite towns like Milan 2, a manicured sprawl of consumer-friendly red-brick dwellings built around an artificial lake with a fountain. A forest of aerials and satellite dishes announces the headquarters of Berlusconi's three national television networks. Berlusconi came to television relatively late. In 1974 the Italian government deregulated television and allowed private local channels to be set up. By 1980 the country's ether was bristling with over 1300 local television stations, a higher number per capita than in the United States. Then as now the majority were cheap, home-made shopping channels that often verge on the surreal. On several occasions I found myself transfixed by a two-hour talk show about the merits of a serrated carving knife. A Neapolitan channel seemed to be devoted to the marketing of a 'sauna-suit' for women, a plastic jumpsuit that made you sweat and therefore, it was claimed by a man in a brown suit and green kipper tie, lose weight. All you could see was a perfectly shaped bottom, gyrating in a wet and clinging pair of plastic trousers. Every three minutes two hairy male hands appeared on the screen, peeled down the trousers and revealed two supposedly shrinking buttocks. A telephone number flashed up on the screen with an invitation to make a purchase.

Starting modestly, Berlusconi bought Telemilano in 1974, a small local station that broadcast cooking recipes and horoscopes for housewives during the day and repeats of dubbed American or Brazilian soap operas in the evening. For the first five years he treated the channel as little more than a hobby. But in 1979 the tycoon made a significant step towards expansion by buying a library of over 300 movies, none of which had been shown on television before. In the early eighties Berlusconi controlled the majority stock of second-rate Italian films, which most of the other local television channels were keen to get their hands on, but weren't rich enough to buy. He rented the films cheaply to local television stations if they broadcast the advertisements made by his company Publitalia. Twenty years later Berlusconi would use a similar deal to promote his political party Forza Italia. Local television stations were encouraged to air the party's election spot in return for Fininvest programmes.

Despite his creative advertising scheme Berlusconi had difficulties moving into national television. Fearful of losing their monopoly, RAI 1, 2 and 3 tried to halt Berlusconi's expansion. In July 1981 the political parties put pressure on Italy's constitutional court to issue a decree stating that only RAI was allowed to broadcast nationally. Berlusconi, who by now had effective control of scores of local channels up and down the country, reacted nimbly. He created a *de facto* national channel by distributing video cassettes of the same programmes to scores of local stations who then carefully synchronised their broadcasts. For instance, at one o'clock on the dot every station would screen the same feature film at three o'clock the cookery programme, and so on. It created the impression of a national channel without breaking the law. The network became known as Channel 5 and Berlusconi faced increasing pressure from RAI. In 1984 magistrates in four cities including Rome issued a court order to stop Channel 5 from broadcasting in their area. Berlusconi responded by calling on his old friend Bettino Craxi. He flew to Rome for a private audience with the then Prime Minister. Two hours later Craxi issued a decree banning the court order. Channel 5 was back on the air and has stayed there ever since.

The tycoon battled the state monopoly in order to set up a

private one. By 1986 he owned Italy's three national commercial stations: Channel 5, Network 4 and Italia 1. Together they captured almost half the country's television audience, and more than eighty per cent of the commercial TV market. Bloated, unimaginative and under the thumbs of the parties, RAI lost more and more viewers to Berlusconi's frothy television diet of cheap game shows, and, most importantly, the big American series that became the cultural hallmarks of the 1980s in Italy – *Dallas* and *Dynasty*. In 1983 Berlusconi scored a *coup de théâtre* against RAI. He snatched the country's most famous television host and housewife's heart-throb, who rejoices in the unlikely name of Mike Buongiorno, from RAI 1, the Christian Democrats' channel. The 'transfer', which cost billions of lire, was dramatic enough to cause a minor government crisis. Fininvest not only stole some of the best television stars, delivered a slicker, livelier, more popular form of entertainment, it also had a much better news service. The news bulletins were free from party control. They were more informative, better written, better presented and less accident-prone than RAI's. In the last decade it was Berlusconi's channels, not RAI, that broadcast the new images of consumption, the new styles of entertainment from Brazilian telenovelas to karaoke sing-alongs which defined popular taste. Berlusconi's advertising created new standards in packaging and promotion.

In the late 1980s the tycoon consolidated his hold on commercial television by buying the listings magazine *TV Sorrisi e Canzoni* (*TV Smiles and Songs*), Italy's most popular publication. In 1986 he expanded to France by buying the ill-fated Chaine Cinq, in 1987 to Spain where he acquired a twenty-five per cent stake in Telecinco, the biggest possible for a foreigner under Spanish law. With his television stations, publishing houses, magazines and advertising companies Berlusconi now owned the second biggest commercial media empire in Europe after Germany's Bertelsmann Verlag. In 1990 he also bought Standa and Euromercato, Italy's most popular supermarket chain. The jewel in his crown became AC Milan, the Italian soccer champion, bought by Berlusconi in 1986 and retrained to become one of the best teams in Europe. Soccer teams have often been the toys of the world's super-rich, like the late Robert Maxwell or the singer Elton John. But in Italy soccer hasn't just been the nation's favourite sport, it has been a secular religion and Berlusconi has become its high priest. The soccer team is to the modern Italian tycoon what the band of *condottiere*, or soldiers of fortune, were to rich and powerful Tuscan *signori* in the fifteenth century: they became the most important symbols of their owner's power and glory.

Until Berlusconi turned AC Milan into the almost perpetual champion in the late 1980s, the undisputed *signore* of Italian soccer was his old rival Gianni Agnelli of Fiat, who owned the Turin team Juventus. Agnelli was the *grand seigneur* of Italian business. The next best thing that Italy has to royalty, he enjoyed almost the same reverence as the Pope. He is untouchable. His is one of the few names in business that has not been dragged into the corruption scandal, although Fiat has been investigated and several of its managers have been questioned by the magistrates. Agnelli's status as the icon of Italy's post-war economic success is sacred. Most Italians would probably prefer to keep it that way. But in 1989 AC Milan displaced Juventus as Italy's premier soccer team. In hindsight this also presaged the transfer of power from Agnelli, the old-style tycoon who influenced politics from behind the scenes, to Berlusconi who occupied centre stage. It also marked a change in style from the dignified paternalism of Gianni Agnelli to the brash self-promotion of Silvio Berlusconi.

The difference was also obvious in the buccaneer way in which Berlusconi expanded his business. Unlike Fiat, Italy's largest private firm, Fininvest, its second largest, was not listed on the Milan stock exchange. It was a private, family-owned firm with a highly secretive ownership structure and opaque accounts. It raised capital by borrowing from the banks, especially from Mediobanca, Italy's most renowned merchant bank. Fininvest had debts of over four billion dollars. Financial analysts are divided about the wisdom of Berlusconi's corporate strategy. Some criticise him for overstretching his empire and jeopardising those companies that are sound – like television and advertising – with others that have become a costly burden. If Berlusconi has run up enormous debts for his own company what does this say about his promises to cure the Italian economy? Others point out that Fininvest's debts are still outstripped by turnover. The Italian economy is in a similar position. The country's budget deficit may be the highest in Europe but its balance of payments is healthy.

The tycoon keeps his personal life very private. His second wife, the former actress Veronica Lario, seldom appears by his side. When she does, the effect is somewhat startling. Mrs Berlusconi is slightly taller than her husband. She is a voluptuous beauty with a broad toothy smile, a very large bust and face whose white, almost Japanese, make-up contrasts dramatically with the Prime Minister's perpetual fake tan. Although she is more than presentable, Mrs Berlusconi only appeared before the cameras during state visits, chatting to Hillary Clinton, or hand in hand with her husband at the G7 summit in Naples. Berlusconi was not breaking with tradition. Italian prime ministers and presidents tend to keep their wives hidden from public view. Some observers have suggested that Mrs Berlusconi was told to keep a low profile because she is the tycoon's second wife, a fact which may jar with his frequent celebration of family values.

By all accounts the Prime Minister's divorce from his first wife, Carla Dall'Oglio, was acrimonious. The couple, who had two children, divorced in 1985, five years after Berlusconi had started an affair with the actress Veronica Lario, and a year after she had given birth to his daughter Barbara. The affair was kept secret for a long time, while Berlusconi maintained his mistress in an apartment at company headquarters in the centre of Milan. The story of how the merchant prince met the actress is worthy of any treacly telenovela, screened on the tycoon's own channels.

Veronica Lario, whose real name is Miriam Bartoli, was starring in Fernand Crommelynck's much-neglected comedy *The Magnificent Cuckold*. Berlusconi was sitting in the front row. The play's denouement involved Veronica Lario taking off her blouse. Her breasts almost fell into the tycoon's lap. After the curtain Berlusconi paid the actress a visit in her dressing room and told her how much he admired her acting. Soon afterwards love blossomed. In one of her rare newspaper interviews Veronica Lario told the interviewer that she didn't mind taking her clothes off on stage, but that she distinguished between gratuitous nudity and necessary nudity. She only took her clothes off when it was absolutely necessary. 'Getting undressed is not my highest ambition,' she continued. 'Personally I like to read, and I take a great interest in current affairs . . . My greatest defect is that I am full of doubts.' The same cannot be said of her husband. Berlusconi has carefully constructed a public image of himself as hard-working, enigmatic, charismatic, devout and supremely confident. He has never tried to be modest. Just as well, when one considers some of the things he has said about himself. Here are some extracts: 'I only know one recipe in life and that is blood, sweat and tears.' Or (repeated again and again during the election campaign): 'I am above all a businessman who makes miracles.' Or: 'I am always right' and 'I always win.' Or: 'I see everything instinctively. As my mother once said about me – I'm a kind of wizard.'

Did Berlusconi follow a master plan or did his political ambitions evolve week by week in the run-up to last year's election campaign? Left-wing conspiracy theorists believe that there was a master plan to put Berlusconi into Palazzo Cighi, the Prime Minister's residence, and that it was hatched by Italian big business in 1992, after it had become obvious that the old political patrons would face the electoral guillotine. Others believe that Berlusconi had devised his own path to greatness well before the collapse of the *partitocrazia*. According to his own advisers Berlusconi decided to get more closely involved in politics in September 1993. He did so at first for commercial reasons, connected with his company. The tycoon feared that Italy's left-wing parties would fill the vacuum left by the collapse of the Christian Democrats and their allies and pass legislation outlawing his virtual monopoly of private television. Berlusconi could not afford to lose the most important and profitable parts of his empire, the three television channels.

Naturally Berlusconi did not say that he wanted to get involved in politics in order to save his own business. His intention, he told journalists in November 1993 at a news conference in Rome's Foreign Press Club, was to save Italy from Communism. This was a preposterous assertion since by 1993 Italy's hard-line Communists had shrivelled down to the small Rifundazione Communista (Communist Refoundation) Party, a splinter group of orthodox ideologues who had broken off from the main body of Italy's Communist Party in 1988. They hardly constituted the Red Peril evoked by Berlusconi. The main successor to the Italian PCI, the Democratic Party of the Left, had ditched Marx and become a Social Democratic Party modelled on the German SPD. Nevertheless, as the elections were to prove, Berlusconi had turned the imaginary Communists into a powerful bogeyman. He had conjured up an enemy that existed in the inner recesses of the minds of millions of voters and proved that the fear of Communism, however atavistic, was still a powerful undercurrent in Italian politics.

Berlusconi's original plan was to forge a centre right-wing alliance of existing parties like the Popular Party, the reconstituted Christian Democrats and the Northern League. He was going to use his Club Italias, or Italy Clubs, a nationwide network of 7,000 constituency support organisations, modelled on the AC Milan soccer fan clubs. Before Berlusconi decided to enter the election campaign directly these clubs were going to be his main contribution to politics. When it became obvious that indecision and bickering prevented the creation of a centre-right alliance, Berlusconi decided to enter the race himself and the clubs became the Forza Italia Party. It was thus one of the quirks of the party's rushed genesis that Forza Italia had a grass-roots network before it had even been created. Berlusconi's move was very bold. He joined the race only two months before the elections. Most political analysts and prime ministerial candidates would have considered this to be a dangerously short time. In hindsight brevity may have worked in the tycoon's favour. Some even believe it was the original intention. Berlusconi, the political product, would be as fresh and enticing as a new brand of cream cheese. However, the only way that Berlusconi could win the elections under a new electoral law was to forge an alliance with other parties on the right.

The new law was introduced after the 1993 referendum on electoral reform in which over eighty per cent of voters had opted to scrap the existing system of pure proportional representation for British-style majority voting. It was hoped that this would inject a degree of accountability and honesty into Italian politics.

The reform campaigners had forgotten or chosen to forget that the 'first-past-the-post' majority system had already been tried at the beginning of the nineteenth century, and was abolished because it gave too much power to local Mafia bosses. After months of debate parliament finally agreed on a classically muddled compromise. Under the new system seventy-five per cent of the seats in the lower house would be allotted to single-member constituencies or electoral colleges. The rest would be elected by proportional representation. A minimum of four per cent of the vote was needed to get into parliament, a threshold which later proved fatal for a number of smaller parties. Although the new system was supposed to limit the number of parties and therefore make parliament less fragmented and government more stable, it had the opposite effect. In the end sixteen parties entered parliament. Because even the smaller groupings like the Christian Centre Party thought they had a chance of getting their deputies elected to parliament, the new system discouraged the formation of large parties like the British Conservatives or the Labour Party. The secret to winning the elections was thus to create alliances of parties which would ensure that candidates from the right, the left or the centre which belonged to different parties would not tread on each other's toes. In short, Italy's agonising experiment at electoral reform left the country with an even more convoluted system than before, giving birth to a number of brittle electoral pacts. The left created the Progressive Alliance and the centre the Pact for Italy. Berlusconi's task was less easy.

The Italian right was ideologically divided between the neo-Fascists of Gianfranco Fini and the Northern League of Umberto Bossi. The federalism of the Northern League was diametrically opposed to the nationalism of the neo-Fascists. At a pre-election congress the outspoken Bossi told delegates: 'With the Fascists' – he didn't even bother with the polite 'neo' – 'Never!' Berlusconi solved this problem by forging two separate alliances, one with the Northern League called the Polo della Libertà – the Freedom Pole of the Alliance – and the other with the neo-Fascists called the Polo del Buongoverno – the Alliance of Good Government. He was able to do this because the neo-Fascists' vote was concentrated in Rome and the south, while the Northern League focused on its own fiefdom in the country's industrial north. This brittle geographical solution, with north and south balanced in mutual political antagonism but forming part of the same majority, worked because Berlusconi became the pivot. The right-wing alliance hinged on him and his party. As for his new-found allies, they now had a partner who could offer them the things they didn't have, like television air-time, a well-oiled publicity machine and the respectability of a successful business tycoon. Although Berlusconi was ingenious at creating this marriage of electoral convenience he was later incapable of solving the alliance's ideological contradictions. Once in power he became a victim of his own coalition partners, the Northern League, who began to regard the tycoon as the greatest threat to their political survival.

Forza Italia became Europe's most 'post-modern' and innovative political movement. The party wasn't so much the political expression of a creed or a mood that had germinated in the electorate, it was similar to the French Gaullist Party: a tool for winning power. The difference is that it used all the modern tools of communication available to a media tycoon with his own television channels, advertising companies and public relations know-how. Forza Italia was launched like a soap powder. In the words of Roberto Lasagna, one of its campaign managers, a former head of Saatchi and Saatchi and now a senator for Forza Italia: 'We discovered a market niche and proceeded to fill it.' The market niche was created by the old corrupt system and by a nation which had grown tired of self-flagellation and muttering *mea culpa*s. It created the strong demand for a brand-new party with brand-new faces headed by a tycoon who was reassuringly rich and felt good about being Italian. In fact the party's name wasn't new at all. In his excellent account of life in Naples in 1944 Norman Lewis describes the emergence of a 'purposeful and sinister movement . . . with fascist leanings', which he, as an officer in the Intelligence Corps, was sent to investigate. He describes the brooding faces of the supporters of Forza Italia, meeting at a rally to express their opposition against the Allied presence. The slick image of Berlusconi's Forza Italia couldn't be further removed from its gruff predecessors but the muscular patriotism is a common theme.

Berlusconi's party represents the genesis of politics in reverse: first came the opinion poll, then came the political party. In his austere but elegant Rome office Forza Italia's national administrator Mario Valducci explained the evolution of the party in three phases. 'Phase one,' he said, sitting back in his swivelling black leather chair, 'involved conducting a poll. We wanted to find out whether Italians would support a completely new party with a right-wing ideology. We asked about 20,000 people and found that the answer was a resounding yes. Then came phase two: setting up a network of Forza Italia clubs all over the country. Finally, phase three: choosing parliamentary candidates and winning the elections.' Modelled on the fan clubs of Berlusconi's own team, AC Milan, the clubs are in essence constituency support associations. There are over 7,000 of them with over one million members. To found a club you paid around 300,000 lire or (230 dollars), which was later reimbursed by the party. This bought you a basic set of tools: posters, rattles, ties, flags, pens and a list of the party's ideological principles, which can be summed up as low taxation, minimum bureaucracy and little government interference, a free market, law and order. Most of the clubs have no more than a dozen members. Often they meet informally in a member's home, which avoids paying rent. During the election campaign they had a multiple task: firstly to recruit potential candidates that could run for election. In the end the party auditioned more than 3000 applicants and chose 267. Secondly to support the candidates during the campaign, by organising rallies and spreading Berlusconi's message of confidence and national pride. And thirdly to develop the party's greatest asset, the personality surrounding Silvio Berlusconi. Festooned with posters of the smiling tycoon, the clubs were not so much classical grassroots organisations where citizens met to discuss politics and get their local candidates elected. They were small units in a vast publicity machine run by the Prime Minister's own company executives. Once the euphoria of the Berlusconi victory had evaporated this became a problem, as some clubs complained about the autocratic behaviour of the party leadership and the lack of internal debate. Indeed Forza Italia's biggest shortcoming is that it is not a political party in its own right. It is quite likely to disappear whenever Berlusconi decides to return to business. Despite their large membership, the clubs have no ideological or social roots.

In two months Forza Italia rose from nowhere in the opinion polls to become Italy's most popular political party. The clubs were one reason for this meteoric rise. The other was the message. Berlusconi used the language of football for political ends. When he entered politics the media tycoon said: '*Scendo in campo*', or 'I'm taking to the field'. The mellifluous male voice at the end of Forza Italia's slick television election spot called on voters to do the same. Berlusconi described his candidates as the *azurri*, or 'the 'blues', the name he normally uses for his football team and which was used for Italy's 1994 World Cup team. He also calls his cabinet *la squadra*, the team. So far there has been an uncanny coincidence between his political successes and the triumphs of his team. On the night that Berlusconi won his first big parliamentary hurdle, the No Confidence in the Senate, where his alliance did not have a majority, AC Milan beat Barcelona 4:0 in the UEFA Cup. Soccer is the message. The most obvious example is the name of the party. 'Forza Italia!' means 'Go for it!' or 'Come on, Italy!' This a rallying cry from the soccer terraces and is usually used by fans to egg on their team. But *forza*, which is one of those untranslatable words, also has other connotations. On its own the word means strength or force. Used as an exclamation it's like the French *courage!* All these meanings evoked a strong Italy with a bright future at a time when national self-esteem was low, and when many Italians were growing tired of the traditional pessimism of the left. The corruption scandal, the recession, the strains on the country's unity, the confusion unleashed by the end of the Cold War, the end of an era of complacent certainty, all these have left Italy in a mood of self-flagellation, yearning for reassurance. Berlusconi's genius was to realise that the Italians wanted to be reassured, that all the debate about secession and federalism stimulated by the Northern League was essentially an expression of national self-doubt in the face of recent political upheavals.

Berlusconi manipulated a wave of surging national pride at precisely the right moment. The nation was already beginning to have a higher opinion of itself. Berlusconi's entry into politics coincided with a shower of gold medals for the Italian team at the Lillehammer Winter Olympics. But patriotism couched in the language of soccer was only one part of the Berlusconi appeal. The other was the promise of an economic miracle, which seemed more plausible than such promises usually do because it was made by a tycoon, who clearly had the Midas touch. 'If Berlusconi can do it for his company, he can do it for his country!' This was the conclusion which voters were supposed to draw, and at least twenty-five per cent of the electorate clearly did. The promise of a new miracle seems to have been particularly effective among young voters who had suffered most from unemployment. Berlusconi was also careful to attract female voters who had been repelled by the male chauvinism of the Northern League. The handsome tycoon went out of his way to court the powerful Federation of Housewives. At one meeting during the election campaign he told over a thousand enchanted housewives that he loved to do the house-cleaning and liked using a feather duster. The audience of mainly middle-aged, fur-lined women squealed with delight at the pious protestations of the former nightclub crooner. Ingratiation paid off: fifty-five per cent of Berlusconi's voters were women.

Berlusconi proved himself to be a magician of electoral engineering. He turned his company into a political party and tapped into the modern Italian mind like a psychiatrist. Football had fine-tuned his grasp of mass psychology. Above all he was a candidate made for and by television. The electronic medium is an integral part of every modern election campaign. Every presidential candidate from Little Rock to Lima times his rallies, press conferences and sound bites to appear on the evening news. Meetings are stage-managed to look good on the small screen. But Berlusconi has invented a new brand of politics created by TV. His election spots, broadcast at least twenty times a day on his own channels, were a brilliant compilation of all the most famous advertisements that the Italian viewer would have been aware of: from the languid shampoo advert to the frantic and exciting car advert, to the reassuring homeliness of the insurance advertisement, to the escapism of a holiday video, all underscored by stirring music. It was pulp fiction but it moved millions of people to vote for Forza Italia. One reason why Berlusconi has given so few television interviews is that he not only feels uncomfortable when faced with the irreverent questions of journalists he doesn't employ, but also because he likes to control the lighting. In his villa at Arcore a special room has been set aside for interviews. Lights and reflectors have been erected to show Berlusconi in a soft golden glow. This gives the Prime Minister the translucent air of a latter-day saint. The television craze is taken to an absurd extreme at party rallies. While the tycoon bonds with his audience on stage his double, ten times the size, dwarfs the audience from a patchwork of giant video screens. Media moguls around the world may want to imitate him and become prime ministers. But they probably need a country like Italy to succeed: an electorate in the midst of a vendetta against the old political order and a public, a media and political institutions that aren't too bothered about the blatant conflicts of interest inherent in the tycoon's campaign. Berlusconi fought an American-style election campaign without any of the checks and balances of the American system.

'No, no, no! Not like that! You hold the microphone like this. Make sure you don't trip over the lead.' Looking a little nervous the Forza Italia candidate explained to the woman in the red suit and with the shrill voice that he had never had to hold a microphone before in his life apart from once at a wedding. 'Try again,' the voice trainer said more softly. The candidate was a businessman from Milan. He was being groomed to become a politician. He flicked back his fringe of greying hair, adjusted his round horn-rimmed spectacles and launched for the fifth time into his campaign speech, trying to imagine that the white wall and the video camera he was addressing were in fact thousands of voters at a rally. 'As a businessman, I promise you, I can assure you. We will lower taxes, we will make Italy work again . . . We will create another Italian miracle . . .' 'No. Not like that! Please!' The voice again, shrill. 'Stress *taxes*, *miracle*. Those are the words you want people to remember.' I wondered whether this candidate would make it. But on the first day of parliament I saw him sitting in the fourth row of the Forza Italia section of the chamber of deputies. The metamorphosis had been successful. In the room next door, equally bare but for some chairs, strip neon lighting, a rubber plant and a video camera, another candidate was learning how to breathe. 'In . . . out. In . . . and out,' intoned the teacher while she placed her hand gently on his expanding and contracting tummy. Down the corridor a group of six were watching a video of themselves being interviewed. None of them had ever been in politics before either.

This laboratory for creating Forza Italia candidates was in the cellar of the Diakron Public Relations building in Milan. One wing on the ground floor contained the printing presses that made the party's posters, postcards and pamphlets. The smiling face of the party leader decked the floor of a store-room, where the posters had been rolled out waiting to be taken away and pasted on the country's billboards. In another wing, eager volunteers assembled the party's gift packages. These included a tie-pin, a badge with the omnipresent smile of Berlusconi, a handkerchief and a rattle, the type given to babies. Presumably this gadget was meant for stirring up support in public. Upstairs the party's managers sat in rooms filled more with aftershave than with smoke, discussing strategy. Where there used to be charts showing the consumer target group for a particular deodorant, there were now charts showing the consumer target group of the Prime Minister's party. The set-up was very convenient because Diakron is the public relations company that belongs to Berlusconi. It had now become a factory for the election of its owner and his party. The media tycoon seconded forty managers from his company to run the election campaign. Thirty deputies and senators of Forza Italia now sitting in parliament are former Fininvest executives.

Candidates were not just groomed to sound and look as confident as their party leader. They also had to be taught the ABC of parliamentary politics. Their teacher was a former general and defence correspondent for a national newspaper. Luigi Caligaris had his office in Forza Italia's Rome headquarters, a splendid palazzo near the Corso in the Via dell' Umiltà. The penthouse had been turned into an apartment for Berlusconi. The rest of the salmon-coloured palazzo was dedicated to party business. 'I am here to oil the weapons of our soldiers in preparation for battle,' Caligaris told me. 'Inexperience is the price of political honesty, that we have to pay. We do not want to be associated with the old political system. There isn't one "old" politician in our party. That means we are untainted. Unfortunately it also means that few of us know anything about parliament. And we have to be ready to fight for our cause once we get elected. Our deputies have to know how parliament works, how the committees work, how legislation works. That's where I come in . . . Together we will create a new generation of politicians.' I was reminded of Peter Sellers's rendition of Dr Strangelove.

Forza Italia found it easier to recruit voters than qualified candidates. In fact only hours before the final lists of candidates had to be presented to the Interior Ministry Berlusconi himself was gripped by panic. Livio Caputo, who was elected senator and became Minister for European Affairs, told me how he was called up at three o'clock in the morning by Berlusconi himself. 'Silvio asked me whether I wanted to run for Forza Italia in a safe seat. "Can't this wait until tomorrow?" I asked half asleep. "No, you must decide here and now. We need people like you, people who speak English, who know something about foreign affairs." ' Caputo was one of Italy's leading commentators on international relations and the deputy editor of a newspaper, *Il Giornale*, formerly owned by the media tycoon. Caputo said yes. He was given a safe seat in Bergamo near Milan, and now he is the number two at the Foreign Ministry, in charge of drawing up Italy's much more assertive and independent foreign policy, especially towards Europe. Livio Caputo had at least been a seasoned observer of politics. But the lack of experience amongst many other Forza Italia candidates forced Berlusconi more and more to recruit help from the old political class, especially the Liberal Party. The free-market philosophy of the Liberals was close to Berlusconi's heart, and despite its being the party of the former Health Minister Francesco de Lorenzo it had been less tainted by *tangentopoli* than the Socialists or Christian Democrats.

During the elections Forza Italia wore its political virginity like a badge of distinction. It did this for a very good reason. Opinion polls conducted by Diakron had shown that many Italians would vote for a party that had nothing to do with the old discredited political system. Being aware of this, even the old parties did their best to change names. The neo-Fascist Social Movement gradually metamorphosed into the National Alliance. The Christian Democrats were reborn as the Popular Party, a name that owed as much to wishful thinking as to the party's historical roots. Italy's first Catholic party, modelled on the German Zentrums Partei, was founded in 1911 as the Popular Party. But Forza Italia applied the Orwellian mantra 'Old is Bad/New is Good' with far greater rigour than the other parties. The novelty message was hammered home relentlessly. And it seemed to work. Whenever and wherever I asked Forza Italia supporters why they had voted for the party, the reply was always the same. 'Berlusconi is new. He is a new man. His party is new. He will renew Italy.' Few bothered to ask themselves seriously whether novelty or indeed honesty were sufficient qualities to run a country. The impression of a new class of citizen politicians was all-important.

Who better then to stand for the party in the Sicilian city of Catania than Franco Zeffirelli, the outspoken film and opera director. He was one of the most illustrious citizen politicians in the Berlusconi camp, keen to prove that the business of politics should be handled by gifted amateurs rather than professional hacks. In that sense Berlusconi's party was both ahead of its time and very old-fashioned, recreating the nineteenth-century ideal of parliamentarians who first made their name and their fortune outside politics, before being qualified to lead their community as elected representatives. I interviewed Zeffirelli in the courtyard of a crumbling baroque palazzo in the stunningly beautiful centre of Catania. The walls were decorated with voluptuous putti, puffy-cheeked, pert-bottomed angels in stone. There were lemon trees and above a brilliant blue sky. Mount Etna was still capped with snow and as a reminder of its hidden force the live volcano exhaled a wispy plume of smoke. Zeffirelli couldn't have staged it better himself.

'Infiltrated by the *who*?' Zeffirelli flicked the ash contemptuously from his long thin cigarette and gave me an incredulous look. 'Isn't there a danger,' I repeated my question again, 'that the Mafia will try to use Forza Italia, which is a completely new political force, as its protector, now that it has lost its old friends. Furthermore,' I continued, 'so many Forza politicians like yourself are new and simply can't know what they're up against.' The Forza candidate for senator in central Catania, the fiefdom of the Mafia in eastern Sicily, became strident. 'Any mafioso who wants to infiltrate' – he spat the word – 'my party in this city will first of all have to deal with *me*.'

Although he is from Florence, Zeffirelli had decided to run in Catania because he felt the challenge was greater. He also had a great deal of affection for the city. He made some of his best films here and he loves the baroque centre of Catania. 'The Via dei Crociferi is the most beautiful street in Europe, darling. Have you been there yet?' I hadn't. The interview was occasionally interrupted by one of the director's three Jack Russells. The tiny sausage-shaped dogs were wearing leather harnesses, studded with Forza Italia badges and the smiling face of Italy's future Prime Minister. They pounced on their owner, affectionately licking his cheeks. Zeffirelli is very good with dogs. Finally Sabrena, his assistant, had to lead the dogs away. A charming and bubbly Roman, she had been reluctantly seconded to politics for the duration of the election campaign. Like hundreds of other Forza Italia campaign workers and even some of its candidates, she had been 'volunteered' into politics by her boss.

'Mafia . . . MAFIA,' the opera director continued airily, 'I can't hear that word any more. I think Sicily has been given a bad press by films like *The Godfather*. There is crime, yes, and banditry and of course drugs. But that's everywhere.' His eyes squinted in the bright sunshine. Forza Italia had rented an apartment in the palazzo. There was a bedroom for Mr Zeffirelli, a small kitchen and three offices. The walls were festooned with election posters showing him lounging in a wicker chair wearing a blue and green flowery silk shirt. His blue eyes had a twinkle in them. The atmosphere in Forza's Catania headquarters bubbled with the same jollity that one might find backstage at a musical, completely alien to the melancholy air that hung heavy over the city. The office was run by a former Socialist with a drooping walrus moustache, to whom the others deferred when the film director wasn't there. I wanted to ask him what he felt about the accusations of Mafia infiltration, especially since he belonged to the Socialist Party of the former Defence Minister Salvo Ando, a powerful Catanese who was forced to resign in 1993 because he was under investigation for links with the Mafia. But in the friendly show-biz atmosphere of Zeffirelli's campaign headquarters the question would have seemed too rude. It would have shattered the suspension of disbelief. I refrained and had another coffee.

Catania is one of the most exotic cities in Sicily. Ringed by the usual concrete sprawl of unfettered construction, the centre is a stunning baroque honeycomb, built by the Bourbon kings of Spain in the seventeenth century. The limestone façades are still translucent despite the film of grime and smog. The detail carved into the stone is voluptuous. Every Saturday there is a fishmarket in a sunken piazza, shaped like a triangle, between the covered market and the town hall. From the marble fountain which marks the entrance to the piazza at the top of some stairs you look down into a hiving sea of activity. The stench is overpowering. The walls echo the noisy chorus of the market. Fishmongers in blood-spattered aprons stand in front of buckets filled with eels, squid and lobster, all squirming, wriggling and wrestling against the odds. A young man is cutting a large swordfish into thick bloody slices on a block of wood. He sees our camera, slits open the stomach, takes out something raw, round, red and disgusting and puts it into his mouth. He chews and then laughs hysterically. At that moment Franco Zeffirelli descends the staircase into the market, his entourage in tow, including Jack Russells.

Franco, who is clearly not put off by the fact that he is better known on the opera and cocktail circuit in Rome, Milan and New York than in Catania's fishmarket, throws up his hands in delight and exclaims: '*Carino!*' ('Darling!') He approaches a mountain of a fishmonger who is currently holding up an octopus for sale and letting its slimy tentacles run through his fat fingers. The man smiles. Franco eats a prawn, lowering it into his open mouth. There is applause. A vote has been won. The opera director is a consummate campaigner and although the fish-mongers of Catania's market may not have heard of him, many were clearly intrigued by this man and his entourage. Policies were barely discussed on the hustings in the market, but Forza Italia's feel-good message of reassurance came across and that's what counted.

Zeffirelli fervently believed in the native genius of the Sicilians. 'All you have to do is get rid of the old parties and all that stifling bureaucracy and you will unleash the creativity of people here, some of the most articulate, intelligent and sophisticated in Europe.' Claudio Fava, Zeffirelli's opponent from the La Rete party and a local Catanese, who should have been flattered by the director's appreciation of the Sicilian character, disagrees. He believed that Catania needs more than just a face-lift and deliverance from the threat of Communism. It needed economic development to reduce the unemployment of almost twenty-five per cent, and youth unemployment that is twice as high. It needs a revolution of the mind.

Claudio Fava was in his mid-thirties. He and his wife live in a modern house in the hills above Catania, surrounded by a high wall and barbed wire. They had two soldiers constantly on patrol in their garden. When Claudio Fava goes to town he travels in one armoured car with two bodyguards. The other bodyguards follow in the second armoured car. They drive at high speeds. The Favas rarely go out at night, and then only with an armed escort. The couple owe their *vita blindata* to Claudio's father Giuseppe. Like Claudio he was a journalist and writer. In January 1984 he was killed by the Mafia for publishing what in those days people only dared think: that the Mafia ran Catania, its construction business, its port, its drugs, its arms, its politicians, the lot.

On the wall of his kitchen Claudio Fava has a photograph. It was taken in 1983 and it shows a group of men clutching champagne glasses at a party. There is Salvatore Coco, the city's mayor. Salvatore di Stefano, the regional head of the ruling Christian Democratic Party, Franco Guarnera, the chief doctor at the local prison, Antonello Longo, the head of the local Social Democratic Party, Salvatore Lo Turco, a Socialist Party deputy in parliament and a member of the parliamentary anti-Mafia commission, are also present. Lo Turco has one arm intimately slung around the shoulders of another man. This is Benedetto Santapaola, or Nitto.

He was the head of the Mafia in eastern Sicily and, after Toto Riina, considered to be most senior mafioso in Italy. At the Maxi trial in Palermo in 1986 Judge Giovanni Falcone, who was later assassinated by the Mafia, asked Lo Turco how he found himself embracing the Mafia's number two. 'Believe me, your Excellency,' said the deputy, 'I would never have imagined . . . that Santapaola conquered me with his gentle manners and kindness.'

In Catania too the Mafia thrived on a potent mixture of myth, rumours and malice. Protected by a conniving political establishment and a warped judiciary, Nitto Santapaola and his clan turned the port city into one of the centres of the international drugs trade. They imported cocaine from Bolivia and Peru, heroin from the Golden Triangle, hashish from North Africa. They exported arms to Yugoslavia and Turkey. At home they created a criminal empire based on extortion, prostitution, gambling, and construction. Santapaola was arrested in 1993. He was found in a farmhouse outside the city.

Fava said his mission was to persuade ordinary Sicilians that they didn't have to be sucked into the lure of organised crime, that the Mafia was an affront to their rights as citizens, and that the Mafia only offered protection from itself. The message was popular but it didn't win Fava the elections. In fact La Rete suffered a humiliating defeat all over Sicily. Palermo, which had elected Leoluca Orlando, the head of La Rete, as mayor in December 1993, suddenly turned its back on the party. Antonio Caponetto, the venerated former head of the city's anti-Mafia pool of magistrates who had received 40,000 votes as city councillor only three months earlier, also failed to get a majority. In almost every case the election was hijacked by Forza Italia and Silvio Berlusconi.

Why, I wondered, did the people of Catania vote for Franco Zeffirelli, a Florentine opera director who romanticised the Mafia as a colourful band of brigands? The opposition claims that the votes were bought by the Mafia looking for new political patrons after the collapse of the Christian Democrats and the Socialists.

The hairdresser in the run-down district of San Cristofero, the principal fiefdom of the mob in Catania, had a Forza Italia sticker on his shop window. His parlour was full of giggling smoking young men who were having their hair cut. Short at the back, long at the front. The hairdresser was a man in his forties who was wearing a yellow silk shirt and deftly held a cigarette while snipping the hair of his clients. Why Forza Italia? I asked him. 'Why not, they are new, they say they'll improve things. They are clever. I like Berlusconi. He's done well. He's a self-made man. He's not like the others!' Had he heard of Franco Zeffirelli? 'Franco *who*?' he replied. I explained. The hairdresser listened patiently. 'If he's Forza Italia, and if you say he's a famous and intelligent man, I'll vote for him. After all, he's Berlusconi's man.' For many Italians, especially on the left, the victory of Forza Italia meant that a genuine chance for reform had been missed, that the 'sweet revolution' started in 1992 had been derailed, that the transformation of Italians from individuals who seek refuge in their family, church or party to citizens who trust a benevolent state would have to wait. They may have expected too much in the first place.

The opposition spent much of the campaign trying to convince voters that the Forza Italia product owed more to skilful recycling than to genuine novelty. They had a point. Berlusconi was linked to the past as much as any of the other *condottieri*. The era of greatest expansion for his media empire was in the 1980s when Bettino Craxi was Prime Minister. The difference is that Berlusconi himself had never been arrested or, as far as we know, investigated for the charges that had disgraced so many others. Now the magistrates attempted to make up for lost time. They questioned his brother Paolo for suspected bribes in a number of real estate deals. They issued arrest warrants for three senior Fininvest managers. Among the three was Marcello Dell'Utri, the head of Publitalia, on suspicion of involvement in the payment of multi-million-dollar bribes for the transfer of football stars by Berlusconi's club AC Milan, the so-called 'Clean Feet' scandal.

One week before the elections, plain-clothes officers from the Digas secret police section raided his headquarters in Rome and Milan and demanded to see the lists of all the Forza Italia candidates and presidents of the Forza clubs in the poor southern province of Calabria. The warrants had been ordered by Maria Grazia Ombroni, a magistrate in the Calabrian city of Palmi, who was conducting an investigation into the links between the local Mafia, Masonic lodges and politics. Berlusconi's spokesmen pointed out that they could have done this by faxing the information department of the Interior Ministry a list of requests. A raid, they argued, was as unnecessary as it was headline grabbing. The President of Italy, Oscar Luigi Scalfaro, sensibly pointed out that the magistrates could not ignore questions of political timing. According to Berlusconi's in-house pollster Gianni Pilo, the episode produced a last-minute swing in favour of Forza Italia.

Two days before, Italy's Interior Minister Nicola Mancino had declared publically that he was afraid Forza Italia clubs had been infiltrated by the Mafia in Sicily. A day later Luciano Violante the respected head of the parliamentary anti-Mafia commission and a member of the Democratic Party of the Left, resigned after having leaked the names of three Fininvest managers under suspicion for links to the Mafia to the press. The investigations misfired and may have cost the left the elections. Instead of bowing to the judiciary, the media tycoon took them on. The raid on his headquarters was the final straw. Berlusconi was incandescent. He called a special press conference in which he denounced 'a conspiracy to prevent us from competing fairly in the elections, inspired by our left-wing opponents.' The mask of serene confidence and the perpetual smile had now given way to a grimace of rage. 'These are totalitarian tactics,' the future Prime Minister thundered. 'This has never happened before in our democracy!'

The claim as well as the response was exaggerated of course. While being careful not to mention the name of Italy's best-loved judge, Antonio Di Pietro, Berlusconi had declared war on the magistrates, on the very heroes of Italy's 'sweet revolution'. It was a shrewd move. The attacks on Berlusconi in the run-up to the elections had all the hallmarks of orchestrated coincidence. The media tycoon suddenly became the victim of the unreasonable forces of law and order. His outcry may have rekindled the innate fear and loathing which so many Italians harbour for a state that makes up for its negligence with sporadic acts of ferocity. The left-wing coalition never managed to dent the credibility Forza Italia had established so rapidly. They themselves had been minority shareholders in the systematic corruption and they were constantly on the defensive, fending off accusations that they had received bribes. Furthermore Achille Occhetto, the leader of the Democratic Party of the Left, looked and sounded like a tired party apparatchik. He made the mistake of assuming that he was the sole occupant of the moral high ground and taking victory for granted after the successes in the local elections of winter 1993. Many Italian voters also clearly relished the seductive tunes of the Berlusconi campaign. They wanted some escape from the dreary routine of *tangentopoli*. Berlusconi, described by Eugenio Scalfari, the editor of *La Repubblica*, as 'the Great Seducer', provided it. Thanks to the tycoon's brilliant campaign, many Italians forgot that he had been as much a product of Italy's sleazy past as the politicians he vowed to replace. They turned a blind eye to Berlusconi's friendship with Bettino Craxi, the most disgraced figure in the *tangentopoli* scandal; they didn't even mind that several members of Berlusconi's entourage were under investigation for corruption. Some were tied up with the alleged bribes to buy football players for AC Milan, others were investigated in connection with the Mammi law, named after a former Minister. This was the notorious law that allowed Berlusconi's holding company Fininvest to retain all three of his private channels despite the fact that they gave him a virtual monopoly. None of this mattered much during the election campaign. Whenever the left-wing parties like the PDS tried to bring up the subject, they were accused by Berlusconi and his men of being 'gossipy intellectuals'. The purveyor of pulp television exploited the anti-intellectualism of a large section of the Italian electorate and portrayed a vote against him as a vote against Italy. Through his campaign with its stirring anthems, television commercials, the karaoke rallies and his sing-along politics Berlusconi suspended the disbelief of a large part of his audience, the Italian electorate.

13

The Men of Providence

A British diplomat in Rome tells the following story. In the summer of 1966 a Roman taxi-driver was stuck in some appalling traffic. When he could no longer bear the heat, the noise, the chaos and the fact that he wasn't moving, he threw up his hands and shouted: '*Duce, Duce! Dove sei?*' ('Duce, Duce, where are you?') In 1513 Niccolò Macchiavelli wrote in chapter 26 of the *The Prince*: '. . . Italy waits for him who shall yet heal her wounds and put an end to the ravaging and plundering of Lombardy, to the swindling and taxing of the Kingdom of Tuscany, and cleanse those sores that for long have festered. It is seen how she entreats God to send someone who shall deliver her from these wrongs and barbarous insolences. It is seen also that she is ready and willing to follow a banner if only someone will raise it.' The yearning for a *deus ex machina* to deliver the people of the Italian peninsula from their torments – be they foreign invaders, internal feuds or, for that matter, Roman traffic jams – has been a recurring theme of Italian history, starting well before the creation of the Italian nation. This constant search for unity and greatness has often been fuelled by the distant memory of empire, glowing dimly amongst the ruins of ancient Rome. In the fourteenth century Cola Di Rienzo tried to recreate the Roman Republic in the lawless, festering city, marked by disease and torn apart by feudal disputes. He failed and died a violent death when he became too powerful and irreverent for the feudal families like the Colonna who were the real masters of medieval Rome. The Risorgimento, the creation of Italy in the 1860s, was part of the nineteenth-century tradition of nation building but it was also inspired by ancient Rome and by a return to past glories. The white marble monument of King Victor Emmanuel II, which dwarfs the Capitol and the Forum, the heart of Imperial Rome, is a prime example of architectural one-upmanship. The fact that Victor Emmanuel is buried in the Pantheon, the best preserved of all Roman monuments, is another example that the architects of the Risorgimento tried to establish a continuity between past and present. Perhaps the most brazen neo-Imperialist was Mussolini. He tampered with Rome's layout by building the Avenue of the Imperial Fora that connects the Piazza Venezia with the Colosseum. When that wasn't enough he tried to recreate the ancient capital at EUR on the outskirts of the city. But above all the Duce described himself as the 'Man of Providence' that would restore Italy to greatness. Of course, he too failed, undermined by his own excesses, by the disastrous decision to go to war on the side of Nazi Germany and by conspiracies in his ranks.

Does Berlusconi fit into this tradition? He himself would strongly deny this. The dramatic failure of the Mussolini experiment and the establishment of Italian democracy has ruined the imperial sex appeal of Italy's past. But in a stark contrast to all his predecessors in office, Berlusconi has spoken of himself as much more than just a prime minister, chosen by parliament. In December 1994, shortly before his resignation, the tycoon said he had been 'spiritually anointed by the Italian people to lead them'. He had received a mandate which no party could break. This was not the case. Unlike in Britain, the Italian electorate does not elect its prime ministers directly. The head of government is chosen by the victorious party or parties, who form a majority in parliament. They advise the President who then appoints the Prime Minister. During the election campaign of 1994 it was, for instance, by no means clear that Berlusconi would actually become Prime Minister after his coalition of right-wing parties had been elected. Strictly speaking only twenty-three per cent of the Italians had voted for Forza Italia and therefore for Berlusconi, the party's leader, a percentage that hardly amounts to a spiritual contract with the nation. Nevertheless in his highly controversial TV addresses, which became more frequent as his troubles mounted, Berlusconi attempted to appeal directly to the voters. At one stage he even called on people 'to take to the streets in silent protest' if he should lose a vote of no confidence in parliament. Critics of Berlusconi like the PDS leader Professor Luigi Berlinguer were outraged by the Prime Minister's 'Peronist behaviour'. They feared Italy's degeneration into a Latin American-style populist dictatorship. Some, like the veteran newspaper editor Indro Montanelli, compared Berlusconi's use of television to Mussolini's use of propaganda. Montanelli, who used to edit Berlusconi's right-wing *Il Giornale* before he broke with the tycoon over editorial interference, had set up his own polemical newspaper, *La Voce* (*The Voice*), at the ripe old age of eighty-four. One of the leading campaigners against Berlusconi's attempts to control all of Italy's electronic media, Montanelli described the tycoon's use of television as 'the electronic balcony', a reference to the balcony in the Palazzo di Venezia favoured by Mussolini for his public addresses.

'He may not know it, he may not *want* to know it, but Berlusconi is a kind of Mussolini figure.' Franco Ferrarrotti, the Professor of Sociology at Rome University who delivers his wisdom with all the nuances and cadences of a Lord Olivier, sat in his study surrounded by towering piles of books and yellowed papers. 'He wants to be seen as the man of providence, the man who alone is capable of uniting the country, of giving it a fresh start and creating a miracle, as only the Italians can dream of one. A miracle to save them from the skulduggery of their daily lives. He wants to be seen as the *deus ex machina*.' Once again there were promises of salvation, of miracles, of prosperity and of sweeping reform. There were also many contradictions and inconsistencies. Berlusconi the champion of the free market who made his fortune thanks to a virtual monopoly of private television and advertising. The devout Catholic and family man who has had an acrimonious divorce. The Prime Minister who has promised to keep Italy united but who at the same time has been planning to promote devolution of the regions and create a federation. There is something for everyone in Forza Italia, just as there had been something for everyone in Fascism. As Mussolini, who embodied the contradictions of the movement that he had created, said: 'Fascism is the synthesis of every negation and every affirmation.'

Ideally Berlusconi would have liked an American-style presidential system. His campaign was highly personalized. Forza Italia's *raison d'etre* was to be a vehicle for Berlusconi's triumph. The party's candidates were cloned in the image of the tycoon in order to remind voters that a ballot for their local candidate was as good as a ballot for Berlusconi. He wasn't just the leading candidate of his party, he was its chief embodiment. In the language of advertising, which so inspired his campaign, there was total brand identification. Berlusconi has also shown that the unabashed celebration of power still exercises its lure. While the old ruling parties were desperate to hide their cellphones, limousines and bodyguards, the toys of power which reminded the electorate of their past excesses, Berlusconi preened himself like the newly crowned king of the jungle. The number of bodyguards milling around him swelled. Berlusconi travelled in motorcades that dwarfed those of the President of the Republic. Wherever he went he was pursued by a swarm of paparazzi and his own personal television cameramen. In Britain or Germany Berlusconi the candidate would have tried to play down his power to appease a public and a media worried about his conflicts of interests. Not in Italy. The ownership of Fininvest only became a public issue four months after the election. In Italy power is not there to be checked and screened, it is above all to be respected and exploited as a source of patronage. As a friend of mine put it: 'If they were giving away Olympic medals for jumping on bandwagons, Italy would win gold every time.'

Berlusconi was not an isolated phenomenon. While he lured voters on a national level, a local politician in the southern tip of Italy provided an uncanny mirror image of the nation's yearning for a man of providence. Taranto is situated on the instep of the Italian heel. Its air is thick with the stench of fish and the acrid fumes wafting from Europe's biggest steel plant. The old city, lodged on a narrow strip of land between the gulf and the lagoon, looks as if it has emerged from the bottom of the sea after decades of submersion. The once luminous yellow stone of the stuccoed houses has become encrusted with the green moss of decay. The peeling walls are festooned with damp washing, hanging out to dry in the rain. The shrill flatulence of mopeds echoes through the dank alleyways. The city's tourist industry has been reduced to one Scandinavian backpacker, who has taken on the shabby appearance of a street urchin, begging for his return fare to Stockholm. While the old city is imbued with the folklore of petty crime and chaos, the steel plant on the other side of the bridge hails from the futuristic thriller *Blade Runner*. Ilva at Taranto is Europe's biggest steel plant. A giant landscape of blast furnaces, billowing funnels and huge metal pipes that look like gleaming intestines, it contains more than fifty kilometres of railway track and 200 kilometres of roads. The pollution descends like a yellow blanket on the nearby olive groves and fruit orchards for which the city used to be famous and in which most of its inhabitants used to be employed before the arrival of steel in 1960. Taranto's 250,000 inhabitants care little about the foul smell hanging over their homes or the continuous roar coming from the blast furnaces. For them the smoke represents jobs. Despite being one of Europe's most efficient steel producers and despite having already scaled down its workforce from 24,000 in 1974 to just over 10,000 today, Ilva must cut another 5000 jobs in the next three years, to meet the European Union's productivity requirements. As they spill out of the factory's main gate at the end of a shift, the workers look particularly glum. Taranto, in short, is a depressing place. An old guidebook reminds the visitor that it was Taranto which gave its name to the tarantula, 'a species of spider whose bite was the reputed cause of a peculiar contagious melancholy madness known as tarantism, which was curable only by music and violent dancing. The hysterical mania reached its height in southern Italy in the late seventeenth century and has left its memory in the tarantella, the graceful dance of the region.'

Faced with rising unemployment, crime and more decay, Taranto is once again in the grip of tarantism. This time the distraction comes not from music or violent dancing but from the city's mayor, Giancarlo Cito. Elected to office last December, he embodies all the confusions, hang-ups and urges that have been unleashed by the collapse of Italy's old party system. For decades Taranto had been ruled by a Christian Democratic administration. As in hundreds of other cases the city government was disbanded at the height of the corruption scandal amidst the

usual flurry of investigations into bribes, rigged construction contracts and large-scale graft, fuelled by steel subsidies from Rome
and from Brussels. For eighteen months Taranto didn't even have
a mayor, an omission which made very little difference to the
running of the city. During the campaign for the municipal elections in November 1993 it was widely assumed that the left-wing
alliance of reformed Communists, unreconstructed Marxists,
Greens, Radicals and the mild-mannered Democratic Alliance
would win. They were running against a dinosaur coalition of the
old ruling parties who had, in the words of one local newspaper,
'changed their suits but not their underwear'. Giancarlo Cito was
the unorthodox outsider, running as an independent candidate
with his own home-made party. It thus came as a shock to many
when the burly proprietor of the local television station was
elected in the second round with a resounding majority.

Mayor Cito was one of the first practitioners of a new style of
television politics pioneered in Italy. In 1984 he sold his construction business and set up the local television station. In 1990 he
formed his own party, the Mezzogiorno Action League. First
he lured his viewers with a mixture of cheap bootleg movies and
soft-focus porn, then he bombarded them with propaganda. Both
the party and the television network were created for the sole
reason of promoting Citizen Cito's message of no-nonsense,
table-thumping government. Crude perhaps, but it worked. Viewers relished the way that Cito harangued, insulted and browbeat
his opponents. Yet Cito was the subject of sixteen separate judicial
enquiries by the parliamentary anti-Mafia commission into
alleged links with organised crime, the dubious financing of his
television station and the illicit funding of his construction business. He was also a member of the neo-Fascist MSI party and
once belonged to an extreme right-wing pressure group.

When I visited the mayor, Taranto's town hall was teeming
with policemen. Some were pacing up and down the vaulted
entrance hall in nervous expectation of the mayor. Others were
lounging on the staircase outside his office. At first I thought that
a senior politician from Rome must be visiting.

We made ourselves comfortable in the mayor's office and examined the etchings and paintings on the wall for glimpses into Mr

Cito's soul. Psychological detective work proved unnecessary with such an outgoing subject. The doors were suddenly flung wide open and a very large man marched in, proceeded by a whirl of secretaries, deputy mayors and bag carriers. Mayor Cito sat down underneath a crucifix. His desk was flanked by two large flags, one Italian, the other one displaying the crest of Taranto. The mayor's grand entrance had been filmed by his own personal cameraman. 'Mimo' follows the mayor like a footman. The most mundane mayoral act, from a meeting with the deputy mayor about a new set of lamp-posts to a meeting with the BBC, is recorded on video and then broadcast that evening on the mayor's own television channel. 'Get us some coffee, Mimo!' The mayor adopted the gentle tone of someone who commands enough authority never to have to raise their voice. Mimo, who was in his early twenties, sported a wispy post-pubescent moustache and bore the scars of a turbulent complexion, recently tamed, it seemed, with pungent antiseptic cream. He lurched to attention and left the room.

Our main purpose was to film the mayor being filmed on one of his inspection tours around the city, at which he revives that crucial contact between the *palazzo*, the rulers, and the *piazza*, the ruled. Unfortunately we had just missed that morning's round of inspection. 'Don't worry! said the mayor. 'What would you like to see? The municipal cemetery, which I have had cleaned up, the Garibaldi Park?' One of the mayor's flunkies, visibly embarrassed, cleared his throat and interrupted. 'Sorry, Dottore, but the workers have gone home. It's raining. Have you seen how it's raining now?' The mayor's swarthy face clouded over. 'Get me Girolamo!' The flunky disappeared. Two minutes later the cellphone rang. The mayor pressed the slimline miracle of modern communication onto his cheek and hollered into it: 'Girolamo! It's me, Cito. Get your boys back out there . . . I don't care if it's raining. I've got the BBC in town. Let's organise something big for them.' The mayor sat a little more upright. His chin jutted out a fraction.

We waited for him as arranged by the gates of the Garibaldi Park. The police had cordoned off the street. Flashing blue lights announced the mayor's cavalcade of two cars. The five municipal gardeners, who had been dragged away from their game of cards, stepped up their pruning. Idle for decades, they were now shearing hedges, mowing grass and raking leaves in a park that was once a sprouting metaphor of the city's decay and neglect. The mayor's entourage included the head and deputy head of the Taranto Parks Authority, the senior local policeman and traffic warden and of course Mimo, the cameraman/footman. Mayor Cito stopped to admire a freshly pruned hedge. Everyone nodded approval. The municipal gardener began to snip even faster. He looked as if he was pruning for his life. Wherever the mayor went, he unleashed feverish activity. Four gardeners in white overalls were raking leaves so vigorously, they were in danger of digging up the lawn. None of them, apart from the foreman, looked up to greet the mayor or even catch his admiring eye. Authority inspires respect in these parts.

The inspection was just about to end, hailed a resounding success, when the mayor and his entourage discovered that someone had parked a rusty blue Fiat Uno between the oleander bushes. The faces of the entourage blushed visibly. 'Who does this *car* belong to?' asked the mayor, casting around him with a stern look on his face. '*Who* does the car belong to?' shouted the chief traffic warden. Finally the chorus was taken up by the entire party. Curious bystanders slunk off quietly. A woman who was carrying a child and had been watching the mayor's procession from her window disappeared behind a curtain. Suddenly a young man appeared from behind the bushes, got hastily into the car and drove off. The mayor smiled, and glanced quickly at us, perhaps to make sure that we had filmed the lesson in authority. His own cameraman certainly had. There was relief all round. The mayor declared himself satisfied and headed back to his armoured car after telling one of his flunkies to order someone else to remove some rotten fruit from the pavement. The *podestà* sped off into the distance, blue lights flashing. The gardeners stopped pruning, the woman reappeared at the window and the deputy head of the Parks Authority looked at me pleadingly and asked: 'Can we go and have lunch now?'

Taranto gave a comical insight into the trappings of power and the deference they produce. During our visit many people in that city seemed to be entranced by their hyperactive mayor as he flitted from pruned hedge to swept pavement. Elements of this absurd cult of activity had resurfaced not just in Taranto but also in Rome. Almost no press conference or television address went by without Prime Minister Berlusconi telling the Italian people how little he slept and how hard he worked for them. 'I work eighteen hours a day,' he once told his audience, 'much harder than when I was a businessman.' As the agony of his government dragged on in December 1994, the tycoon looked increasingly exhausted. The harder he worked, the more he created problems for himself. He should have learnt from his predecessor Giulio Andreotti, who declared wisely that 'power only exhausts those who do not possess it'.

But how powerful was Berlusconi as a Prime Minister? Heads of Italian governments have never been strong. The tycoon leads a brittle coalition of northern regionalists and neo-Fascists that was conceived as a shotgun marriage of convenience and fell apart in December 1994, forcing Berlusconi to resign after only seven months in office. He would no doubt have preferred to control one large majority party. It took him many months to learn that you can't dominate a parliamentary coalition like a company boardroom. Umberto Bossi and Gianfranco Fini did not see themselves as salaried managers but as majority shareholders. The cantankerous Bossi saw opposition to Berlusconi, his own coalition partner, as the only way of ensuring his own political survival.

Silvio Berlusconi followed in the tradition of Julius Caesar and Benito Mussolini, strong men toppled by palace coups because they had become too powerful. The tycoon was forced to resign by Umberto Bossi and the rebels of the Northern League because he was too ambitious, owned too much and thus upset the delicate balance of power at the heart of Italian politics, the *trasformismo* of old times. The recipe for staying in power is not to coerce but to juggle conflicting interests, be they factions within one party, or different parties within one coalition. Like the ringmaster in a circus tent one should crack the whip and wear the glittery uniform of power, but the horses, lions and clowns are so well trained they would jump over the gate and through the hoops anyway.

The illusion of control is more important than control itself. Crack the whip too hard or too often and the performing beasts will turn on the ringmaster and trample him into the dust. Berlusconi had failed to respect that rule. So had Mussolini but, a brilliant if impotent analyst of his own demise, he was only too well aware of the fact: 'It is not impossible to rule the Italians,' the dictator once said, 'it is pointless.'

14

Own Goals

If Roberto Baggio, the Italian striker, had not missed his penalty shot in the tie-breaker of the 1994 World Cup Final, would the country's political development have been radically different? The question is less flippant than it sounds. Silvio Berlusconi had achieved the perfect if crass marriage between soccer, television and politics in his Forza Italia Party. For two weeks in the summer of 1994, as the whole country was gripped by World Cup fever, one couldn't be sure whether Italians shouting 'Forza Italia' were egging on the national team or the Prime Minister's ruling party. This was precisely the intention, when Berlusconi named his movement after a rallying cry from the nation's favourite sport. It was a brilliant idea. Unfortunately its success depended in part on the ability of the national soccer team to score goals. At 23:30 on Sunday 17 July, when Italy's streets and piazzas were deserted because the entire nation was glued to the television, Baggio missed the shot, losing Italy the cup, albeit in the most unfair way. A collective groan of despair echoed through the country. World Cup-weary Italians, who had hoped to celebrate all night, lurched home, their heads bowed, their flags rolled up, their rattles silent. The 'Forza Italia' cry had begun to sound hollow, in soccer and, as it turned out, in politics.

Had Italy won, some of the footballing glory would have rubbed off on the Prime Minister, whose club had supplied most of the players on the national team. The tycoon would have laid on a spectacular coming-home party. His popularity ratings would have shot through the roof. Mr Berlusconi would have felt confident enough to threaten his unruly coalition partners with fresh elections. At this crucial juncture in his political career, the tycoon may have been able to consolidate his power. But above all if Italy had won the World Cup, the fans may have forgiven Berlusconi a series of 'own goals', as *La Repubblica* put it, which revealed that the tycoon-Prime Minister had not yet mastered the craft of politics. Is this attaching too much importance to soccer? Perhaps. But for the Italian public football is a religion and Berlusconi, the soccer and TV tycoon, regarded it as the modern equivalent of bread and circuses. Five days before the game against Brazil, in fact at the very time when Italy was rallying to defeat Bulgaria in the Semi-Finals and the country was in the grip of a euphoria bordering on hysteria, the Berlusconi government tried to pull a fast one on the country. It hurriedly issued a decree which almost caused its own downfall barely one hundred days after taking power. The Decreto Biondi, named after Alfredo Biondi, the Justice Minister, stipulated that all suspects being held under preventive detention for crimes relating to corruption as well as a number of other minor offences would be released from jail and put under house arrest. The government justified the decree as a necessary measure for reforming the country's judicial system.

More than half of Italy's prison population – about 27,000 inmates – were routinely kept in jail without being tried or even charged. They were effectively detainees without trial, a fact which Amnesty International had regularly criticised in its reports. This included the 2000-or-so suspects in the *tangentopoli* affair. The director of Rome's Regina Coeli, Queen of the Heavens jail, a gloomy ochre-coloured institution which was built in the 1860s for 500 inmates and now houses around twice as many, was overjoyed by the decree. 'We have released five hundred people in the last three days. There has never been so much space.' Inmates, who were forced to sleep four to a cell designed for two, were finally granted some breathing space. Tension in the prison declined. The government had accused the judges of using their sweeping powers of arrest to extract confessions. The Italian situation was clearly unacceptable, but so was the way in which Berlusconi tried to remedy it.

The Prime Minister had taken on the Milan judges, partly out of revenge for their earlier attempts to humiliate him during the election campaign, partly because he rightly feared that the noose of investigations into his companies would tighten. The battle between the Prime Minister and the Milan judges, between the Italian executive and part of the judiciary, between Italy's most popular politician and its most popular judge, was only possible in a country where the dividing line between the institutions was notoriously fuzzy. *Tangentopoli* and the election of Berlusconi muddied the waters even more and produced a bizarre reversal of roles: the politicians accused the judges of behaving like politicians. The judges attacked the government for meddling in the judiciary. Both were right. The decree to end preventive custody, issued in July 1994, was Berlusconi's first serious salvo against the judiciary. His spokesman, Giuliano Ferrara, a former talk-show host on one of the Prime Minister's channels with an acid wit and a Falstaffian girth, said the decree was an attempt to end the injustice of Italian justice. 'We are one of the few democratic countries which has no *habeas corpus*. Our legal system is based on the principle of guilty until proven innocent rather than the other way round.' Anyone who has been subjected to the terrifying whims of an Italian judge and who has been locked up for months without being charged would agree. Unfortunately Berlusconi, burdened by his conflict of interest and by the criminal investigations into his companies, was not the ideal man to change the system. What should have been a legitimate question of judicial reform, turned into a fierce political battle.

Antonio Di Pietro, the judge-turned-national-hero, saw the decree as a direct challenge to his authority. After all, he argued, had it not been for preventive custody, none of the suspects in the corruption scandal would have confessed. The Christian Democrats and Socialists would have continued to extract bribes from business as before. In an unprecedented move Di Pietro and three other colleagues went on prime-time television the day after the decree was issued and said they wanted to be removed from their posts. Without the powers of preventive custody 'their conscience did not allow them to continue working on the corruption probes'. The burly Di Pietro looked ashen-faced, almost moved to tears. His somewhat sanctimonious address was a direct appeal to the Italian people to back him in his battle against Berlusconi. They did. The tycoon had underestimated the popularity of Di Pietro.

Even more serious was the fact that Berlusconi had failed to see the consequences of his actions. He had not bothered to ask himself what the public reaction would be to the release from jail of some of the country's most disgraced politicians. On leaving jail Francesco De Lorenzo, the former Health Minister accused of having taken bribes in return for bumping up the price of medicines, was greeted by an enraged crowd of Neapolitans, spitting and throwing coins – a traditional sign of disrespect for convicted thieves, considerably helped by the fact that coins of fifty or a hundred lire are worth next to nothing. Within days of the decree being issued, almost 2000 suspects were released. Most of these had, in fact, little to do with the corruption scandal. They were petty thieves, drug addicts, dealers and the doctor of Toto Riina, who had been held on suspicion of links to the Mafia. But the impression was created that Berlusconi, who was elected on promises to clean up the country, was freeing some of its most lurid offenders.

Berlusconi had also failed to see the suspicion that surrounded his motives for passing the decree. Newspapers and café gossip bristled with the obvious questions. Did he pass the decree to protect family and friends? Bettino Craxi, for example, was languishing in self-imposed exile in Tunisia at the time. He was the main defendant in a corruption trial concerning Milan's metro. He had sent a fax to the judges claiming to be too ill to turn up at court. However, pictures of him tossing a volleyball on a beach at the Tunisian resort of Hammamet cast some doubt over his claims. Would Craxi now discover a miraculous cure and return to Italy in the secure knowledge of not going to jail? Another potential beneficiary of the Biondi decree would have been the Prime Minister's younger brother Paolo. The forty-four-year-old head of the family's property business Edilnord had already been indicted on charges of bribery. Now a nationwide probe into the peccadillos of Italy's Financial Police, the Guardia di Finanza, had cast the net of investigation over Berlusconi's business empire once again, with the finger of suspicion pointing once more at Paolo.

In the face of mounting pressure from the public and from his own coalition partners, Berlusconi was forced to abandon the Decreto Biondi and come up with a draft law that would address the serious issue of judicial reform. The judges got their revenge by pressing ahead with the investigations into widespread tax fraud, casting their net slowly but inexorably over the Prime Minister himself. First an arrest warrant was issued for Salvatore Sciascia, the head of the Fininvest tax department, as well as a handful of other executives from the Prime Minister's company. Under questioning Sciascia confessed to having paid 200,000 dollars to the Financial Police on two occasions to ensure a 'favourable' reading of the books of three Berlusconi-owned companies. Then an arrest warrant was issued for him too, specifying that the Prime Minister's brother must stay in jail because of legitimate fears that he might tamper with the evidence. This was adding insult to Berlusconi's injury. After two days of negotiations, during which Paolo had gone into hiding, a deal was finally struck between his lawyers and the magistrates. Paolo Berlusconi would not have to suffer the indignity of jail. He would be questioned in Milan's Palazzo di Giustizia

After a hearing that lasted seven hours Paolo was smuggled out of the courthouse in the back of a flower van and his lawyers spoke to the press. The Prime Minister's brother admitted that his company had created a two-million-dollar slush fund for bribing the Financial Police, 'to keep those officers at bay who had become a nuisance'. His lawyers put it in a familiar way: 'Paolo Berlusconi,' they said, 'had been the victim of a system of corruption from which neither he nor any other entrepreneur could escape.' Here was the excuse that had become so familiar in the last two years: universal corruption neutralises personal culpability. Meanwhile the Guardia di Finanza, the very organisation that was supposed to enforce the law, was still reeling from the fact that forty of its officers including one general had been arrested. Three officers implicated in the scandal committed suicide in one month. When the allegations continued, the commander of the force sued the judiciary for libel. The 'revolution' had degenerated into farce: one branch of the police force was libelling the judiciary who were engaged in a full-scale war with the Prime Minister, whose brother had admitted paying bribes. Everyone blamed someone else. No one was completely above suspicion.

Meanwhile the shadow of suspicion fell on the Prime Minister who was elected partly because he promised to clean up Italian politics. From the public's point of view, the arrest of Paolo Berlusconi and the Fininvest tax scandal confirmed their suspicions that the Prime Minister was trying to save his next of kin by issuing the decree on preventive custody. Suddenly all the questions and conflicts that had hung precariously over the Prime Minister's head and had been partially ignored by the public crashed down on him. His aura of invincibility had been shattered, and gave way to the suspicion that his political problems were exclusively of his own making. Berlusconi, 'the Great Seducer', had become his own worst enemy.

The episode of the Biondi Decree and the investigations into the Financial Police also gave the Italian public an alarming insight into Berlusconi's impatience with the laborious process of democracy. From their very first day in parliament Berlusconi's team of manager-deputies began complaining about the tedium of debates, voting procedures and other parliamentary formalities. The eleven deputies and senators who had been employed by Fininvest before they were volunteered into politics all bore the same expression of glazed boredom when they sat in parliament. They had a point of course. The Italian parliament is notoriously time-consuming. Its machinery is slowed down and sometimes brought to an abrupt standstill by the fact that every piece of legislation has to be approved by both chambers, and will be tossed from one to the other in a kind of parliamentary ping-pong until the right deal can be struck and the law can be approved. The inherent fractiousness of coalition politics doesn't help either. In order to overcome these obstacles Italian governments have often resorted to decrees rather than to laws. Although decrees should only be invoked in 'exceptional and urgent circumstances', they have almost become the norm. The government of

Prime Minister Ciampi issued eighty-eight decrees, ranging from privatisation to tax reform.

A government decree comes into force as soon as it has been published in the parliamentary gazette, which is usually the next day. It then has to be approved or thrown out by parliament within sixty days. Most of the decrees announced by the Ciampi government were widely accepted as the bitter but urgently necessary medicine of economic damage control. In fact they made the government headed by an unelected central banker with a cabinet of professors the most effective, resolute and even popular administration since the era of Prime Minister De Gasperi in the 1950s. But Berlusconi issued a number of decrees, none of which were deemed essential, but all of which were tinged with the suspicion that they could benefit his own business interests. A decree on legalising unauthorised construction could theoretically have helped Berlusconi's construction company Edilnord, which has been prevented from building a number of holiday villages in Sardinia because the local authorities refused to grant planning permission. Another decree created a virtual amnesty for water polluters. Companies that polluted rivers or lakes with waste were now allowed to pay a flat fine of three million lire, about £1400. Although it was still illegal for them to pollute rivers, they would no longer be taken to court. This measure helped to clear a massive backlog of cases, but with such a low fine it also gave companies a financial incentive to pollute. A decree about copyright – hardly an issue worthy of 'exceptional and urgent' circumstances – extended the copyright that Italian publishing houses have on an author from fifty to seventy-five years. Since the Prime Minister's publishing empire Mondadori owns twenty-five per cent of all Italian copyright, it is natural that his motives came under suspicion. By dint of his own policies the tycoon managed to highlight the fundamental problem bewitching his government. Silvio Berlusconi was too rich for his own good.

Belatedly most of the Italian public, the media, parliament and the Prime Minister himself discovered the blindingly obvious: the constant conflict of interest created by the dual role of Berlusconi as head of a government and head of a widely diversified company. The potential conflict of interest existed on so many different levels, that it was difficult to think of a single piece of legislation that would not somehow have come under suspicion. The reason why this conundrum took such a long time to dawn on the Italians was that during the election campaign Berlusconi's business power was not seen as a liability but as an attraction. It was proof of the tycoon's Midas touch. Only a handful of opponents from the former Communist Party warned about the conflict of interest. The majority of the country was infatuated. Berlusconi had already given up the management of his company in January when he entered politics. That was enough for most people.

Berlusconi would probably have been able to keep his conundrum a public secret had it not been for the fact that he himself gave the game away. At the point of utmost political sensitivity when his decrees were being questioned by the press and by his coalition partners, and when the magistrates were homing in on his company, the tycoon decided to host a dinner in his villa in Arcore. Among the guests were his brother Paolo, the Minister of Defence Cesare Previti, who used to be Berlusconi's private lawyer, the Under-Secretary of State for the government – effectively Berlusconi's chief of staff – Gianni Letta, a former executive manager of Fininvest and Fedele Confalonieri, Berlusconi's oldest friend and now the chairman of his company. Salvatore Sciascia, the head of the Fininvest tax department who had just been issued with an arrest warrant in the investigations concerning tax fiddles and bribes to the Financial Police, was represented by his lawyer. 'Just old friends meeting for a chat,' Confalonieri angrily told reporters who had heard about the meeting. 'This country is worse than Stalin's Russia, if old friends can't even meet socially,' he thundered. The kitchen cabinet, which spans business and politics, had been convened to discuss a common strategy regarding the 'legal problems' of Paolo Berlusconi. It is hard to imagine an equivalent, because nothing like the Berlusconi situation has ever existed in any democracy before. Even the government spokesman Giuliano Ferrara described the meeting as 'foolish'. Yet again the Prime Minister revealed himself to be a stranger to the concept of accountability in public life. He still thought he was running a deferential boardroom.

Berlusconi's blunders have become text book material for any tycoon contemplating a life in politics. Another lesson which the Prime Minister had to learn the hard way was how to use his own television and his own in-house opinion polls. The television channels which the Prime Minister had used to great effect in the run-up to the elections, broadcasting his own campaign messages and giving live coverage of his party rallies, became a liability once he was in power. Afraid of being bombarded with hostile questions from journalists who were not on his payroll, Berlusconi preferred to appear on one of his own channels, fielding questions from his favourite anchorman, the oleaginous Emilio Fede. Too smooth to be real, Fede is not so much a newscaster as a master of ceremonies in the television court of Prime Minister Berlusconi. He has complete editorial control over the news on Rete 4, which means the Prime Minister can rely on favourable coverage; he also directs the news bulletin from his chair – on air – as if he were conducting a circus. Fede walks around the studio impatiently if stories are late; two terrified subs sit on either side of him, staring into a computer and supplying their master with news updates. Fede treats them like his children. 'Gianni,' he is prone to shout, 'what's the latest Reuters! . . . What do you mean, they haven't come up with the story yet?' All this is live on air. Fede's introductions to news stories are laced with opinion, delivered in a godfatherly fashion. 'The really important thing about this story is . . .' or 'Look out for . . .'

Emilio Fede is the anchorman the Prime Minister turned to in times of trouble. At the height of the crisis caused by the Biondi Decree in July 1994, Berlusconi's only interview on national television was with Fede. While the newscaster braved such irreverent questions as 'What's troubling you, President of the Council of Ministers?' or 'It must be very hard to govern under these circumstances!' Berlusconi poured out his anger and indignation like a wounded animal with a bruised ego. The Great Seducer looked ruffled. The rigid mask of haughty composure had cracked. His voice was hoarse with anger. His hurried justifications sounded insincere. The whole spectacle produced in the viewer a most profound and delectable sense of *schadenfreude* as one of the mightiest egos in modern politics was deflated. The

Prime Minister had been made to look ridiculous on his own television channel. He had only himself to blame.

A few weeks later he still hadn't understood that as the Prime Minister he would have to be careful about how he used television. In order to regain some popularity and credibility, Berlusconi commissioned a series of advertisements which reminded the weary viewer of the government's achievements. The spots were broadcast on RAI as well as on Fininvest channels, incurring the wrath of the opposition in and outside the ruling coalition. After four days Italy's media watchdog banned the advertisements apart from one on taxes, which was considered a useful public information broadcast. The episode was another embarrassment for Berlusconi and another demonstration of the conflict of interest.

Berlusconi's second mistake was that he relied too much on opinion polls, especially his own opinion polls. Like many other heads of government the Italian Prime Minister makes no important move without first consulting his polls. The difference is that he owns the polling organisation. It's part of his characteristic distrust of the world outside his company and his inner circle of advisers. The Prime Minister's chief pollster is a young executive who used to work for Rete 4. Gianni Pilo was one of the thirty managers who helped to orchestrate Berlusconi's election campaign and one of the eleven who ended up in parliament. In September 1993 Pilo and a partner brought Diakron, a Milan-based polling company. Nominally Diakron is independent but almost all of its business is with Fininvest. Diakron's offices are located in a Fininvest building on the outskirts of Milan and were used as the campaign headquarters during the elections. Here the symbiosis between Berlusconi's politics and his business was perfect. Pilo employs a staff of 150 telephonists who question a daily sample of 500 Italians on the political issue or issues of the day. Although the sample is relatively small it is carefully chosen from different regions, age groups and professions. Pilo assured me that the frequency of the polls produced an accurate trend of opinion. On the day that I interviewed Pilo, whose radically short hair, boyish looks and dark blue suits make him look like a reformed skinhead, he told me that he had conducted two polls.

'We asked people today whether they feared that the presence of the neo-Fascist National Alliance in any way threatened democracy; the answer was a resounding "No". We also asked them what they felt about the Northern League as a coalition partner. The majority were not happy.' Pilo was quick to point out that Berlusconi doesn't follow his polls slavishly. 'Sometimes he follows his instincts, even if the polls point in a different direction.' But the danger, surely, is that the polls begin to blunt the instincts, especially if the surveys become a daily confirmation of the Prime Minister's popularity. At the height of the decree crisis Berlusconi insisted on referring to results of his own polls, which needless to say endorsed his policies, even while other independent opinion polls indicated that the country was turning against him.

While in office Berlusconi consulted Pilo and his polls every evening at 6:30. Five hundred years ago Berlusconi would have been consulting the stars, or reading cards; two thousand years ago he would have been staring at some pig's entrails. The polls are nothing more than the daily ritual of trying to predict the future. First comes the poll, then the policy. If legislation and decrees are drafted and issued on the basis of Berlusconi's in-house polls the nature of the questions in the surveys becomes an essential part of government. In the case of the decree concerning preventive custody, which allowed hundreds of corruption suspects to leave jail, Gianni Pilo had clearly asked the wrong type of question. Apparently he asked his sample whether they were in favour of judicial reform in Italy. The answer was of course a resounding 'Yes'. But the question should have taken into the account the consequences. 'Would you be in favour of judicial reform if it meant releasing the suspects in Italy's corruption scandal?' The answer to that question turned out to be a clear 'No'.

At the end of August 1994 Berlusconi had demonstrated two things: firstly that he was better at winning elections than at governing the country, and secondly that he couldn't tell the difference between the two. There were several reasons for this: his will to rule was not matched by the political means at his disposal. Although the right-wing Freedom Pole had an over-whelming majority in the lower chamber, it narrowly lacked one in the upper chamber. Every piece of legislation could theoretically be stalled by the opposition. Secondly Berlusconi gave the impression that he wanted to create tyranny of the majority. Whenever the tycoon encountered a political hurdle or some sharp criticism in the newspapers or on state television he would accuse his detractors of 'going against the will of the majority'. Berlusconi appeared to be convinced that once he had been endorsed by a narrow majority of the Italian people he was free to wield power as he wished. This system works in Great Britain or the United States where the institutions are strong and independent, but not in Italy, where they have been weak and politicised. The solution here has traditionally been a *modus operandi* where the opposition has been encouraged to become a minority shareholder in the system of power. Compromise was a means of taking the sting out of one's opponents. Berlusconi tried to break with this tradition. But his declared desire to establish a British-style democracy with an alternation between government and opposition was not only frustrated by Italy's fragmented political landscape but also by his own conflict of interest.

The most alarming illustration of Berlusconi's interpretation of majority rule was his attacks against RAI. In June 1994 Berlusconi said 'the fact that state broadcasting repeatedly criticises the government, which is after all the expression of the majority of the Italian electorate, strikes me as an anomaly'. The real anomaly was of course that the Prime Minister already had a virtual monopoly of commercial television. A week later Berlusconi stepped up the offensive, threatening RAI with sweeping cuts and reforms. Few people doubted that these were necessary to drag the bloated, overspent, overstaffed and underachieving excrescence that is RAI into the late twentieth century. But Berlusconi, the media tycoon, was the wrong man to launch the attack. The entire five-man board of directors at RAI resigned. Berlusconi tried to appoint his own men and women, but was stopped by his coalition partners. After several weeks of haggling RAI had a new board of directors. They included a medieval historian, an estate agent, a stockbroker and the owner of a small news agency. None of them knew anything about television or radio. They were apparently chosen for their business and management skills. The most important fact, however, was that the directors mirrored the constellation of the right wing-majority in power. Two were appointed by Forza Italia, two by the Northern League and one by the National Alliance. Under the old regime RAI reflected the consensus of the *partitocrazia*. The Christian Democrats controlled RAI 1, the Socialists RAI 2 and the Communists RAI 3. Under Berlusconi and the new RAI management, this consensus had been sacrificed. Although the government made some attempt to put men and women from the right-wing parties into new positions of management at RAI, it failed to satisfy the demands of the Northern League for their own TV channel. The most obvious and easiest solution would have been to give the neo-Fascist AN and the League RAI 1 and 2, which used to be controlled by the Christian Democrats and the Socialists, and allow the Left to hold on to RAI 3. This way some degree of balance would have been achieved, keeping the largest number of political parties happy.

As a business tycoon who was used to getting his own way Silvio Berlusconi did not suit the times. Italy is not yet ready for a 'Thatcherite' leader, as Berlusconi likes to describe himself. It may never be. But here's the riddle: if Berlusconi was elected because he embodied power and patronage, why was he prevented from exercising them? The most obvious answer is that his ruling partners didn't let him. The tycoon had come up against the bitter reality of Italian coalition politics, which is the art of surviving conspiracies. Berlusconi looked like an Emperor whose ship of state was no more than a rubber dingy with a puncture. Most of the opposition to the Prime Minister came from his own partners, especially from Umberto Bossi, the cantankerous head of the Northern League, whose party had lost support to Forza Italia. Bossi's political survival depended on his ability to oppose Berlusconi within the coalition without being blamed for its demise. By attacking the tycoon, he was defining his own features as a politician. This explains the fact that he became a constant thorn in the Prime Minister's skin. Berlusconi obliged him with his string of mistakes and miscalculations. Gianfranco Fini, the leader of the National Alliance, pursued a similar policy although in a much more subtle way. Fini too opposed the Prime Minister because that was one way of showing how his right-wing party differed from Berlusconi's. But as the street-fighter and the bruised tycoon locked horns in the arena of parliament, the neo-Fascist leader gazed on the spectacle below him with princely disdain. At the height of the coalition crisis in December 1994 I interviewed Fini in his small office at party headquarters filled with Christmas presents and cards, many of which seemed to have been sent by the Carabinieri, Police Federation and the armed forces. While his allies looked more and more exhausted and ashen-faced from the daily political battles they fought, Fini sported a winter tan and self-satisfied smile. The jolly image was underscored by the pattern on his multicoloured tie, which was of frolicking dolphins. On the table in front of him was a chess board and after the interview, in which Fini had produced the usual litany of bland reassurances, he challenged me to a game. I was beaten after only ten minutes. Considering how badly I play chess this was hardly surprising. But what did strike me as unusual was that the leader of one of Italy's ruling parties found time to play games while the political establishment was collapsing around him. Fini was rewarded for his cool. In the summer of 1994, he began to overtake Berlusconi as the most popular Italian politician. By the end of the year every opinion poll put him at the top of the list, well ahead of his rivals.

Ideological differences over privatisation, taxation, subsidies, the Constitution, the federation, abortion and a host of other issues meant that Italy's right-wing ruling coalition was in constant danger of neutralising itself after it came to power. If so many policies automatically lead to a coalition crisis then it is better not to broach them at all or water them down so much as to render them ineffective. This is precisely what happened before 'the revolution'. The difference then was that the ruling parties enjoyed the near-certainty of staying in power, however often they fell. The same government reconstituted itself Humpty-Dumpty style over and over again. The system was deeply unsatisfactory but at least it created the illusion of change. The danger with the present coalition is that it is not strong enough to govern and not weak enough to be removed by the opposition. Meanwhile it is busy doing what all previous ruling coalitions have, which is to carve up or 'colonise' the state as much as possible, and thus spread the virus of ungovernability to important sectors of the economy and administration. Italy's vast state holding conglomerate IRI is a case in point: the board of IRI, like the board of RAI, echoes the fine balance within the ruling coalition. It contains members from all the three main parties, creating a perfect political equilibrium between the various forces of government. But when substantive issues are discussed, the board comes to blows.

The right-wing coalition that was elected in 1994 turned out to be much more fractious and paralysed than many of its predecessors. After years of agonising electoral reform and soul searching about a new, more efficient political system the coalition often seemed like little more than a cruel joke. Ideally both the Northern League and the neo-Fascists wanted fresh elections in the summer of 1994 to feast off what they thought was the rotting carcass of Forza Italia. But such thoughts of revenge turned out to be premature. Although it had cut Berlusconi down to size by opposing him on key pieces of legislation, the Northern League still could not be confident that it had reversed its decline. A protest movement deprived of its principal object of protest, the Northern League degenerated into a kind of multiple sclerosis. The movement became increasingly schismatic with one wing keen to stay in power at all costs and carve out a part of the patronage cake for itself. Meanwhile the other wing was yearning for constitutional reform to turn Italy into a federation. Like the Bavarian Christian Social Union (CSU) one part wanted a strong regional identity even if it meant less power, the other wanted more power in central government at the cost of identity. Eventually the two will become incompatible. The League is likely to split.

Meanwhile the neo-Fascists needed more time to prove that they were clubbable and had ditched some of their more embarrassing ideas and bedfellows. The longer they could be associated with government, the more respectable they hoped to become. They too had a vested interest in putting off fresh elections. The result was a government in office but not in power. Like some ancient fable warning about the excesses of vanity and the futility of change, Berlusconi had been politically emasculated. His miracles began to sound like hollow promises. Berlusconi became the victim of a combination of arrogance and naivety. As a tycoon who is used to the unshakeable loyalty of his boardroom he underestimated the deep current of betrayal that runs through Italian politics.

Although the Italians like to think of themselves as great individualists, they are essentially creatures of the tribe. They like to huddle together in clusters whether on beaches, motorways, in the piazza or in politics. The bandwagon is their favoured mode of political transport whether in victory or defeat. Berlusconi, who had himself done so much to nurture the consumer herd instinct with his television, his advertising, his cinema and his publishing empire, first became its beneficiary and then its victim. As he is struggling to assert himself and consolidate his power he may remember that the Italians have always been ruthless in ditching their leaders even as they are still intoxicated with the sweet sounds of flattery. Betrayal, when it happens, is sudden and brutal. Benito Mussolini was ousted by his fellow Fascist chiefs at a meeting of the Grand Council in July 1943. In 1992 Bettino Craxi was still confident enough to demand the Prime Ministership either for himself or one of his lieutenants. A few months later he was spat at by crowds outside his hotel and ousted by the party he had ruled with a feudal grip for sixteen years. As he was pushed from power he too muttered the word 'betrayal'. In Italian politics no one is indispensable.

Furthermore the Italians are ruthless with losers, especially in politics and soccer. One day Roberto Baggio, the Buddhist striker with the pony-tail who missed Italy's last penalty in the World Cup Final, was hailed as the 'God of football', the 'saviour', the 'magician', and the 'Little Buddha'. The next day he was called a 'wet lame rabbit', 'a sour disappointment', a 'failure'. The knives were out for Baggio in the same way that the knives were out for Berlusconi, only one hundred days after he had become Prime Minister. When Berlusconi was reeling from his first bitter lesson in politics, feeling abandoned and abused, he decided to seek solace from some of the people closest to him. One Saturday afternoon in August the Prime Minister took his helicopter and flew to the training grounds of his favourite possession, the AC

Milan football team. He watched the practice and then joined the players in the canteen for lunch. 'You are my only encouragement and hope,' he told them tearfully, like a late Roman emperor socialising with his favourite gladiators in his greatest hour of loneliness. Four months later, on 22 December, Berlusconi was forced to resign. Rebels from the Northern League led by Umberto Bossi had finally pulled the plug on the ruling coalition, threatening it with a vote of no confidence supported by the left-wing opposition. Berlusconi pre-empted the inevitable result by resigning before the vote had taken place.

The tycoon Prime Minister had been undermined by his conflict of interest and by the criminal investigations into his media empire which had gathered an alarming pace. At the end of November Berlusconi received an *avviso di garanzia* – a notification that criminal proceedings had started – on the very day that he was hosting an international conference on organised crime in Naples. With shrewd timing the judges had dealt Berlusconi a bitter blow laced with stinging irony. The Prime Minister's earnest protestations in the conference chamber that Italy and his government were at the forefront of the fight against the international Mafia were deflated – to say the least – by the fact that Berlusconi himself would have to be interrogated by the judges. His response was emotional. In public he swore 'on the heads of my five children' that I have never corrupted anyone. Almost in the same breath he admitted that illegal payments had been made to the Guardia di Finanza. But like so many before him, Berlusconi described himself as a victim of extortion. 'I, like tens of thousands of other Italian businessmen, was subjected to a system of extortion' – he used the word *concussione* – 'which we were powerless to oppose.'

But this left several questions unanswered. Firstly, why did Berlusconi not alert the press, the judiciary or the regular police to this extortion when his companies made the payments in 1989 and 1991? Secondly, what were the benefits in unpaid taxes for Fininvest? As his rival Carlo De Benedetti had admitted a year before, extortion was immensely profitable. The investigations reached their humiliating climax when Berlusconi was summoned to the forbidding Palazzo di Giustizia in Milan, where he was questioned by the magistrates for almost eight hours. Instead of giving a press conference, as his advisers had promised, Berlusconi was driven under tight security to his favourite habitat: a television studio in one of his own channels from where he launched a stinging, televised attack against the judges.

However, what finally toppled Berlusconi was neither his conflict of interest, nor his legal problems, nor even his humiliation at the hands of the judiciary. It was betrayal by his own allies, the rebels of the Northern League. Berlusconi's time in office had lasted barely eight months. Instead of creating an economic miracle and a million jobs, as he had promised, the number of unemployed rose by 400,000. Between the time that Berlusconi took office and gave it up, the lira had lost thirteen per cent of its value to the Deutschmark and eight per cent to the dollar. By all accounts the tycoon's Prime Ministership had been a resounding failure. And yet, even before he had resigned, Berlusconi was already pressing for fresh elections as soon as possible. He was convinced that his trials and tribulations had created a sympathetic groundswell of support on which he could capitalise. Was this merely the final example of a deluded ego or was this extraordinary confidence based on fact? To many commentators' surprise, independent opinion polls confirmed that if new elections were held Berlusconi would be re-elected. It seemed as if the former Prime Minister had succeeded in portraying himself as a victim. His legal problems and his conflict of interest, which would have disqualified a similar candidate in the United States or Britain, did not seem to deter the majority of Italians from voting for Berlusconi. The revolution which had sought to turn the Italians into responsible citizens and make the country's rulers more accountable still had a long way to go.

15

Coitus Interruptus, or
A Revolution
without Climax

The Italians take their porn queens seriously. When Moana Pozzi, the queen of queens, died suddenly of cancer in September 1994 she was mourned with full honours not only for her matronly looks but also for her intellect. Miss Pozzi was the thinking man's porn queen, appealing to the lecher and the intellectual snob alike. '*Addio Porno Diva, Intelligente*', sobbed the earnest *La Stampa* on the front page. '*Ciao Moana*', wailed the politically correct *Il Manifesto*. *La Repubblica* mourned 'an Italian icon'. But the *Espresso* magazine upstaged everyone when it eulogised '*Santa Moana Vergine*' – St Moana Virgin – and pointed out that she had died at the same age as Jesus, thirty-three. Columnists earnestly discussed the *de facto* canonisation of the author and star actress of films such as *Moana – Deep Hole*, *Wet Ecstasy* and *Orgasmissima*.

But in Italy you don't have to be dressed to be an intellectual. Miss Pozzi had received an excellent education courtesy of the Ursuline sisters. Her library had been stacked with the tomes of Italo Calvino, Primo Levi, Marguerite Yourcenar, Alexandre Dumas and many other hard-core literati. Her deathbed literature was nothing less weighty than *The City of God* by St Augustine of Hippo. Not surprisingly the Archbishop of Naples, Michele Giordano, was moved to speak at Sunday Mass about 'our poor daughter, Moana Pozzi', who 'had demonstrated how often faith dwells in the hearts of human beings like a spark under the ashes'. Italy may be the home of the Vatican and boast more saints per square mile than any other Catholic country, but it is also one of the least prudish societies in the world. Public servants may have been hounded out of office for their fiscal irregularities, but on the carnal front they are free to frolic. When he was still Foreign Minister Gianni De Michelis, a divorcee, made no attempt to hide his philandering. Surrounding himself with beautiful and at times dubious models was a manifestation of power. Luigi Rossi, an eighty-seven-year-old deputy for the Northern League and a friend of the late Winston Churchill, is the leading force behind a campaign to legalise Italy's brothels and prevent the spread of Aids through illegal roadside prostitution. 'I lost my virginity in a brothel,' he told me. 'It did the trick and the embarrassment was minimised by the anonymity of the act.' Mr Rossi describes himself as a practising Catholic.

There are historical reasons for this lack of prudishness, from which men have, needless to say, benefited more than women. The Church has long ceased to be a moral authority in Italy, a fact which senior clergymen would blame on the permissiveness of modern society. But in Italy, the Church also has itself to blame. The experience of the Papal States, which ruled central Italy in conditions of feudal deprivation for four centuries, has left a deep seam of anti-clericalism. As hosts to the Popes the Italians have always known the papacy as a political institution, as much dictated by the *realpolitik* of power as any Bourbon court or ruling party. Likewise, the very teachings of the Church, especially the comforting notion of original sin, have made the Italians remarkably tolerant towards their own and other people's temptations. Italy's ambiguous relationship with the Church helps to explain the 'canonisation' of a dead porn queen; but the main reason is that the Italians are living in a sumptuously decadent country, where the end of an era happens to coincide with the end of a millennium. Faced with such doom, anything goes – even Saint Moana Pozzi.

Two years before her death the porn queen tried to take advantage of Italy's feverish spirit of sexual tolerance and occupy what she felt to be her rightful place in the Italian parliament. After all, she was merely following in the footsteps of La Cicciolina, 'the Little Bunny Rabbit', who was elected as a deputy for the maverick Radical Party in 1987. The Partito del Amore or Love Party, was Miss Pozzi's contribution to Italy's political transition.

It was founded in 1992 and was committed to the free market – in love. According to the party's manifesto, Italians should be allowed to relieve stress and tension by making love in their lunch hour. For those too far from home, special love parks would be opened where office workers could copulate between shifts. La Cicciolina was the party's guiding spirit and its Honorary President. Real power was concentrated, however, in the manicured hands of Moana Pozzi, who became the party's General Secretary, and Barbarella, the Secretary for Propaganda and External Relations.

The founding congress took place in one of Rome's largest discothèques, a cluster of pink domes built around a green fountain made of cherubs in erotic embrace. The discothèque had been hired by the Love Party's secretariat for one evening in February 1992. Pink heart-shaped invitations beckoned supporters to pledge their signature and thus help legalise the party in time for the elections. It was here that I managed to beat a path through the throng of reporters, supporters and titillated teenagers to put my question to Miss Pozzi. What had made her dabble in politics? Moana fixed me with her large green eyes and launched into a brilliant exegesis. 'Italy is going through a profound transition. The rigid structure of party politics, which prevailed in this country for four decades, has been shattered by corruption and by the end of Communism. The breaching of the Berlin Wall and the end of Communism,' the star of *Moana's Wet Dreams* confided in me, 'have deprived the Christian Democrats and their allies of the reason for perpetual re-election. What you are witnessing in Italy today is dramatic, unique.' Her bosom heaved. She took a deep breath. 'The danger,' she continued, 'is that this so-called revolution of ours will fizzle out . . . in a coitus interruptus.'

Miss Pozzi was ahead of her time. In 1994 it did indeed seem as if Italy's ethical cleansing had stopped in its tracks and been denied a climax. The 'revolution' was, after all, nothing more than foreplay. The country had opted – once again – for a typically Italian Catholic solution: collective confession, *mea culpa*, penitence and absolution, woven into a soothing blanket of forgiveness and compromise. Proposals for a general amnesty that had almost brought down governments two years before were now being made by the very judges who had spearheaded 'the revolution'.

Antonio Di Pietro, the magistrate-turned-folk-hero, was so overwhelmed and exhausted by the sheer volume of corruption cases that he suggested wiping the slate for existing charges and imposing tougher sentences in the future. Later he resigned from the pool of magistrates he had helped to make famous, cast off his gown in anger and contemplated a career in politics. For all the high drama of arrests, subpoenas and resignations, the Italian judiciary had very few convictions and prison sentences to show for their efforts. In October 1994 Sergio Cusani, the most famous *tangentopoli* defendant to reach the dock, was preparing his first of two appeal trials and suing the judges for negligence. It was now the judiciary's turn to fend off a smear campaign. Bettino Craxi still languished in sundrenched exile in Tunisia, ignoring his eight-and-a-half-year prison sentence and claiming that he was too ill to appear at the other trials awaiting him. Francesco De Lorenzo, the former Health Minister who had been charged with fraud, bribery and extortion involving millions of dollars, was released from preventive custody. He was photographed with a friend of his emerging from lunch in a restaurant called 'I due Ladroni', 'The Two Thieves'. Gianni De Michelis, the former Foreign Minister, was busy giving interviews in court about China, his new passion. The dodgy Doge had become a 'cultural consultant' for Italian businessmen, seeking stronger ties with China. It seemed as if the bloodcurdling morality play that was *tangentopoli* had been rewritten after Act Two to become another light-hearted operetta. A country that had bayed for the blood of its rulers was already bored.

The anaesthetic of corruption fatigue had begun to work. In October 1994 magistrates discovered that the Guardia di Finanza, the Financial Police, and SECIT, the Italian state tax auditors, had turned a blind eye to financial irregularities in return for handsome bribes. Over seventy officers of the Financial Police, the very body that is supposed to ensure that the Italians pay their taxes, were arrested. Three committed suicide in the space of two months. The businesses involved ranged from a number of branches in Fininvest, the Prime Minister's company, to Milan's fashion houses. On one damp Saturday in September 1994 the designers Giorgio Armani, Gianfranco Ferre and Krizia all filed into Milan's austere Palace of Justice to be questioned by Antonio Di Pietro about the system of bribery with the Guardia di Finanza. Krizia admitted to paying 100,000 dollars in bribes to the Guardia in 1990. Giorgio Armani's lawyer told reporters that the eternally tanned High Priest of Haute Couture had paid 60,000 dollars to the tax authorities, and the corpulent Gianfranco Ferre, the chief designer of Christian Dior in Paris, said that he 'simply loved the judge's cashmere jacket'. All the designers said they had become the victims of extortion, that their businesses would have been closed down if they hadn't paid the money to the tax authorities. The latter, however, have claimed that the so-called extortion had spared them in taxes: and therefore it was in their interest to be 'extorted'.

A few months later the same argument would be used by none other than Prime Minister Berlusconi who told the nation during a special TV address – how else – that he too had been forced to pay money to the Financial Police 'like hundreds of thousands other businessmen'. This was an absurd statement, especially from a head of government who had vowed to clean up politics. But instead of unleashing a torrent of outrage his admission was greeted with a quiet nod of understanding. Despite his undoubted mistakes Berlusconi and Forza Italia continued to lead the opinion polls in a triumph of hope over experience.

The media tycoon embodied a nation, in which, it seemed, every individual from prime minister to fashion designers, from tax inspectors to taxi-drivers, cast him or herself as a victim of a flawed human nature, rather than one of its practitioners. In Catholic Italy original sin has become a kind of opt-out clause for personal responsibility. As the sociologist Franco Ferrarotti has put it: 'If human nature is hopelessly flawed and perfection can only be achieved in Paradise, there's no point in trying too hard while trapped in the mortal coil. This profound sense of human imperfection has not plunged the Italians into a deep depression, or driven them to self-improvement, no, it has freed them to be selfish and pragmatic. It is obvious from the way we drive, the way we park, the way we dodge our taxes, distrust the state and every one of its representatives.' The spirit of pragmatism has spawned its own very Italian term: *possibilista* – or literally 'possibilist' – in other words, everything can be achieved with the right degree of compromise After 1945 the Communist Party concentrated on good local government rather than advancing the cause of proletarian paradise.

Perhaps its leaders realised at an early stage that Italy, fragmented into an archipelago of interest groups from families, tribes, regions, cities, and village fraternities to trades unions and political parties, is quite simply unfit for revolution. This undergrowth of associations, loyalties and affiliations has resisted the imposition of the state in the interests of society as a whole. It has undermined civic responsibility and obstructed reform, especially on a national level. But it has also prevented Italy from degenerating into anarchy.

Considering the wholesale collapse of the old regime, the arrest of thousands of politicians, bureaucrats and business leaders, the eradication of entire political parties, the calamity of a prime minister accused of conniving with the Mafia, of secret service agents plotting against the state and the Everest of bribes that financed this system of corruption, Italy has remained suspiciously unruffled. My Italian friends used to boast about their *dolce* revolution. But this placidity had less to do with the self-restraint of an outraged people and more to do with the cynicism of a country that had always expected its politicians to sin. It tolerated their peccadilloes as long as they provided patronage, jobs, welfare and a blind eye over tax fiddles in return. When they continued to take the bribes but stopped delivering the goods this working relationship broke down. However, another damning indictment for those who claim that the last few years produced 'revolution' or even reform is that the political debate has been dominated by personalities rather than issues and principles.

Italy has been called the laboratory chamber of European politics. The British historian E. P. Thompson coined the term in an article in which he described the rise of Mussolini in 1922 as a taste of things to come in Germany and Spain. Italy has certainly experimented in recent years. Its laboratory has frothed and fizzed with media tycoon prime ministers, Fascists resurrected from the dustbin of history wacky self-declared regional republics. As five decades of rigid *partiticrazia* collapsed, Italy filled the void with experiments and became a magnifying glass for nascent developments in other Western countries. The last three years have witnessed the decline of the political parties and philosophies that have ruled much of the Western world since 1945, the fragmentation of the nation-state into regions, the rise of citizen politicians, the invention of a new political language based on TV, soccer and consumer culture and the branding of the *partito azienda*, the business conglomerate turned political party. I wonder how many international tycoons have been inspired by Silvio Berlusconi to turn their companies into electoral movements? Shortly after Berlusconi's election victory in 1994 a delegation of Japanese businessmen came to Rome to study the genesis of Forza Italia. They were exploring the possibility of setting up a Forza Japan party. Regionalists, devolutionists and secessionists around the world may have been inspired by Umberto Bossi's Northern League with its make-believe passports, its currency and its historical pageantry. Italy, once the cradle of civilisation, has become the whirlpool of decadence.

Italian politics can inspire, frustrate, amaze or entertain. But Italy is too idiosyncratic to be a model for any other country. Its experiments are best ignored. Because this country has achieved the near-perfect separation of state and people, because what happens on the political level barely impinges on the life of the voters, Italy can afford to dabble in experiments that would be dangerous elsewhere. Imagine the consequences of *tangentopoli* in Britain, where something as trifling as the poll tax unleashed violent riots in Trafalgar Square. In Italy the poll tax would either have been ignored or briefly paid by those who were sufficiently intimidated. In Britain *tangentopoli* would probably have led to the collapse of the monarchy.

The fact is that with its innate conservatism, its fragmentation into millions of resilient family units, its petty provincialism, its inherited distrust of the state, its mystical dislike for logic, its unwillingness to respect the laws of cause and effect, Italy is simply not made for collective change. The country is unfit for revolution. This is an insurance policy against extremism and should reassure anyone who is worried about the rise in neo-Fascism. However, it is also a pity because Italy is still a long way from facing up to the real if mundane challenge: to re-invent the relationship between the citizen and the state. The consequences of *this* 'revolution' could be felt in a thousand tiny ways. It would shorten queues in banks, deliver letters on time, open museums, improve the traffic and the health system. If it could do that, Italy, with its culture, weather, beauty, humanity, humour, industriousness, inventiveness, unselfconscious eccentricity and delicious food, would surely be the closest thing to paradise on earth.

Index

Prime minister is used where this office has been achieved.